D1503236

DOING BUSINESS IN TODAY'S INDIA

DOING BUSINESS IN TODAY'S INDIA

Douglas Bullis

QUORUM BOOKS
Westport, Connecticut • London

Library of Congress Cataloging-in-Publication Data

Bullis, Douglas.
    Doing business in today's India / Douglas Bullis.
      p. cm.
    Includes bibliographical references and index.
    ISBN 1–56720–136–9 (alk. paper)
    1. India—Economic conditions—1947– 2. Economic forecasting—
India. 3. Investments—India. 4. Business etiquette—India.
5. Negotiation in business—India. I. Title.
HC435.2.B87 1998
658'.049'0954—dc21   97–1705

British Library Cataloguing in Publication Data is available.

Library of Congress Catalog Card Number: 97–1705
ISBN: 1–56720–136–9

First published in 1998

Quorum Books, 88 Post Road West, Westport, CT 06881
An imprint of Greenwood Publishing Group, Inc.

Printed in the United States of America

The paper used in this book complies with the
Permanent Paper Standard issued by the National
Information Standards Organization (Z39.48–1984).

10 9 8 7 6 5 4 3 2 1

To
Ravi, Vijay, Nathan, Raj,
Arul, Dexter, and Richard
the best team The Crew could have

Contents

Acknowledgments

This is one of those new books showing up that relies on the Internet and E-mail interviews for information more than traditional printed publications. The magazines, journals, and books listed in Appendix B: Additional Readings were useful sources, but many were already dated.

It is difficult to write a bibliography in this situation. The nuisance of the ephemeral and all too copious that is inherent in online communication rears its head. In this book the defects on online sourcing are perhaps less an issue than in a more traditional scholarly work, for this is not a scholarly work. It is intended for business people who want to know what business in India these days is about. Hence the absence of citations and notes in the text. There are so many they would have cluttered the pages to the point of being a distraction more than an aid.

This said, there are many thanks to be extended to so many people. An important influence for this book came from Barbara Crossette, the former *New York Times* correspondent in India, and author of the landmark book *India: Facing the Twenty-First Century* (Indiana University Press). If there is one single book a prospective business visitor to India should read, it is Barbara's.

Business leaders and government officials whose information contributed to this book include P. B. Sawant, chairman of the Press Council; Nancy Shroff of Bexim's International USA; S. L. Rao, former director of NCAER and now advisor to the *Business India* Group; R. C. Bhargava, managing director of Maruti Udyog; Parvinder Singh, chief managing director of Ranbaxy; Anand Mahindra, deputy managing director, Mahindra & Mahindra; Subhash Agrawal, president of the consultancy Business foundations in New Delhi; Edward Milward-Oliver, director of *Inasia.com* (Intermedia Corporation, Hong Kong); J. Venkatadas, CEO of the Canbank Venture Capital fund; Thomas Thomas of Indus Venture Management; Vinod Haritwal, senior vice president of IL&FS Venture Corporation; David Loseff, managing director of Bank of America's Global Equity Investment Asia Group; G. Sabarinthan of the Technology Development and Information Company of India; Vivek Bharat Ram, chairman of DCM-Benetton; Sanjay Bhowmick, vice president of Creditcapital Venture Fund (India); Jonathan Bond, director of HSBC Private Equity Management India; Pradip Shah, managing director of Indocean Venture Advisors Private, Ltd.; Kiran Nadkirni, managing director of Draper Internatioal (India) Pvt. Ltd.; Roshan Verghese, chief manager of investment funds of ANZ Grindlays; J. Vishwanathan senior investment officer at the Investment Corp. of India; Philip Banks, vice president of AT Kearny, Inc.; Ron Lemmens of McKinsey & Co., Delhi; Byung Mun Pak of Samsung India Electronics; Muktesh Pant of Reebok India; David Bell, chief executive of the *Financial Times* Group; Peter Denis Sutherland, chairman of Goldman Sachs International; attorneys L. Rao Penna, H. P. Ranina, and Nisith Desai; environmental activist and attorney M. C. Mehta; Samir Arora, founder of NetObjects; arts consultants Anita Rathnam, Arshiya Lokhandwala, and Shireen Gandhy; Malaysia's Vinayak Chatterjee of Feedback Ventures Malaysia, and the president of Mauritius, the Honorable Salwan Uteem.

Numerous writers in India and Southeast Asia contributed information through their articles and via E-mail. First and foremost, daily online readings from *The Hindu* and the Web sites listed in Appendix B provided a constant stream of leads and information, much of which was without author attribution; my gratitude and best wishes to all those anonymous contributors whose work cannot be given more personalized acknowledgment here, much as I would like to. Authors of full-length books include Manoj Pant, author of *Foreign Direct Investment in India: The Issues Involved*; Madhaw Godbole, author of *Unfinished Innings*; Bhabani Sen Gupta of Delhi's Centre for Policy Research and author of *India: Problems of Governance*; Sevanti Ninan, author of *Through the Magic Window: TV and Change in India; Tarjani Vakil, author of Achieving Excellence: Case Studies of 6 Indian Export Companies*; V. M. Dandekar, author of *The Indian Economy: 1947–92*; Sarvepalli Radhakrishnan, author of *The Hindu View of Life*; Bhupesh Bhandari and Arjan Rana, authors of "Midnight's Companies," a history of modern business enterprises in India which was published in part in *BusinessWorld* 16–29 October 1996.

Journalists and columnists whose information proved useful include *Asian Business* writers Sanjay Kumar, Sid Astbury, James Leung, Brian Mertens, and Karan Sawhny; *Asiaweek* writers Shirish Nadkarni, Arjuna Ranawana, Ajay Singh, and Matthew Fletcher; *Business India* writers Vikram Doctor, Latha Kuttappan, Neera Bhardwaj, Madhumita Bose, Ganga Subramaniam, Namrata Datt, Devina Dutt, Sudipt Dutta, K. G. Kumar, Hormazd Sorabjee, N. Chandra Mohan, I. Satya Sreenivas, Indranil Pan, Hema Rajashekar, Sarah Abraham, Aloka Majumdar, Sushila Ravindranath, Bodhisatva Ganguli, Mayank Bhatt, Nandita Jhaveri, and Anjan Roy; *Business Today* Internet columnist Vivek Bhatia and writers Jairam Ramesh, S. Ramesh Kumar, Adite Chatterjee, Pareena Kawatra, Archana Rai, Rohit Saran, and Bhakti Chuganee; *Business Week's* Manjeet Kripalani; *BusinessWorld* writers Shuchi Bansal, Niranjan Rajadhyaksha, C. N. Mukeiriea, N. Sriram, Bhupesh Bhandara, Mahasweta Ghosh, Indranil Ghosh, Mainak De, D. N. Mukeriea, Arun Jethmalani, Nandan Chakraborty, S. V. Kumar, Subramaniam Sharma, P. Hari, and Pyaralal Raghavan; the *Economist's* nameless Everybody; *Far Eastern Economic Review* writers Neel Chowdhury, Jonathan Karp, Lincoln Kaye; *Frontline* writer T. K. Rajalakshmi; *India Today* writers Stephen David, Uday Mahurear, Rawash Vinayak, Vijay Menon, Robin Abreu, Saurav Sev, Samar Harlarnkar, Navneet Sharma, Manoj Mitta, Shefali Rekhi, Rohit Parihar, Bharat Desia, G. C. Shekhar, and Smruti Koppikar; and *The Times of India's* Jug Suraiya.

Finally personal gratitude: My long-time associate editor Diane Freburg in the USA graciously pre-edited much of this manuscript so it wouldn't be such a horrifying mess for Quorum Book's editor Eric Valentine. Colleague and confidante Frank Gorin provided many valuable Web sites and E-mail contacts. Kuala Lumpur Associate Wong Siewlyn dispensed sage advice that kept me sane during the most vexing times when computers and E-mail systems seemed to conspire against this ever being completed. Sometimes in moments like this that one looks back and realizes just how many good friends one has.

Introduction: A Sixth of Humanity

India's nearly 1 billion people are indeed a sixth of all humanity. And, to give one statistic a helpful nudge towards significance with another, India is the fifth largest economy in the world, a quarter of the earth's urbanized populaces, a third of the world's people living in democracy, the second largest among the developing economies, and the first massive, complex developing country to successfully transit from a socialist to a market economy without massive help from somebody else. India is a modern industrial state whose ancient roots still condition a collective vision of life in which thousands of years ago were only yesterday, and will shape much of tomorrow as well.

Even though India is among the oldest continuous civilizations, it has a dynamic modern attitude toward business, sophisticated and literate entertainment, a virile and self-examining media, and a legal and accounting system that conforms to global standards. Visitors will feel quite at home in India's business community, yet will be ever reminded they are in a land of exotic cultures and ideas. There was, and is, much innovation in India, yet India's roots have much to teach.

India's history is unique, formidable, powerful. Despite millennia of conquests and colonizations, India has preserved its sense of cultural continuity. It has an uncanny knack for calmly absorbing the useful ideas of the newly arrived while discarding their excess baggage like so many sacks on the heap of history. So deep and yet so resilient are India's social and religious ideas that practices one sees everywhere are depicted in carvings and paintings more than 3,000 years old. Ideas that came to show

India a thing or two have ended up as debris. Every attempt to change India into something else has failed. Village life remains very much the same as one reads in the great epics of thousands of years ago. Even in the fast-paced modern cities like Mumbai and Delhi, beneath the facade of international lifestyles are age-old obligations and symbols of loyalty. As Daraius Ardeshir, managing director of Nestle India put it while explaining the difficulties marketers face when understanding the facade of Indian modernity, "Indians are capable of living in several centuries at once. When I visit my father's house I still kiss his feet."

For new arrivals, diversity is India's most obvious hallmark—diversity of languages, religions, races, cultural styles. This is to be expected given a country of India's size. From Kashmir in the far north to the southern tip at Cape Comorin, India's vertical span is as long as Sweden to Spain, Ireland to Italy, the Canadian to the Mexican border. Widthwise it is Lisbon to Prague, San Francisco to Chicago.

Within that span India embraces three major racial groups: the Indo-Aryans (72 percent), Dravidians (24 percent), and Mongoloids (3 percent). Each of these has multiple subgroups and sub-subgroups. India's people and history are like spending all day watching the sea: a myriad of events are each a marvel of delight to the eye, yet when is all said and done, what you remember is the unity of the sea that they are.

It is difficult to generalize about India's peoples. Attitudes in the north can vary significantly from those in the south, the west of the country is very different from the east. There are enormous differences in values, language, food, dress, and cultural ways between each state and region, not to mention within India's many religious, *jataka* (occupational), and *jati* (birthright) classes. The Hindus alone have more than 3,000 castes to keep track of. Each state has its own ethnic culture and often its own language. Indians are as loyal to their regions as they are to their ethnic and religious communities. The result is a fragmented heritage in which identity comprises region, religion, language, cuisine, garb, work, class, caste, skin, the liquors of the shapes of the eyes. Yet a common mind called India transcends them all.

More than 82 percent of the country's population is Hindu. About 11 percent are Muslims. The rest are Christians, Sikhs, Buddhists, Zoroastrians, Jains, or followers of shamanistic tribal religions. India is home to the third largest Muslim population in the world after Indonesia and Pakistan—indeed, at over 100 million, India has far more Muslims than any Middle East nation.

Historically, Hinduism provided a broad sense of social unity, though it has never been dominant enough to forge a political and economic unity. Nor is it likely to do so today, despite the posturings of the *hindutva* or Hindu nationalist politicians. The Hindu caste system is one of the most complicated, and thus divisive, features of modern Indian life. It originated over three thousand years ago as the attempt by a priest class to perpetuate their superiority. They tied their views of social behavior to the behavior of the ancient gods, turning all life into a formal religion. Eventually the religion became social, with four distinct *varnas* or classes, each with its prescribed set of rules for conduct and behavior.

Caste is no longer used to determine one's *jataka* or traditional occupation, but most affluent Indians tend to be from one of the higher castes and most workers from one of the lower. Historically, the lower castes gave little or no opportunity for education and advancement, thus ensuring people would be unable to break out of their *jati* or birth-determined social level. Government programs today have sought to rectify this imbalance by providing special quotas for the Scheduled Caste (*dalits*), but this has provoked fierce backlashes.

Rural India accounts for 70 percent of the population and remains traditional and provincial. Strict—even suffocating—traditions have changed very little through the centuries. The rural middle class, large as it is in total numbers, is still only about 30 percent of India's rural population. Even the most educated rural people cling strongly to traditional patterns. Marriages continue to be arranged within castes and regional communities, ensuring a level of social and economic homogeneity. Rural women continue to be restricted by severe traditions of social behavior, although the treatment of women tends to differ dramatically from area to area depending on the area's level of educational and economic advancement.

Indians have a great deal of respect for family and elders. All of the Indian languages have specific respectful terms for each older family member. Members of the younger generation will call older Indians *chancha* for "Uncle" and *amah* for "Auntie," whether or not they are related. Indians are relatively quick to accept outsiders into their family, particularly friends of their children or adults with whom they share common interests.

The modern India attitude about nationhood has been shaped in large part by its colonial experience and the resulting Independence and *swadeshi* ("self-reliance") movement, which promoted economic self-reliance, particularly in science and technology.

The introduction of satellite television throughout India and its portrayal of Western affluence has awakened people to their country's economic stagnation under paternal socialism. New ideas, concepts, lifestyles, and products are routinely presented by the media the way everyone should live. Modernization and Western pop culture now permeate the surface levels of Indian city life. As a result, the Indian people are now eager to catch up materially, although Western cultural influence has contributed to confusion about cultural values and roots. Buxom voluptuousness is celebrated in ancient temple art but abhorred on beauty contest candidates even in bathing suits. Some respond with a virulent rejection of the West and everything it stands for—especially cultural icons which are already bizarre to start with, such as those beauty contests' preoccupation with swimsuits over brains and the yellow mammaries of Macdonalds. This can result in hilariously overwrought symbols such as trying to shut down a Kentucky Fried Chicken outlet because two flies were spotted in the rubbish pail of the kitchen.

Until fairly recently, many Indians viewed the earning of money, profit, and commercial activities as "dirty." If questioned, the attitude would soon come out that it was not money itself that was considered evil, but how one got it. Many people assumed that a person had to be unscrupulous in order to succeed. This attitude was evident by the fact that the petty-merchant *vaisya* varna was a low one in Hinduism while the more philosopher-priest *brahman* varna at the very top and aristocrat-warrior *ksatriya* varna just beneath.

Today this attitude has eroded as Indians accept the view that material attainment provides more food for the children than spiritual attainment. As a result, the aversion to wealth as "dirty" now stems more from frustration at one's inability to easily achieve it than anything intrinsically wrong with it.

This view is being embraced fairly quickly with the rise of India's middle class, now approximately 100 to 300 million strong (depending on which economist is defining the term "middle class"). Changes in government policy are encouraging people to become independent business owners. The TV-inspired belief that everyone can participate in the "Indian Dream" has done much to change Indian people's anti-materialist attitudes over the last decade.

Indians, for all this, still tend to think in insular, provincial ways, even if they live in a "metro" or megacity like Mumbai, Chennai, Calcutta, or New Delhi.[1] They tend to view their own particular community (which can be a tiny patch of a suburb) as the center of the world. Indians tend to be more critical than supportive of each another—a predilection that often leads to culture shock in newly arrived advocates of the market economy who have never looked seriously at the absence of historical seasoning in the system they want to switch everyone to.

Most Indians are most certainly not averse to the benefits of the market economy. They feel that a goodly number of Western products and ideas are better than Indian ones. The average Indian is not merely hospitable but quite welcoming to foreigners. Indeed, Indians are often friendlier to foreigners than to other Indians.

Education is very important in India. It has long been seen as the best method for achieving social and economic advancement. Certain professions, especially medicine and engineering, have acquired very high status because they are perceived as guaranteed paths to economic stability. After the tenth standard (grade), students take highly competitive national exams to determine their eligibility to study the "arts" or "sciences." Once a student enters the arts or sciences line, he or she cannot switch to the other. Exams after the twelfth standard determine eligibility into medical, engineering, or other professional colleges. Children are routinely tutored outside of school to prepare them for these exams.

Both Hindu and Muslim Indians have a strong belief in fate. Hindus, Jains, and India's tiny contingent of Buddhists believe that one's whole life is determined at birth. This imposes a limit to what a person can do to change his or her life. In practice, fate, the will of Allah, or karma all have the habit of inducing people to behave in ways appropriate to their social station. This is one of the sources of India's tremendous cling to the traditional.

Women are still considered to have the ultimate responsibility for the home and children, men for income and security. Where tradition holds sway, Indian women are not treated or even thought of as equals of men. This, too is changing fairly quickly with the advent of TV and consumer advertising, and many women have access to higher education. Many have achieved distinction in fields such as medicine, engineering, and teaching. With the economic reforms begun in 1991, more women seek—and find—lucrative opportunities in business-related fields.

India has changed dramatically in the last six years, especially so since the 1996 elections. The crisis atmosphere of mid-1991, which saw Indians aghast as they watched their nearly last precious gold reserves disappear into an airplane for London, galvanized them for change that came quickly and dramatically. Forty-five years of socialism and self-reliance went out the window, and in came market interdependence and the global economy. Progress was neither easy nor simple, but it was definitive. In five years

India transformed its economic attitudes irreversibly. India is not the same any more.

The 1996 elections brought the same kind of sea change politically. Forty-five years of Congress one-party rule expired in a dismal wheeze of internal rot, to be replaced by a youthfully fractious, feisty, vibrant coalition that is sure to provide Delhi-watchers with years of fascination.

But the change underneath was deeper than the squabbles in the Lok Sabha. The state coffers are—every single one—nearly or actually broke. People are appalled at the antics of the country's fake "godmen," trading the ascetic serenity of the wandering gurus and yogis of the past for all-too-modern wheeling and dealing, monumental cheating, amid the company of film stars and stock-market manipulators. The populace has awakened to the world on Hong Kong's Star TV, and Rupert Murdoch is not noted for pulling his punches.

All of this has fairly momentous international implications. Today's aging intellectual and political leadership saw all problems in East-West or North-South terms. They failed—or didn't want—to notice that powerful and effective movements for the environment, human rights, and the equality of women were growing in the industrialized nations. India's intelligentsia is dumbfounded by the Western reality that culture is not created by the ancient Indian distinction between labor by brawn versus labor by brain, but rather created by product and knowledge. They revere India's admittedly vast institutional memory but forget that memory isn't where creativity happens. Still swathed in its old merits and scorning those new, the last fifty years of India's history is yet another speck of dust hovering in the air as India's great procession now moves again beneath.

NOTE

1. Bombay changed its name to the ancient name for the locale, Mumbai, in 1994. Madras made a similar switch to its pre-colonial name Chennai in 1996. Both the old and the antique names are still used interchangeably (notably in the press) but it seems likely the new ones will catch on over time. We will use the new names throughout this book, with occasional reminders for readers who may be dipping in at random.

DOING BUSINESS IN TODAY'S INDIA

1

Political and Economic Outlook

INDIA IN THE WORLD ECONOMY

India has veered sharply away from its former command-economy path to pursue market economics. The change has been bumpy but steady. It is likely to continue, despite misgivings from some quarters and opposition from others, gradually increasing in strength as the benefits of market economics manifest themselves in the real incomes of more and more citizens.

Market economics is likely to change India more dramatically than any other economic theory in recent history. The main reason is not so much that more people are becoming more content, but that it is removing their economic fate from the hands of politicians. Economic liberalism means deregulating the economy at home and more investment—and ideas—from abroad. Even after only a half-decade after adoption, the results have been impressive: the rapid rise of a middle class that largely ignores caste boundaries, an economy stabilizing at a new and much higher level, and the eviction from office of the corrupt remnants of political ideals gone sour.

From the overseas investor's point of view, India has emerged as the most promising mass market in Asia, surpassing China's in sophistication, openness, internationalism, and transparency. India's institutional structure and national psychology is based on political and economic freedom tempered with more limited social mobility. The country has an uninhibited press, a judiciary that can (and often does) overrule the administration, a modern if slow legal system, international standards of accounting, and a strong research and academic infrastructure. India's itchily competitive private sector is the backbone of its economy. Private business is 75 percent of the GDP. There is considerable opportunity for partnerships, joint, and share-based ventures, although sole proprietorships owned by foreigners are presently more limited.

India's economic future transcends the parochialisms of the country's political parties. So separate are business and politics that Indians see little conflict when its communist parties invest surplus funds in the shares markets.

The Liberalizing Economy

In 1991, India inaugurated a wide-ranging program of economic reform. Significant changes were made in the conduct of trade, industry, foreign investment, finance, and taxation, while more modest changes were applied to the public sector. Their goals were macroeconomic stability, higher domestic savings and investment, a stronger private sector and capital market, more diversified industry, and agricultural self-sufficiency. Regulation of investment and production was considerably relaxed.

Today, private enterprise is encouraged in all but a few industries. The largest infrastructure industries such as the posts, road, rails, and ports are still government-administered, yet even there a phased program of public-sector divestment and restructuring is underway. Telecommunications are already liberalized. Foreign investment is considered equal to—and as welcome as—domestic investment. Import barriers have dropped radically and are in line for yet more cuts. Capital markets freely court foreign investments, and get it. Banking controls have been eased. Private investment—supported by India's personal savings average of 22 percent of the GDP (1996)—is strongly encouraged. Much of it finds its way into capital markets via shares acquisition and unit trusts. The tax structure has been simplified and its rates reduced. The Indian rupee is convertible in both current and capital accounts.

India is the fifth largest economy in the world. On the leveled playing field of purchasing power parity (PPP), India's economy is the second largest among the developing economies. In November 1996, the GDP (PPP) was $1.294 trillion, or $1,385 per person for the populace of 934 million. The economy averaged 4.2 percent annual growth between 1982 and 1991, and 5.8 percent after 1991. Inflation fluctuated between 8 and 13 percent over the same period. As of late 1996, foreign exchange reserves were a comfortable $18 billion, the foreign debt $85.2 billion, and the current account balance was minus $5.1 billion, or 7 percent of the GDP.

Real per-capita GDP growth was 7.0 percent, exceeding population growth (at 2.1 percent per year) by 333 percent.

Growth was not likely to accelerate through 1997 because of tighter monetary policies and the political realignments brought about by the 1996 national election. For 1997—1998, assuming continued political stability and no agricultural calamity, growth is expected to stabilize at 5.7 percent by the end of 1998.

Key business and economic statistics reflect India's confidence. As of November 1996, the per-capita GNP was $335 and the per-capita GDP was $1,384, a 4-to-1 ratio compared with Singapore's 1-to-1, South Korea's 1.2-to-1, Thailand's 3-to-1, and China's 6-to-1. The inflation rate dropped from 13.5 percent in 1991 to 8.8 percent in 1996. Inflation is predicted to decline steadily to 6–7 percent by 2000. India's high FDI (foreign direct investment)-to-GDP ratio reflects considerable investor confidence in the country.

In sum, India's 1991 reforms largely accomplished their goal of rejuvenating the country's business environment and opening the economy to foreign investment. Their success signaled a sea change in thinking that is unlikely to be shunted aside by parochial political issues. On the other hand, India has a long way to go, as anyone who arrives in Mumbai's dirty, crowded, service-poor, everyone-for-oneself airport will attest.

The government has to juggle two basic economic philosophies:

- Progress between 1991 and 1996 has been remarkable and has clearly shown that the wave of the future is the continuance of market reforms, even if it means serious medium-term social unrest as the inefficient public sector is converted to private enterprise.
- Too much private enterprise will exacerbate India's already serious rich/poor disparities, leaving the poor with no social safety net and turning them into a huge and chaotic political force.

Both of these have merit, and the second issue is often too much minimized by free-marketers who have not lived in India and do not realize how deeply rooted is the value system of everyone being taken care of. India still lives with a strong legacy of castes, tribes, clans, and families, all of which have strong inbuilt social protections. Democracy has shifted the responsibility for fulfilling these expectations to politicians, who transfer the burden to government, which all too often shifts it to debt. There is considerable pressure on the government to maintain a more "pro-poor" image and increase populist spending despite its obviously corrosive consequences. The political imperatives resulting from the 1996 election are likely to resist economic reforms that endanger public welfare. The government will be very sensitive to charges raised by the opposition party (whomever it happens to be). The affect will be government economic policies that are slowed down and "fudged" (an Indian term meaning that decisions are made but nothing is done—the equivalent to America's "unfunded mandates").

The Probable Pace of Reforms from 1996 to 2000

Foreign and Private Investment Continues to be Increasingly Welcome. No backtracking on reform is expected. Substantial progress has already been made, although some slowdown is likely through 1997 as the government focuses on other priorities such as straightening out the states' finances. No political party is seriously opposed to private or foreign investment, although there may be more selectivity in approving it as party politics uses overseas investment as a whipping boy.

Public-Sector Reform Will Remain Sensitive. The government still balks at large-scale privatization since it involves the sale of the state-owned public-sector units (PSUs) to the private sector, resulting in considerable job redundancies. The government prefers the indirect route of privatizing industry by opening up public-sector monopolies to private investment, and then diluting its stake in the PSUs via share sales in the capital market. Up to now, this policy has been used largely to raise funds for budgetary needs and has not resulted in the elimination of government management in the restructured units. This situation is unlikely to change in the immediate future.

Labor Reform Is Also Likely To Be Slow. There is still little talk of a government exit policy that would enable inefficient enterprises to close down or convert to other enterprises. Plant closures and layoffs will continue to be political hot potatoes. The fact that state governments are often involved will make reform even more difficult. The multitude of parties in power in different states across the country and their varying political commitments make labor reform a complicated issue. Progress is likely to be slow despite the generally reformist charter given by the 1996 elections.

Exchange Rate Reform Is Likely To Be Put on the Back Burner. While foreign exchange reserves are comfortable, the economic fundamentals are not yet stable enough to support capital-account convertibility. The problems of inflation and a widening current-account deficit need to be tackled before exchange rate reform can proceed.

Foreign Trade and Indirect Tax Reform Are Expected To Be Rapid. The commitment to trade reform remains high. As long as the reserves position remains comfortable, the government faces little trouble in sustaining reform. There is also little resistance to tax reform.

India's Future as a World Economic Power

India's moves to liberalize its economy and welcome foreign investment have reversed its backward image in a surprisingly short time. In foreign affairs India has much improved its relations with its former antagonists, notably China and the United States. The East and Southeast Asians express few public opinions about India's international policies, but they have an avid interest in the proximity and size of India's market, although there have been few overtures to integrate India into APEC and/or East Asian Economic Caucus (EAEC) agendas. Regionally, India still plays big brother to its lesser neighbors, resulting in ethnic and religious conflicts in Pakistan and Sri Lanka, whose origins are largely traceable to Indian meddling.

Today's Indian government is faced with neighborly fence-mending tasks equal to its task of introducing market economics at home. Memories are long in India. As the country's consumer manufacturing sector develops, the United States and other Asian investors are wary of product piracy, recurring problems of the Enron and Kentucky Fried Chicken type, equitable access to politically protected markets, and India's tendency to dominate regional trade. It remains to be seen what India's reaction will be if investors (particularly from Southeast Asia) begin to see the potential of Sri Lanka, Bangladesh, and Nepal as cost-efficient manufacturing centers for their own consumer products if the ultimate destination of those products is India.

All of this takes place on a more worldly stage than India has been accustomed to. India's development into a market economy coincides with a period of unexpected problems in economies that once regarded themselves—as in the case of Japan, Korea, and Singapore—as invincible. World trade volume is forecast to grow 8.5–9 percent a year through 1998. The World Bank estimates India's 1994–2003 growth rate to be 5.5 percent, compared with East Asia's 7.6 percent and the G7 countries' 2.5 percent. U.S. growth is expected to be around 2.5–3 percent, as the dollar stimulates exports and counteracts a further tightening of monetary policy. European

Union (EU) growth is predicted to be about 3 percent per year through 1999.

Amid this international economic environment, India's economy appears stable enough to sustain steady GDP real growth averaging 5.5 percent a year between 1996 and 2000.[1] This expansion will be driven by export and investment growth as India's reforms gather momentum. The most important effect for overseas investors will be rapidly increasing import demand, especially for capital goods. The balance of payments will thus show some deterioration, with the trade debt rising from $3.2 billion in 1994 to $7.5 billion in 1997. On the other hand, in percentage terms, the current account balance is predicted to remain about the same as its 1995 rate of minus 2.2 percent through 1997. India should not have the pressures financing its current account debt that Malaysia and Thailand have.

The need to finance such a sizable budget deficit will fuel inflation. However, at a time when fiscal restraint—particularly in the public sector—is needed to curb excessive demand and rising interest rates, Indian politicians have consistently demonstrated that they will set aside economic restraint in favor of political promises.

ECONOMIC REFORM AND THE FUTURE OF DEMOCRACY

To read the news accounts, over the past few years India has become more difficult to govern. Scare headlines abound about Enron, KFC, air disasters, strikes, and political leaders being investigated. While it is inevitable that corruption stories will get more press than the innovative but dull details of India's remarkable economic turnaround, governability is indeed a divisive issue for India's social conservatives and economic liberals alike. Both point to a common set of symptoms:

- politicization of the bureaucracy;
- corruption of the electoral process;
- decline of the effectiveness of Parliament;
- low confidence in government and elections;
- powerless policies of the unfunded mandate type;
- criminalization of political power.

Note that these are all political in origin, not economic. Some critics say that these failings demonstrate that India will go the same way as coalition governments elsewhere, that a significant improvement in the quality of governance will forever elude the country. Others say that the political system will degenerate to where India becomes the Italy of Asia, paralyzed by chronic political instability, an ineradicably corrupt ruling elite, and the economic performance of a world backwater.

Others offer a more optimistic outlook. They see India's tackling corruption through the court system as the beginning of an Italian-style "Clean Hands" shakeup. They see India rejuvenating its historical role as a center of ideas and influence uniquely its own, and point to the intellectual ideas and expressive art coming from India's globalized new middle class as the first swallow of India's spring.

Note again the political character of the pessimist argument and the moral/cultural character of the optimists'. Some analysts outside either of these camps interpret the political fallout from economic reform quite differently in a scenario interpreted as a federalizing reaction to the centralization of the last five decades:

- The states will acquire much more power and autonomy.
- Larger religio-ethnic groups will develop their own accountable self-governing councils.
- A network of self-governing democratic institutions will span districts and villages.

There are common features to all three of these interpretations of India's future:

- They are idealistic and vague to the point where partial success can be claimed as achievement.
- They hearken back to the ancient days of the Vajjian republics of 700 B.C. when much of India was a string of self-governing units.
- They can be seeds of great rigidity and conflict if translated into partisan terms.

Combined into one theme, these three features are a picture of a polity that idealizes a far-distant past era of peace and wisdom that was later corrupted by institutionalized power. This in a nutshell is one of the fundamental themes of the Indian view of history as it really works. It appears as far back as the *Vedas* and *Upanishads* of Hinduism, in the philosophy of the Buddha, in the more recent Vedanta movements, and in the ideal state proposed by Nehru.

This theme can also be found in the present government. The National Front–Left Front (NF–LF) coalition embraces many reforms in principle, but must yield to the power grasp of two of its constituents. The Janata Dal faction opposes giving priority to foreign investors in key areas such as infrastructure building; they want the multinationals to supplement and not supplant the state's leading role. The Janata Dal favors restricting entry of multinationals into India and opposes "indiscriminate globalization."

The Communist Party (CP) wants to reverse what it calls "unbridled liberalization" by opposing the privatizing of the public sector, which happens to be its power base. The CP believes that there should be an end to preferential treatment for foreign investors, and that the entry of foreign capital should be decided on the basis of national priorities and technology needs.

Even within the reformist spirit of today's government, there are powerful factions that still think in terms of an idealized past creating a future power base for themselves.

Reading Between the Lines of India's Common Minimum Programme

It is important that the foreign business person learn how to read the subtle signals emanating from India's leaders. There are several recent examples of the kind of clues to watch for.

Foreign institutions will continue to be encouraged to invest, although the highest preference—as has been the case for 5 years now—is for FDI in the core areas of technology and infrastructure. Although the CPM seems to discourage FDI in low-priority areas such as consumer goods, existing projects are free to expand. While infrastructure and technology will certainly make the greatest impact on the long-term structure of India's economy, a consumer boom is likely to have longer term consequences, most of them social.

Indian economists have an unworded fear that savings will drain out of the economy to such a degree that it forces the government into financing by debt and equity instruments with which it is unfamiliar. Nearly all of the political groups favor increased foreign investment specifically because Indians are saving less and spending more than they used to. Unlike the economies of East and Southeast Asia, where the savings rate approaches 40 percent of the GDP (sometimes, as in the case of Singapore, by government-enforced savings plans), the Indian savings rate has fallen from an estimated 24 percent of the GDP to 22 percent between 1991 and

1996.[2] There has been an upsurge in purchases among even the lowest income groups, but there has not yet been a commensurate upsurge in their earning power.

Against this, Finance Minister Chidambaram has fought hard to insert into the Common Minimum Programme policies that will result in more efficiency and competition in the economy. In the past such policies were not hard to implement because they targeted domestic businesses. But if they target workers in the state-owned sector and vested interests such as the *babus* (traders) and farmers, the coalition can easily have problems.

The farming sector is India's perennially indulged child. India's land reforms are based on simultaneously implementing industrial liberalization and promoting agribusiness and horticulture. The ultimate effect will be a more advanced industrial state than Manmohan Singh dared propose. Mr. Gowda's pledge was to "review immediately and abolish all controls and regulations that are in the way of increasing the income of farmers." No one was defined on a region-by-region basis exactly what these were. The Common Minimum Programme says only that it will step up the rate of investment in agriculture to "ensure that farmers get a decent price for their products." If high value-added agricultural production increases and exports of farm products are boosted, the consumer revolution that has already modestly begun in rural India could transform the countryside dramatically.

That is the theory. The reality is that the farming sector has been notoriously unreliable at turning its government-given largesse into increased productivity. More subsidized irrigation water seems to go into the soil than into fruit and rice. India's rural sector, especially in the north, is plagued with a politician/rich farmer/thug-enforcer coalition that has turned Bihar, for example, into one of the great wastelands of humanity. For nearly all of low-caste rural India, the phrases from the Finance Ministry might as well be from another planet.

Given Gowda's 1996 electoral sops to rich farmers in the form of subsidies and higher procurement prices, it would appear that there is a danger of tilting the terms of trade too much in favor of an agriculture sector that has girded itself against meaningful change. Yet Mr. Gowda knew how to deal with these people. He stirred a hornets' nest in 1995 when he sought to unilaterally amend land-ceiling legislation in Karnataka. Tucked away in the back corners of his speeches were subtle statements about "stepping up outlays on rural development for casual wage employment," "poverty amelioration programmes," and "attracting FDI to rural infrastructure." These are code for private-sector investments in rural India. The government knows that agrarian populism will bankrupt state treasuries and stoke national inflationary fires. Hence the Common Minimum Programme is an aptly self-effacing name for a program that, between the lines, has much subtle dynamism. Investors and arriving business people simply need to learn the code.

A Dramatically Changing Media Scene

Recent changes in India's media are a hidden revolution in a country long immured to a puppydog press.

Indians take great pride in intellectual attainment. Having a reputation for being well informed carries as much cachet in business circles as a degree from a good school. Despite the 50–million size of India's television-owning populace, Indians in the know get their knowledge and facts from the newspapers and weeklies. The quality and vivacity of India's political and business writing comes as a surprise to first-time visitors. Daily news and commentary fare are matched in the West only by *The Economist, Financial Times, Le Monde,* and *Allgemeine Frankfurter.* In-depth coverage and analysis in India's business press far exceed anything emanating from the government-dominated presses of Southeast and East Asia.

While the explosion of satellite and cable television has received much attention in the Western press, its influence in India is largely imagistic— again the preference in India for the fancied to the fact. The print media, on the other hand, have undergone a quieter revolution. Much of it is related to their growth and economic performance. Many established players such as *The Times* are far larger and richer than they were a decade ago. Yet it seems that every aspiring tycoon now wants a publishing arm. New entrants have flourished, and more are mooted regularly in the business press.

Economic liberalization has brought its changes here, too. India's serious press, in the main, was talking reform long before the politicians were, so it is not surprising that they have made the most of it once it arrived. The most notable change is that the press is becoming more politically independent as it gets more powerful. It is also jettisoning self-imposed restraints that once lay at the heart of its aloof institutional image. In the past, eminent journalists interpreted the thinking of "the Centre" (in this context meaning the cabinet), "South Block" (the Ministry of External Affairs), and political heavyweights. Editors wrote stuffy analytical pieces that were heavy with academic jargon and references. Lighter articles tended to be anecdotes about government or military service.

This is now being seen as passé, even stodgy. The change of editorial posture is part of a larger course of changes in India's media culture all across the board. As the English-language press moves away from its cozy relationship with the political and bureaucratic establishment, its traditional dominance is being challenged by the rise of Indian-language newspapers, notably in northern India's vast Hindi-speaking belt. The total circulation of Hindi-language dailies moved past that of their English-language counterparts in the early 1990s, and appears set to pull further ahead.

Most of the big English-language papers were started or acquired decades ago by rich *Marwaris*—members of the Rajasthani *babu* (trading) community that dominated trade and informal banking early this century. They respected the profession of journalism. Journalists enjoyed a social status almost akin to that of professors. It was often said that the editor of *The Times* was the most powerful person after the prime minister.

The early newspaper owners were also close to politicians, their links having been forged during the struggle for independence. The late G. D. Birla was a close friend and financial supporter of Mahatma Gandhi. Today his son, K. K. Birla, is both proprietor of *The Hindustan Times* (New Delhi's biggest-selling English daily) and a Congress party member of the *Rajya Sabha*,[3] Parliament's upper house.

A brief look at some of the details of recent developments in the Indian media establishment paints a vivid picture of the world view being adopted by India's business community as a whole.

Change has come quickly to the press since 1991. A new generation of proprietors has taken direct control in the three biggest media conglomerates: Samir Jain at Bennett, Coleman & Co., the owners of the Times of India group; Vivek Goenka at the *Indian Express*; and Shobhana Bhartia (K. K. Birla's daughter) at *The Hindustan Times*.

Samir Jain's distinctive stamp is the most obvious signal of the new era in India's newspaper industry. He shook up rivals by cutting the paper's cover price in New Delhi. After failing to organize a distributors' revolt, his competitors were forced to follow suit. He also closed venerable but unprofitable publications such as the *Illustrated Weekly of India*.

Much more future-forward was Jain's recruitment of marketing executives into senior *Times* editorial slots. Today's editorials in *The Times* and *The Economic Times* are sprinkled with marketing phrases like "brand extension" and "franchise." *The Times'* editor, Gautam Adhikari, has inaugurated other improvements as well. The paper now prints well-researched social exposes, notably a series on child labor. *The Times'* pages now carry more business news and more foreign news from international wire services.

One result is that *The Times* is no longer considered the newspaper to read for the most authoritative reports on government and politics, nor do many people feel that it leads the market in op-ed pieces and book and arts reviews. *The Times'* most successful circulation-booster is a weekly color insert called *E-Times*, which is full of gossip about film stars and the coming week's cable-television programs.

Whether this switch to a market-oriented format will show up on the bottom line is debatable. Jain cannot point to profit surge to justify his approach. In the decade 1948—1994, *The Times'* profits multiplied 110 times over revenues that had grown seven times. Yet the smaller *Hindustan Times*, which dominates English circulation in New Delhi, showed pretax profits of Rs 608 million ($17.4 million) on revenues of Rs 1.82 billion ($52 million) in 1994—without a *Times*-style change of face.

Business readers also have the *Business Standard*, published by the Calcutta publishing house Ananda Bazar Patrika (ABP)—which publishes a best-selling Bengali newspaper with the same name. Editorial quality is a *Business Standard* high point. ABPOs owner is Aveek Sarkar, whose English daily, *The Telegraph*, competes with Calcutta's *The Statesman*. He has steadily updated all of his papers with high-quality writing and news probity. Sarkar's business editor is T. N. Ninan, who previously built up the *Economic Times*. His tenure at *Business Standard* has seen the putting together of what many overseas businesspeople consider India's sharpest business and economic reporting team.

Circulation growth in the English papers has apparently plateaued somewhat and has become cannibalistic in the process. *The Economic Times* competes with *The Times of India* in New Delhi. Smaller papers include *The Pioneer*, brought to Delhi from its former home base in Lucknow by entrepreneur Lalit Thapar, and the *Business and Political Observer*, which Reliance Industries started in the 1980s. However, both of these have endured that common phenomenon in India—losing money after a promising initial success. *The Telegraph* evenly divides Calcutta's English readers with rival *The Statesman*. In most other cities, growth is stagnant or moderate, as with the *Deccan Herald* in Bangalore and *The Tribune* in Chandigarh.

Magazines were the fastest growing sector of English publishing in the 1970s and 1980s, notably with Ashok Advanit's *Business India* and Aroon Purie's *India Today*. New magazines are still coming into the market. The highly regarded editor Vinod Mehta started a weekly magazine called

Outlook with backing from Bombay real-estate and cable-television tycoon Rajan Raheja. South Indian corporate takeover specialist P. Rajarathinam is trying to revive the *Illustrated Weekly* (whose title was bought from Bennett, Coleman).

The fastest growing magazines specialize in the shares (stock) market. This reflects the astonishing amount of conversation one hears on the street on the subject of shares trading. An average ricksha-wallah will likely converse more authoritatively about the shares market than he will about India's cricket or popstar scenes. A big period of magazine growth in this sector came between the second half of 1993 and the second half of 1994—the Bombay-based *Capital Market*, for example, boosted its audited circulation 48.4 percent, to 82,000 copies.

General-purpose magazines, on the other hand, are under strong pressure from new television channels and the more interpretive, more imagistic, and less stodgy daily press. Established giants such as *India Today* and *Business India* have grown through translation into other Indian languages and diversification into video and audio entertainment.

The overall picture is saturation in the English press markets and increases in the regional languages where circulation growth parallels the rise in literacy. The growth in the regional-language press has been phenomenal. The Gujarati-language *Sandesh* expanded its circulation from 172,000 to 439,000 in 10 years. Bombay's Marathi-language *Navakal* was not even audited before 1988, but since then its sales have skyrocketed from 52,000 to 350,000. India's best-selling vernacular newspaper is *Malayala Manorama*, publishing 800,000 copies daily in the Malayalam language from the sleepy town of Kottayam (where local timber yards still use working elephants).

Supported by advertising from their regional governments, the vernacular papers do very well in their linguistic homelands. By contrast, newspapers in "stateless languages," such as the Urdu used by Muslims in northern India, have languished. The old elite in the north Indian Hindi-speaking belt conducted business and read the news in English, but a large part of the masses who spoke only Hindi were illiterate.

Indian-language papers are also less and less beholden to state politicians. State government advertising, once a lifeline that could be withdrawn at a politician's whim, is now a nuisance for the big papers, although it still can make or break many small papers in poorer states. The chief problem is that states want to pay very low, "old" rates (sometimes one-third or less of the current ones), and then are slow to pay.

The most financially powerful English or non-Hindi regional newspaper groups have seen the need to move beyond their core business. In 1995, *The Hindustan Times* established a television–software joint venture with Britain's Pearson group and Hong Kong's TV5. *Business India* has launched a 24–hour multichannel satellite-television service. The Tamil-language *Eenadu* has booked a satellite transponder and acquired rights to a library of old movies. In a noteworthy example of cross-media thinking for the future, *Eenadu* is setting up a "film city" outside Hyderabad.

Malayala Manorama is extending its empire beyond the confines of Kerala's Malayalam language. Its successful annual review sells 400,000 copies in English, Malayalam, Bengali, and Hindi. The group's English-language *The Week* is now the best-selling weekly magazine in India, with 77,000 copies sold. (Rivals such as *India Today* are fortnightly.) *Manorama* has plans to launch a new magazine aimed at farmers, and its women's magazine, *Vanitha*, will be translated into Hindi. Overall, the strategy of the vernacular press is to attack a market instead of waiting for it to come.

How This Press Sees Reforms

Although political views tinge everyone's interpretation of the 1991 reforms, there is a broad consensus about their historical significance. This is generally the picture being painted in the press about reforms today.

Two events forced Prime Minister Rao's reforms in 1991: an ideological shift among elite sections of Indian society in favor of reform, and a specific cash-flow crisis that demonstrated the consequences if reforms were not inaugurated. During the 1980s, many Indian economists, bureaucrats, politicians, and journalists began to call for an overhaul of India's command economy. The collapse of the Soviet Union devastated many people's faith that socialism would solve history's economic disparities.

In 1991, India's government had been expanding more or less continuously since Independence. It had taxed as much as it could. It had borrowed as much as it could. By 1991, the point had come where India might have to default on its international obligations. Foreign exchange reserves were next to zero. The budget deficit had soared. Inflation was rising.

When reforms came, they came hurriedly. Prime Minister Narasimha Rao's finance minister, Manmohan Singh, devalued the rupee and largely abolished the "License Raj," in which anyone desiring to set up or change a business had to get a government license. He slashed import tariffs from a maximum of 300 percent in 1991 to 50 percent four years later and abolished most import-licensing. He ended the monopoly of the public sector in power, roads, ports, aviation, and telecoms by inviting private and foreign investments. He liberalized foreign investment rules. His policy was to reverse the old Nehruvian obsession with self-sufficiency and integrate India into the interactive world economy.

Prime Minister Rao appointed locally based committees to propose reforms on the financial sector, the public sector, and taxation. Although those proposals in fact followed World Bank–IMF suggestions, Indians felt they were debating Indian proposals made by Indian committees.

Opposition parties and the populist media denounced these measures as an IMF plot. They claimed that India would suffer a "lost decade," as had happened in Africa and Latin America in the 1980s. Instead, India's growth slumped its way through 1991 but then quickly rebounded. The rapidity of its recovery made it easier for fence-sitting politicians to hop down on the side of reform.

When the Rao reforms began, many people realized that it would not be enough to reform the central government alone. Much economic activity in India came under the jurisdiction of the states. Some were ruled by parties espousing command economy or socialist policies. Yet these also saw the need to reform. One reason was that their own finances were as bad as the Centre's (and they still are). Some states began privatizing industries under their jurisdiction.

However, political pressures ensured that subsidies in many troublesome areas were maintained. The result today is that India's liberal consensus is intact but muddled. Still, all three of India's major parties are now united behind three propositions they see as politically inviolable:

- Liberalization must continue in order to attract private and foreign investments; without them, the state the public sector will no longer be able to control the economy.

- To survive politically, India must continue subsidizing the causes of influential lobbies, acknowledging that these could inadvertently bankrupt the exchequer.

- India cannot significantly liberalize its labor policies, allow firms to lay off unneeded workers, or close loss-making firms.

Unhelpful as this mix is likely to be in turning India into an economic tiger, there is a political (if not economic) expediency binding all three elements to the medium future.

However, such political accommodations mean that almost all of India's states will not have enough revenue to invest in education, health, and nutrition. As the East Asian tigers have shown, this trinity is vital for growth. Without expanded education, India cannot create a more productive workforce; without rural investment, agriculture will not flourish. If public investment in roads, power, bridges, water supply, and irrigation suffers, so will industrial development.

Normally these would be considered ideal opportunities for the private sector. Indeed, the private sector is stepping in with power plants and telecoms, and often getting badly burned in the process. This means that it will be more difficult to interest the private sector in areas like rural roads, power, and new classrooms and books.

It is the third point in the above consensus—no sackings—that poses the biggest problem. An enormous amount of capital is tied up in unprofitable factories, and most are in the public sector. In most burgeoning market economies, these are remorselessly liquidated and their assets, labor included, redeployed more productively. However, the Indian government is terrified of antagonizing trade unions, who are voluble, volatile, media savvy, and have no hesitation in whipping up the blind emotions that undergird so much of India's labor activity. Hence the government has done nothing to liberalize labor laws or speed up exit procedures.

Presently India's public sector ties up more than one-half of the country's industrial capital. Ironically, the competition brought in by reform will drive more of them toward insolvency—raising the very likely prospect that "foreigners" will be blamed for India's social ills. While the 1991 reforms made the private sector more dynamic and efficient, they also revealed the dreadful inefficiency of the public sector. The implication for foreign investors is that they are likely to be blamed for India's social problems, yet not likely to be given due credit for its improved economy.

Are Reforms Reversible?

In June of 1996, India's voters sent a clear message to the country's political leaders: They did not want any one party dominating the political scene. The majority of Parliament members they voted in were in favor of reforms. Their message was: Whichever group holds power, and whatever the rhetoric, the reforms must continue.

The voters had reached the end of their patience with corruption. They were aware—probably more than most politicians—that reducing fiscal profligacy is the government's biggest challenge. That could only be done if there is more transparency and decentralization in economic policy.

Today the majority of Indians concede that continuing the reforms begun in 1991 is mandatory. The record of center-left parties in government suggests that they are less unfriendly to business than their words might suggest. A clue to their real behavior is that the states ruled by these parties have aggressively implemented reforms to attract greater foreign direct investment. West Bengal, Andhra Pradesh, Bihar, and Karnataka—all ruled by parties that would dominate a center-left coalition—have in fact implemented reforms related to (a) privatizing state-owned enterprises, (b) privatizing infrastructure, and (c) deregulating laws governing restrictions on land ownership.

To take an example, the success story of the software industry in Bangalore is partly the result of Deve Gowda's pragmatic socialist policies during the time he was chief minister of Karnataka state. His record suggests that there is a clear understanding within the NF–LF of the value of developing and nurturing business, especially companies through which India can compete on a global level. Before the 1996 elections, the Marxist-led government of West Bengal was more aggressive in implementing reforms than even the Congress-ruled states.

The Gowda government said that India needs foreign investments of at least $10 billion a year to sustain its GDP growth of 6 percent or more. Whether that was actually the case or not, no government can afford to jeopardize inflows of FDI. Even a Marxist-led coalition will be responsive to market conditions in India and abroad.

Hence the momentum of India's growing integration into the global economy may be momentarily slowed by temporary conditions up to and including a change in prime ministers; with the size of growing consumer demand, the consumer voting bloc, and the middle class's dominance of the media, it is very unlikely to be halted or reversed. No government can survive without addressing the consumerism of Indians of all income levels, despite the pain that reforms engender.

Discrimination against Western firms might possibly occur, but that will not deter other Asian companies, certainly not the investments to which Japanese and South Korean firms have committed themselves. With Japan being India's largest aid donor and New Delhi's "Think East" foreign economic policy finding favor with all of the political parties, ties with entrepreneurs from ASEAN countries and Japan, South Korea, Taiwan, and Hong Kong will continue to strengthen.

That no single party won a clear mandate in the 1996 elections introduced a force of pragmatism in politics that will exert a sobering pressure on any particular faction that threatens to get out of hand.

Can Economy Threaten Democracy?

India is highly unlikely to become an economic tiger of the Southeast Asian–type. It is much more likely to muddle along with its current growth rate of 5–6 percent. It is not impossible that Indian politicians might one day take the easy way out and disengage themselves from sustained reform. If today's bad habits like parties buying themselves votes with populist giveaways continue, there looms almost certain bankruptcy combined with stagflation.

This possibility raises the Indian voter's view of the relationship between economy and democracy. Already some businessmen and reformers blame democracy for their woes. While their excuses may be intricate, the fact is that they do not know how to live without being coddled. Since political pressures related to India's long history of coddling create the largest demand for subsidies and specialized treatment, some analysts feel that Indian democracy may be vulnerable.

On balance it appears that such thinking is alarmist. India has several long-established self-centering mechanisms that keep consensus on the rails—rocking, reeling, and screaming all the way, perhaps, but still on them. For one, India allows all parties a chance at power, and the post-1996 political line-up gave even the sharpest of political pundits some surprises. It would have seemed unimaginable, for example, six months before the votes were counted that Deve Gowda's face would be smiling from the windows of 1 Janapath Marg, New Delhi.

In addition, since 1991, there has been a consistent record of parties attacking reform in opposition and then embracing it once in power. The same democracy that competes so vigorously in election-year giveaways also sets limits on the process after the votes are in. Once in office, politicians suddenly become acute to the clap of doom that awaits if they lose control of inflation.

Most people have by now concluded that, while India's political system may produce slower growth than some of the authoritarian countries of East Asia, democracy will in the long term provide the surer foundation for Indian-style growth. In the short term, India's volubly populist democracy may impede growth. But political populism is directly proportional to political pluralism. In the long term, all of those "p"s in "political populism" and "political pluralism" are likely to merge into the one "p" in "pragmatism."

SOCIAL ISSUES

Demographic Trends

The main contributor to India's population growth has been the country's sharply declining death rate. Life expectancy has increased by 50 percent, from 41 years in the 1950s to about 59 years in 1996; it is expected to rise slowly but steadily to about age 60–61 by the year 2001.

More of this population lives in towns and cities than ever before. In 1951, only 17.3 percent of the population was urban; in 1991 (the year the last national census was taken), it was 25.7 percent. By the year 2001, an estimated 30 percent of the population will live in cities.

The 1991 population was 51.9 percent male and 48.1 percent female. As with much of Asia there is a strong Indian preference for male children, especially in the rural areas, since boys are supposed to grow up to be providers for their parents in old age while girls are supposed to have little time for anything but their husbands. This is one reason why the rural market is poor for products for young girls, good for domestic nondurables for housewives, and quite good for products that ease the travails of the day.

For the next few decades, the population will increase most among the 15–59 age group, India's prime consumers. This group is expected to grow at an average rate of 2.7 percent per year between 1996 and 2001, at which time it will comprise 57.7 percent of the population. The next largest group, from birth to age 15, is surging because of declining birth rates and greater life expectancies. Its proportion is expected to age upward from 36.8 percent of the population in 1992 to 35.7 percent in 2001. The 60–and-over group will grow about the same rate as the overall population and thus retain its present proportion of 6.2 percent.

The economic condition of the average Indian seems destined to improve no matter which political powers hold office. The origins of what they are able to buy, on the other hand, are vulnerable to the political winds. Per-capita real GDP growth increased to 3.5 percent in the 1980s, 2.5 times the 1.4 percent rate of 1951–1980.

Growth of about 6 percent per year is anticipated in quality-of-life aspects of the economy. India's populace is increasingly a younger, more affluent, and more educated one—with the glaring exception of the already poverty-stricken countryside. In general, though, literacy rates increased to 52 percent in 1990–1991 from 18 percent in 1950–1951, and there was a sharp drop in the poverty level from 48.3 percent of the population in 1978 to 28 percent in 1991, with a corresponding increase of affluence in the cities. Per-capita income in the countryside is likely to rise more slowly than in urban areas. Since low literacy is related to population pressure on the school system, low employment will continue to burden rural sectors the most.

These facts translate to a rural consumer market that is dominated by intense price competitiveness among rapid-turnover nondurables—almost exactly the opposite as the urban picture. Given that India's middle class and its rural sectors have approximately the same aggregate amount of disposable cash, yet with a 100 million to 600 million size differential between them, product marketers are faced with a fundamental choice about which sector they should focus on.

The Demographics of Urbanization

India's population density is high, at an average of twenty-five persons per square mile. Large areas of the country are heavily populated, many overly so. Approximately 75 percent of the population still lives in rural areas, scattered throughout more than 500,000 villages, but urban centers have grown dramatically in recent years. City growth has been exceptionally high. The population of greater Mumbai rose from some 6 million in 1971 to over 13 million in 1995. Over the same period, the population of New Delhi doubled to approximately 8.5 million, and Calcutta increased by one-third to 12 million. Chennai, Hyderabad, and Bangalore each have approximately 5 million inhabitants.

With gradual improvements in the standard of living, changes in India's demographic profile have been taking place rather quickly. An increasing proportion of the population is entering the productive age group. Better medical facilities and higher educational standards have contributed to an increase in life expectancy and a drop in infant mortality rates. Given the size of the population, improvements will continue to be gradual, with different parts of the country developing at different rates. Government resources are inadequate to meet the social welfare needs of the large and growing population.

The benefits of development will percolate down, but the process will be slow. Poverty will continue to affect large sections of the population. Population growth and illiteracy will continue to be major concerns. This problem is probably more acute than the overall growth rate indicates, because the population growth rate is faster in the poorer sections of society, where there is likely to be little softening impact from education and social change.

Population growth will continue to eat into the benefits of economic development. This will make it more difficult to alleviate, let alone eliminate, poverty. India's democratic structure makes it difficult for the government to enforce population control. Coercion and incentive programs have backfired in the past, and the government has little choice but to resort to education and gentle persuasion to achieve changes in attitude. Attitudes are very hard to change in a land where children are seen to be a blessing and also one's chief protectors in old age.

Over time, as education and medical standards improve and the standard of living goes up, the attraction of large families will diminish. Urbanization and the trend toward later marriages and a nuclear family will contribute to bringing down the birth rate, but substantive improvement will be gradual at best. Population growth is expected to raise India's population surpassing China's at 1.3 billion each about 2015.

Development is likely to be increasingly skewed toward urban areas now that investment is no longer being forced into less-developed areas by government licensing policies. Gujarat, Karnataka, Maharashtra, and Tamil Nadu are likely to continue developing more rapidly than other states. There are already wide differences between states in levels of income and education, which only concentrates development in areas with more of both.

Infrastructure development also varies considerably between states. Investment will flow more and more into the states that provide the most investor-friendly environment, meaning overall living conditions and the availability of trained manpower in addition to infrastructure excellence. State policies aimed at attracting investments vary in strength and nature from state to state, with Orissa, Andhra Pradesh, and Rajasthan being less effective in attracting investments. As the more developed regions become saturated and the cost of doing business in them increases, business investments will move to the lower cost regions. This may turn out to be a very gradual phenomenon.

Agriculture is and will continue to be the main source of employment in rural areas. Urbanization will continue despite the problems of overcrowding and congestion in the cities, and indeed, worsening them considerably. This will aggravate unemployment and the already onerous problems of urban squatting, and with these urban crime and unrest.

Nevertheless, the basic structure of Indian society and its historical reliance on family values will provide a degree of stability that makes the threat of disintegration very unlikely. The exploitation of caste-based politics by politicians in many states will probably continue to keep class and ethnic tensions simmering along despite economic change. On the other hand, the remarkable nonviolence of the 1996 elections is a very encouraging sign, since these could have easily been fanned into flash points. The fact that the 1996 *hawala* (bribery) scandal erupted just before them and tarred just about every party with the same brush may have had a lot to do with the benignity of the elections. Indeed, some wags commented on Doordarshan TV that what the nation really needed was more illustrative scandals.

The Caste System

Many divisions exist within Indian society, due largely to linguistic, caste, ethnic, and religious differences. The constitution recognizes nineteen regional languages, although English is the official business, legal, and political language. Hindi is widely spoken in the north. Over 80 percent of the population is Hindu, with Muslims forming the largest minority at 11 percent. Other minorities include Sikhs, Buddhists, Jains, Parsees, and Christians.

The caste system is a social hierarchy that transcends religious and economic differences. Indian society divides into upper caste Brahmins and Ksatriyas, through Vaishyas and Shudras in the middle, down to a huge underclass of laborers known as untouchables. Although the system has been officially outlawed for more than 30 years, caste still exerts a powerful influence on Indian life that neither the growth of mass education nor the spread of radio and television has been able to erode. People classified as lower caste are most prevalent in the south of the country, where they make up an estimated 75 percent of the Hindu population, compared with a national average of 52 percent.

The system presents the lower castes with a choice: They can either accept their social status or they can make the best use of their "backwardness" to take advantage of the complicated affirmative action programs that have been in force since the early days of Independence. Six levels of "backwardness" are recognized, and a percentage of government jobs and places in higher education are reserved for each. The Supreme Court imposed a total reservation ceiling of 50 percent in 1990, but this has not prevented state politicians from manipulating the system to lure the votes of the lower castes.

However, their gains have not been of much benefit to the mass of untouchables who, in general, remain in a state of extreme poverty and who have garnered less than a 10 percent share of the government jobs.

The Increasing Electoral Power of the Scheduled Castes

The 1996 election reinforced the growing political assertiveness of the lower castes. The election of Phoolan Devi—the so-called "Bandit Queen"—was a highly mediagenic example of a fundamental shift of voting pattern. There are several reasons for phenomenon like Devi's election, well beyond her admittedly formidable personality and quasi-legendary status (she gang-murdered twenty-four upper caste men who gang-raped her). They are certainly a result of a weakening of Congress's organizing capacity in the country and hence its ability to mobilize its supporters—the lower castes took many a leaf from the Congress notebook on local political organization.

Another is the cross-cultural character of the *dalit* political message. The party has always seen itself as representing a purely secular tradition that seeks to replace the interests of different religions and sections of society with economic unity. Until 1996, to many Indians the *dalits* stood for big government and large-scale patronage, which Congress had amply proven to be a fount of corruption.

Separatism

Regional strife remains a constant threat to the tenuous national cohesion that binds India together. These are of largely academic interest to business travelers, since they are rarely allowed into India's political hot spots. The case of the five European backpackers who were captured and displayed by a previously unknown terrorist group and who were eventually murdered is something the Indian government does not want to see repeated.

The far northern region of Kashmir between India and Pakistan has been a thorn in the side of Indian governments virtually since Independence. Attempts to quell armed insurrections have intensified the alienation felt by the local population.

Insurrections in Assam and the surrounding northeastern states began in the early 1970s. A negotiated settlement with Assamese nationalists was reached in 1992, but sporadic violence still persists.

In the Punjab, Sikh pressure for greater autonomy prompted an eruption of violence in 1984. The prime minister, Indira Gandhi, responded by using government troops to storm the holiest of Sikh shrines, the Golden Temple at Amritsar. Fighting intensified and, in October 1984, Mrs. Gandhi was assassinated by her Sikh bodyguards. In recent years, the situation in the Punjab has calmed considerably and an uneasy peace now prevails.

More recently, an upsurge of Hindu militancy among supporters of the opposition Bharatiya Janata Party (BJP) in late 1992 led to the destruction of a Muslim mosque in Ayodhya in Uttar Pradesh. (This incident is often referred to as "the Babri Mosque" in the press.) This led to large-scale religious rioting throughout the country and a series of bomb blasts in Mumbai. Presented with India's most serious political crisis since Independence, the government immediately dismissed all BJP-controlled state governments and banned three Hindu organizations associated with the party. The BJP has since been successful in state elections, suggesting that sustained, and violent, Hindu opposition to the government is unlikely to recur.

Human Development

At current rates of progress, India is expected to reach 1996 levels of human development by about the year 2100. Presently, India's ranking is 135 out of 174 in the United Nations Human Development Report of 1996, barely ahead of the African countries but behind most other Asian countries.

Approximately 400 million people have no access to clean water. More than 400 million live below the poverty line of income necessary to maintain a survival caloric intake. About 30 percent of babies are born with low birth weights, compared with 12 percent in Thailand and 17 percent in Ghana. India spends less than 1 percent of its gross national product on health care, compared with 2.4 percent in Brazil and 2.8 percent in Jamaica. Indians own about 78 radios and 7 television sets per 1,000 people; in neighboring Sri Lanka, there are 191 radios and 31 television sets per 1,000; in Mexico, there are 241 radios and 120 televisions. There is no social security system or comprehensive national health service. Small district hospitals function in intense heat without air-conditioned operating theaters or intensive care units.

To put India's economic condition into consumer-class terms, about 200 million people live in reasonable comfort, 200 million live uncomfortably reasonably, and the rest live in hell. There is no political linkage between economic growth and human development. The fruits of growth do not trickle in the direction of human development—it is, after all, difficult to develop when there is a need to accommodate 17 million new people in the school system alone.

A higher economic baseline is critical to the country's humanity baseline. Unless India can provide a minimal baseline of health, nutrition, and physical well-being among its people, it will not be able to contain the social disruption that is inevitable with the 1991 and 1996 reforms. Countries like South Korea, Malaysia, and Poland, who improved the physical quality of life of their people to a higher threshold, did so because they successfully reformed archaic laws and bureaucracies.

Virtually all successful developing countries have seen the relationship between higher economic growth and slower population growth. As *Business India* editorialized in August 1996, "Participating in a borderless world economy makes no sense with a largely illiterate, ill-fed, and ill healthy workforce." Between 1975 and 1989, although economic growth in India averaged 5 percent, employment growth lagged at only 2 percent. Today India has entered a faster growth track of 7 percent per annum, but the majority of jobs that have been generated are still largely in agriculture and in the urban unorganized sectors.

India has excellent economists, but they rarely talk to the poor. There is little government concern with the future of the great majority of India's people. India's political and business establishment is bent on burnishing India's technological, middle-class image, but is leaving the largest part of India's populace out of the future. A few intellectually elect will enter the bright utopian future, while the rest are doomed by embarrassment over their ignorance. It sounds like Calvin talking about heaven.

To the investing business person, India's unseen majority should not be left out amid their plans and projections. The population is growing fastest in areas where caste/money/land tensions are the worst, and technical prowess tends to exacerbate these tensions instead of offer solutions to them. A steadily enlarging pool of unemployed youth is manipulated by politicians to intimidate voters by swelling cheering crowds at their own rallies and jeering crowds at opponents'. India's youthful mobs are becoming larger, more ubiquitous, and more unruly. As *The New York Times'* India correspondent, Barbara Crossette, put it in her excellent study, *India—Facing the Twenty-First Century*, "The thousands of boys and young men trucked into Delhi by the Congress Party to march in Rajiv Gandhi's funeral procession in May 1991 turned the somber cremation site into a travesty of grief, jumping on the pyre platform to wave at television cameras and causing dignitaries and friends of the Gandhi family to scatter."

India's low level of per-capita income cannot be turned into yet another excuse for not trying to reach even the minimal thresholds of human development.

The States' Dire Straits

Virtually every state in India is close to fiscal insolvency. The reasons are mainly their failure to cut administrative expenses, ballooning subsidies promised before elections, and the chronic losses of state public-sector units (PSUs). The worst affected are West Bengal, Uttar Pradesh, Orissa, Kerala, and Rajasthan, where the expenditure/revenue gap is between 10 and 18 percent. Some signs of the extent of their troubles are as follows:

- Between 1991 and 1995, the overall debt of the states doubled to Rs 212,029 crore ($606 billion), nearly one-fifth of India's GDP.
- The states paid out interest of Rs 22,304 crore ($6.4 billion) on loans from the Centre and financial markets; this averaged 36 percent of state revenues in 1995–1996.
- As of June 1996, the states were unable to meet their administrative and other day-to-day expenditures from their earnings and were compelled to borrow funds for their current consumption; 26 percent of all state borrowings are now used for administrative purposes, up from 7 percent in 1985–1986.
- Budgets for 1995–1996 of all the states indicate that, on an average, their tax and nontax revenues fell 7 percent short of their budgeted expenses for government salaries and maintaining social and education services.

The states have five main sources of income. Their taxes contribute 35 percent of their revenues. Nontax state revenues (charges for electricity, earnings from state PSUs, and the like) contribute another 12 percent. Seventeen percent comes from their share of the Centre's income tax and excise duties. Grants and loans from the Centre make up another 26 percent. Market borrowings (4 percent) and miscellaneous sources account for the rest.

The expenses of India's states are high. They must bear the cost of running their own governments and providing essential social and economic services such as health care and electricity. They are also required to invest in infrastructure. Until about 1985–1986, they raised enough income to meet their expenses—most, in fact, enjoyed modest surpluses. After that, taking the lead from the Rajiv Gandhi government's "expenditure-induced growth" notion, the states began ignoring fiscal prudence. Overspending at the Centre was imitated by profligacy at the state level. Surpluses declined, forcing them to borrow more to meet their budgetary targets. By 1991–1992, all of the states were in debt.

Instead of reining in their administration costs, they allowed them to increase by 21 percent per year, against income growth of only 17–18 percent. Bihar, Punjab, Uttar Pradesh, and West Bengal diverted Centre funds intended for nonadministrative services to pay their staff salaries.

The two main reasons for their problems are reckless populism and mismanagement. It is difficult for state political leaders to increase taxes after so many promises of handouts. Moreover, the states are burdened by pressures from various lobbies. This prevents them from fully utilizing their tax potential. In Maharashtra, the government lost revenues of about Rs 250 crore ($71.4 million) by abolishing additional sales and turnover taxes after pressure from the persistent demands of chambers of commerce and industry associations. Promises to convert the existing sales tax into a value-added tax have borne neither fruit nor revenues.

Another reason for mounting state expenditure is a sharp upswing in the salaries and allowances of state government employees. Overall, salaries and allowances of state employees increased by approximately 11 percent in 1995–1996. In the remote northeastern states and Bihar, state employee wages and allowances were 120 percent of their revenues.

Most states have made little attempt to raise their revenue targets. In 1994–1995, they raised 41.4 percent of the resources they were supposed to raise during the eighth plan period (1992–1997). Their tax revenues—about one-third of their total incomes—grew at a slower pace; in fact, revenue growth slowed from 16 percent in the 1980s to 15 percent in 1996.

One obvious consequence is that state governments pay higher interest rates on market loans—12 percent versus 9.6 percent on Centre loans—adding further to their debt burden.

The states allege that they are in these straits because the Centre prefers to give income-tax concessions and raise administered prices instead of increasing the excise duties it must share with the states. Receipts from 1995–1996 excise duties increased only by 10 percent while those from customs duties surged by 32 percent—not surprising, charge the states, since these are fully assigned to the Centre.

Although Kerala has tried to set its house in order, most states claiming to have reduced the gap between their expenditures and incomes have simply cut back on essential social services. Little attempt has been made to slow down subsidies, wage bills, and maintenance expenses, nor has much been done to streamline tax policies. The upshot is that both the states and the Centre can point the finger at each other instead of making sorely-needed changes to their own fiscal structures.

The States' Credit Ratings

India's states' credit ratings are based on models that loosely follow Moody's parameters. They are based on overall political and economic factors such as budget deficit, solvency, and the degree to which the state is encumbered by guaranteed commitments made on behalf of municipalities.

The practice of rating the states began in 1993, when Gujarat's Sardar Sarovar Narmada Nigam Ltd. wanted to market bonds to raise Rs 300 crore ($85.7 million) in 1994. Then the Rajasthan Industrial Development Corporation entered the market. Since then, three other state agencies have done the same.

The Investment Information and Credit Rating Agency (IICRA) completed its research on all states in November 1996. (Their ratings are replicated below.) The Credit Rating Information Service of India Limited (CRISIT) has now rated four states.

CRISIT has also been commissioned by the U.S. giants General Electric and J.P. Morgan to assess the creditworthiness of India's states.

The methodology for the rating the states is still being defined. Some economists believe that infrastructural and fiscal parameters should be given equal weight. Others give equal weight to political and economic risk factors. Whatever the methodology, with ratings beginning to matter more to investors, states will have little option but to be more open. With state governments tapping the capital markets more frequently, the need for these ratings is certain to increase in the future. (Table 1.1).

Table 1.1
Credit Ratings of India's States

All India:	AA–
State	**Rating**
Assam	BB
Rajasthan	BB
Orissa	BB
Madhya Pradesh	BB
Uttar Pradesh	BB
Bihar	BB
Andhra Pradesh	BBB
West Bengal	AA–
Maharashtra	AA
Karnataka	AA
Gujarat	AA
Tamil Nadu	AA+
Punjab	AA+
Kerala	AA+
Haryana	AA+

AAA = Highest safety; AA = High safety; A = Adequate safety; BBB = Moderate safety;
BB = Inadequate safety; B = High risk

State Finances and Economic Federalism

Stagnant revenues and galloping expenditures have led to a dramatic rise in the budget deficits of the twenty-six state governments. A 1995 research project conducted by the Reserve Bank of India on the state of the states' finances revealed that while their revenue deficits rose by 35.6 percent, the gross fiscal deficits of the states had surged by 17.5 percent over the same period, with the share of the former in the latter rising from 26.5 percent in 1994–1995 to 30.6 percent in 1995–1996. The consequences of these deficits are likely to be a fall in investments and a vicious circle of increasing debt.

By 1995–1996, the rate of growth of capital expenditure by the state governments had fallen to a mere 3.5 percent, compared with 18.6 percent in the previous year. Meanwhile, the combined debt of the state governments by the end of March 1996 was 15.2 percent higher than in 1995.

Between 1984–1985 and 1994–1995, the rate of growth of the revenue expenditure of the states was two percentage points higher than the rate of growth of their revenues. While the rate of growth of revenue expenditure rose from an average of 6 percent per annum between 1973–1974 and 1983–1984 to 6.8 percent between 1984–1985 and 1994–1995, the rate of growth of capital expenditures plummeted from an average of 7.6 percent per annum to 1.2 percent during the same period.

A systemic bottleneck throttles the buoyancy of revenues: The Constitution of India allows the states to levy a sales tax on goods but not on services. Even on goods, the state governments can levy a tax only at the first point of sale. Nontax revenues (which are typically charges for economic and social services, and dividends on their investments) are being eroded by rising costs and falling revenues.

How can the state governments pull themselves out of their debt/revenue cycle? Researchers at the National Institute of Public Finance & Policy have proposed five reforms that could rescue the states' finances by 2005:

- There must be a 2 percent cut in the growth of the state governments' expenditure by 2000.

- There must be an increase in the state sales tax base by switching to a value-added system and abolishing the sales tax on interstate sales.

- There must be a revision in the pricing of social and economic services to cover their costs. At present, the recovery rate in the case of state-provided social services is 3 percent of their costs; in the case of economic services, it is only 30 percent of the cost of provisions.

- Sinking funds must be set up by each state for the amortization of market loans irrespective of their revenue account positions; the amounts allocated to these funds should be invested in securities.

- A common pool of divisible taxes between the Centre and the states must be created so that the latter can benefit from the buoyancy in tax revenues.

The pattern of these suggestions implies that federalism is not merely a political ideal but an economic necessity.

Achieving Macroeconomic Balance

India's reforms thus far have only vacuumed the periphery of a house that really needs to be cleaned.

In 1991, the agenda for reform came under two major heads: macroeconomic balancing and economic restructuring. These mainly affected the private sector—organized industry, international trade, financial services, and taxation. Macroeconomic balance—meaning reductions in the fiscal deficit, improved controls on public expenditures, long-term inflation control, stable foreign exchange, and interest rates—have thus far eluded government.

This is primarily due to the inability of the government to control its spending, which in turn makes it difficult to proceed with further reforms in the financial sector such as denationalizing insurance. So long as government has easy access to these sources of finance, no amount of good intention will be implemented through policy.

An area of reform that could have helped improve macroeconomic management would have been a systematic attempt to improve the performance of state-owned enterprises. This would have required large-scale privatization and using the proceeds to reduce the public debt, which would have helped bring down interest costs. Instead, there has been marginal disinvestment of government equity in public enterprises, whose proceeds are used to bring down the government's deficit.

Small-scale industry also needs urgent attention. The adversarial relationship between small business and monopoly-seeking corporate behemoths continues. Little has been done to improve the quality of the infrastructure for small-scale industries, or to encourage them to become larger. Hence they have tended to develop in clusters. The result is industrial towns like Surat for chemicals and Bangalore for computers. Government policy has encouraged small-scale industries to split into amoeba-like new units when they reach the limits set by government for their incentives.

Agriculture has benefited by higher output prices for the major crops and the lifting of many movement restrictions both domestically and for export. However, many restrictions on imports, and continuing high tariffs on products like edible oils, have resulted in signals to farmers to grow crops for which their land is not always well suited, but whose prices are kept high. These price distortions have tended to move farmers to water-intensive crops because of the extremely low prices charged for water and the cheap power for agriculture. The result is depletion of ground water.

The infrastructure has also received poor attention. The delays in private investment taking over from public investment due to corruption and muddled government policies are well known. Little has been done to speed up road construction—an important barrier to private investment. Nor have major new ports received enough attention. This severely constrains India's ability to expand exports, in turn constraining industrial growth.

Above all, there has been no attention paid to reforming government itself. Government decision-making processes and delivery systems continue to be cumbersome, slow, and, at best, inefficient, if not corrupt. There is a plethora of ministries, departments, and agencies, resulting in poor decision making and implementation. For example, health, family welfare, and pharmaceuticals come under different departments of government, with poor coordination between the three. This is repeated on a much larger scale when it comes to agriculture, where both the Centre and the states have a multiplicity of agencies dealing with different aspects of the same problem.

There is no doubt that 1991 marked a revolution in India's economic policies. It has given a new sense of freedom to Indian entrepreneurs and industry. It has expanded the market. Tax collection has improved. The entry of new foreign and domestic investors must be leading to improvements in productivity, which will benefit the economy in the long run. By the standards of many other countries, Indian reforms have tapped only the fringes of what needs to be done if the country is to achieve its full potential.

POLITICAL OUTLOOK

In 1991, the Indian government abandoned several decades of social and economic protectiveness. Complaints will be vociferous for some time to come as vested interests fight to maintain what is left of their dwindling privileges. The Congress party has seen its monopoly of power erode inexorably since Independence, starting with the death of India's first prime minister, Jawaharlal Nehru, in 1964 and the assassinations of his daughter, Indira Gandhi, and her son, Rajiv Gandhi, in 1984 and 1991. The 1996 elections saw Congress out of power again, after two periods in 1977 and 1989, when the party lost to coalitions of regional and left-wing parties. Democratic rule itself faltered in 1975–1977, when Indira Gandhi suspended the Constitution and ruled by emergency decree.[4]

The 1996 general election resulted in three developments that are likely to have a substantial bearing on the shape of Indian politics over the next few years: (a) the declining influence of Hindu nationalism and the BJP party, (b) the rising power and influence of the *dalits* or Scheduled Castes, and (c) the gradual shift in decision-making influence on business investment matters from the national government to state governments.

The Dwindling of the BJP and Religious Parties

The 1996 elections saw a very brief 12 days in the sun for the Hindu nationalist Bharatiya Janata Party (BJP), which assumed the prime ministry and then as quickly receded into the opposition party. The BJP's candidate for prime minister, Atal Bihari Vajpayee, was invested and held office, and was ignominiously defeated in a no-confidence motion after a mere 12 days in office—India's briefest prime ministry in history.

The BJP was founded by militant Hindu activists and has had a sometimes violent history. Originally, it sought to overthrow secularism and turn India into a Hindu-dominated state espousing *hindutva* Hindu hegemonist values. After 1991, it modified its overt militancy and toned down some of its more extreme religious and cultural aims. Many felt that these merely lurked beneath the surface. (It is useful to recall that the crocodile was one of India's early fear totems.)

A more immediate cause was the BJP's association with the Shiv Sena party, an association of often quite violent Hindu activists who were behind the 1991 razing of the Babri Mosque in Ayodhya. The BJP's image was not improved by the negative international and local press response to the bombast of Bal Thackary, who was unelected figurehead of Shiv Sena and apologist for the so-called "saffron brigade," a following of saffron-robed Hindu "holy men" whose crowd style mixed rabble-rousing with baby-kissing, and which would, many felt, prefer to turn back the clock to the lovely days of the Gupta dynasty. Mr. Thackary claimed that Hitler has "some good ideas" and similar Nazi-isms, enunciating them in such a way that the injudicious might conclude that the BJP covertly was behind them.

Mr. Thackary's 15 minutes of fame actually lasted 15 months. It happened to culminate about the same time as news stories broke about the alleged involvement of the BJP's leader, Lal Krishna Advani, in a 1995 *hawala* corruption scandal, which had a substantial effect on the 1996 election. The BJP's seeming invincibility was further tarnished by a fractious, rebellious, mudslinging local contest in Gujarat just before the 1996 general elections, which demonstrated to most observers that the BJP was as venal and deceitful as any other party. The Gujarat insider's revolt has now affected even the BJP's strongest pocket borough, Uttar Pradesh. The ignominious 12–day prime ministry of Mr. Vajpayee after the 1996 elections seems in retrospect a swan song for a party whose volatility was excessive in a time when the electorate wanted not a change of faces but a change of behavior.

There are important lessons to be noted from the BJP's decline. The BJP was a party of northern India where Hindu culture is strongest. It did not command much support among the peoples of the south. Moreover, most Hindus put economic interests ahead of religion when it comes to voting. There is also the undefinable factor of a national television news sensibility on local politics. It was one thing for a local BJP orator to rant about the sacred cow of Mother India before a batch of illiterate farmers in Bihar; it was another thing to see him deporting thus on Doordarshan TV. Where is the milk of the sacred cow when most people buy it powdered by Nestlé's?

Even if the BJP does carve out a national role for itself, it is not likely to seriously effect economic reforms. Indeed, the BJP supported economic liberalization provided it kept out undesirable outside influences such as foreign fried chicken. The BJP welcomed foreign investments into states that it governed, but on the state's terms, not the foreign investor's—as Enron found out the hard way. Its spokesman in the Lok Sabha, Jaswant Singh, had long endorsed the principle of foreign investment in India. The fried chicken issue had overtones of the vegetarian lobby's objections to introducing new reasons to kill animals—a fact that did not receive proper mention in the international press. Consumer aspirations have resulted in formidable spending growths. The BJP may have to soften its stance regarding foreign access to the consumer market if it is to keep what power base it has.

All of these factors make it likely that the BJP's power will narrow to where it largely affects state government issues in its influence areas, and it will probably never again exercise national power at the prime ministerial level.

INDIA'S RELATIONS WITH THE REST OF THE WORLD

Pakistan

Although India regards itself as having a wide range of world interests, much of its foreign policy is dominated by relations with Pakistan. This has been the case since partition in 1947. The disputed northern state of Kashmir remains a thorn in the side of both countries and has been fought over twice. India maintains that Kashmir is an integral part of its territory, while Pakistan insists that the predominantly Muslim state should be given the option to join with it. Neither India nor Pakistan regards an independent Kashmir as an option, although this is the solution favored by most Kashmiris. Since 1990 Kashmiri militants have conducted an armed revolt against the Indian authorities in which 17,000 people have died. India accuses Pakistan of arming these militants as well as being responsible for fomenting dissension in India itself.

The destruction in early 1995 of the historic Chrar-e-Sharief mosque in fighting between the Indian army and Islamic militants has led to a sharp increase in Kashmiri hostility toward India and a further rise in tension between India and Pakistan. The incident came at a particularly inopportune time, as many Kashmiris were beginning to waver in their support for the militants, and India's then-prime minister Narasimha Rao had planned to hold a state election in Kashmir in July in the hope of restoring peace to the region. This is now unlikely to occur.

Enmity between the two countries has also prevented either from signing the Nuclear Non-Proliferation Treaty (NNPT). India carried out a nuclear test explosion in 1974 and Pakistan admits to a nuclear weapons program. India's stance on the NNPT has complicated its relations with the United States, which fears that the situation in Kashmir could escalate into a nuclear conflict.

SAARC and South Asian Trade

The South Asian Association for Regional Cooperation (SAARC) includes India, Sri Lanka, the Maldives, Pakistan, Bangladesh, Nepal, and Bhutan. Although they should be ideal trading partners, up until now trade between SAARC nations has not been enormous—trade with SAARC countries is only about 4 percent of India's total. One reason is that so many SAARC products are similar from member to member.

The two most relevant developments in the field of SAARC economic cooperation have been the South Asian Preferential Trade Agreement (SAPTA) and the SAARC Chamber of Commerce and Industry (SCCI). Influenced by ASEAN's Preferential Trading Arrangement (PTA), SAPTA promotes reciprocal mutual trade and economic cooperation among the member countries. Preferential trade is to be negotiated on a step-by-step basis on all commodities. The emerging prospect of an Indian Ocean Trade Cooperation Area, supported by India, South Africa, Mauritius, and Sri Lanka, also offers further prospects for trade.

SAARC has its problems. The official 1994–1995 intraregional trade among SAARC countries as a percentage of their total world trade was only 3.4 percent. This compares sharply with 63.4 percent equivalent trade among the nations of the European Community. Political factors are one cause of India's neighbors not trading with each other; similarity of products is another. However, the most important feature of SAARC trade is that so much of it is unofficial. According to Amit Mitra, secretary-general of the Federation of Indian Chambers of Commerce and Industry, "Indian exports to Pakistan total some $650 million, of which only $150 million is official. The rest is routed through a third country or is unofficial."

Unofficial trade results in higher transportation costs, delays, and quality-control problems. For example, Pakistan's demand for textile-producing machinery is high. Most could be imported from India, but often the consignments originate in India and end up in Pakistan via Europe.

This points up the type of side effects that Indo-Pakistani political difficulties exert on other nations in the region. The World Trade Organization's dismantling of trade barriers was supposed to help countries work more closely on trade matters. The estimated increase in India's textiles trade was expected to be about 60 percent. SAARC countries are mostly textile exporters. Unless they pool their resources, they will compete against each other. But past hostilities with Pakistan have resulted in Pakistan not granting most-favored-nation status to India. Pakistanis in turn suffer inordinate delays in getting clearances from India. When Pakistan wanted to exhibit its goods at the Delhi SAARC Trade Fair in January 1996, the goods had to be moved by road, but the Indian government gave permission so late that they barely arrived in New Delhi in time. So far India has not gone to the WTO over Pakistan's denial of MFN, preferring to retaliate by irritants such as these.

Nor has India granted other SAARC members meaningful concessions on many trade items. The result is a value of concessional imports of just 6.2 percent of the intraregional trade of member countries. India's actual policy appears to be to extend concessions only bilaterally with its partners. Pakistan has concessions on only 35 items, a pittance compared with the 578 items in its bilateral agreement with India.

Another problem with SAARC trade is its members' low levels of development. Agriculture remains the mainstay of all of their economies. Only India has a mature and diversified industrial structure. The result is significant imbalances in trade, weighted toward India. Bangladesh resents the bilateral trade surpluses run up every year by India. In 1985, its deficit was $75 million, which ballooned to $224 million during the first six months of 1994–1995. To redress this imbalance and try to lessen the substantial volume of illegal trade, Bangladesh wants special and more favorable treatment, including the removal of nontariff and other barriers on a nonreciprocal basis. Bangladesh fears that with freer trade, its nascent industrial structure might be destroyed.

Bhutan, Nepal, Maldives, and Sri Lanka, on the other hand, strongly advocate across-the-board tariff cuts and feel that SAARC should gradually eliminate all tariff and nontariff barriers within the region. Nepal, too, argued in a similar vein. Bhutan is strongly dependent on intra-SAARC trade. All point to the statistic that India accounts for three-quarters of the collective GDP of SAARC. India's trade with other SAARC countries grew by 22.2 percent in 1993–1994 to Rs 3,169 crore ($905 million), but while exports were worth Rs 2,818 crore ($805 million), imports amounted to only Rs 351 crore ($100.3 million). India's tiny neighbors worry about being swamped by its might or excluded from trade, depending on India's whim.

The SAARC/SAFTA issue would remain a comparative sideshow in India's future except for the fact that the arrival of consumerism in India is likely to dramatically change demand for many products that Indian businesses are not entirely able to supply. This is likely to be exacerbated as India attempts to upscale itself on the value-added ladder, shedding low-technology high-labor production to its poorer states. Not without due prescience have Japan, Korea, Malaysia, and Singapore been investing much more heavily in technology-related ventures in India since 1995 (and sharply so since 1996).

This will create a legitimate claim on the part of Sri Lanka and Nepal in particular to be accorded preferential SAARC tariff rates on items that they can manufacture more effectively than India. So far India has shown no signs of recognizing the ability of its neighbors to under-price Indian-manufactured goods. It is a looming trade issue spoken about far more often in Colombo and Kathmandu than in New Delhi.

The burden of shifting SAARC trade policies is falling to the SAARC business community, which most wants to cash in on the limited but available opportunities. As yet there is no database on what sort of products, services, and technologies are available within the region. Nor is there a comprehensive list of businesses that would most benefit from SAARC trade. Business people in the region have more foresight than their governments in the matter of the SAFTA free-trade area. It appears that they will be the first ones to make an international case out of it.

Southeast and East Asia

India and China have moved steadily toward a *rapprochement* following their border war in 1962. The two countries signed a peace agreement in September 1993, which substantially demilitarized their 4,000-kilometer border without compromising their respective territorial claims. As India has liberalized its economy, it has sought closer economic relations with other Asia-Pacific countries. It is keen to join the Asia-Pacific Economic Cooperation (APEC) forum and has recently signed cooperation agreements with Singapore and Vietnam.

Reduced Links With Russia

Another key thread in India's foreign relations was effectively broken following the end of the Cold War and the fragmentation of the Soviet Union. The two countries had signed a wide-ranging treaty in 1971 that covered mutual defense agreements, arms sales, and a bilateral trading arrangement which facilitated the exchange of Soviet oil, minerals, and capital equipment for Indian consumer goods. The break-up of the Soviet Union has made the defense pact meaningless and trade (now conducted in hard currency) has virtually collapsed. However, arms sales and a shared interest in curbing the spread of Muslim fundamentalism provide enough common ground to continue links on a lower level. The Indian government has kept open its options by seeking to strengthen ties with the new Central Asian republics.

The West

India's relations with the major Western powers have improved in recent years. The European Union (EU) occupies increasingly prominent positions in Indian foreign policy. The EU is India's major trading partner and a significant foreign investor.

India's relations with the United States have moved from testy (due to U.S. support for Pakistan and India's friendship with the Soviet Union) to a more cordial stance. India is unhappy with the close, and some feel arbitrary and racist, singling out of India on certain human rights issues. On the other hand, foreign investment by U.S. firms has risen rapidly in the wake of economic reforms, and military cooperation is growing.

How India Views Asia's Other Capitalisms

Indian businesses distinguish several distinct paths Asia's economic tigers have followed to their capitalist development. Indians see three broad ways in which Asia's capitalisms differ. First, some are much more open to foreign direct investment. Second, some are much less prone to try to second-guess the markets through government-directed industrial policies. Third, some have been much quicker to allow financial markets to develop.

The distinction is clearest over East and Southeast Asian attitudes toward foreign direct investment. The Japanese and the South Koreans were determined to build up national champions. They made it difficult for foreign-owned companies to set up shop. The tigers of Southeast Asia, on the other hand, built their booms by welcoming foreigners. Singapore, which practically invented this strategy, now has an economy dominated by multinationals. The export industries of Thailand and Malaysia rely heavily on foreign firms while insisting on large equity holdings by local partners.

The distinction between East and Southeast Asia is more blurred when it comes to industrial policy. There is much admiration in India for the Japanese and South Korean governments' effective sponsorship of steel, shipbuilding, and other heavy industries. Both Indonesia and Malaysia have tried nurturing winners, in aerospace and cars, respectively, but Indians see their efforts as peripheral. Some Indian economists admire Indonesia, where the framework for growth was established by a determinedly orthodox group of economists who concentrated on macro-economic stability and opposed subsidies.

Southeast Asian countries were quick to let financial markets flourish. In the early stages of South Korean and Japanese industrialization, businesses in search of credit had little option but to go to the banks, whose lending decisions were influenced by government. In contrast, the stock markets of Thailand, Malaysia, and Indonesia were cleared for early take-off, allowing companies to raise money without heavy borrowing. Southeast Asians have also been more willing to let foreigners invest in their stock markets. There is clear respect for this kind of thinking in India's moves in the same direction.

Asian countries approach the relationship between technology investment and development in quite different ways. Korea relies on its thirty-odd *chaebol* families to fund research and development via their corporations. Being disinclined to court foreign investment, which would dilute their own holdings, their strategy has been to invest in home-grown technology and improve on existing designs. The result is Korea's strength in heavy industry and industrial monopolies, shedding labor-intensive low-tech operations offshore and imposing tight import policies.

Hong Kong and Singapore avidly court foreign technology by hosting foreign investments. Hong Kong tends to leave the mechanism to the free market while the Singapore government closely shepherds the process. The chief factor in common is that both encourage businesses to value-add from outside sources. The fact that they encourage in quite different ways seems to make little difference.

Taiwan is the most liberal of all, on the one hand courting the wealth of knowledge in its expatriates working in places like Silicon Valley, and on the other by funding research-and-development parks like Hsin Chu to do research for anyone who commissions it. Taiwan's development paradigm is a plethora of SMI companies given a very free hand to value-add with little government oversight.

If India and China manage the kind of economic miracles achieved in other parts of Asia, they seem likely to do it the Southeast Asian way. Both countries have set out to court foreign direct investments. India got into the game much later, but even its nominally Communist politicians are now eagerly scouting the world for foreign investors. Both countries still have large state sectors. But both now see their nationalized industries primarily as a burden that must be reformed before they can be a fulcrum for economic strategy. Finally, both India and China, like the Southeast Asians, have encouraged companies to raise capital through their stock markets.

Such emulation stems partly from choice and partly from circumstance. In the inward-looking economies of India and China in the 1950s, 1960s, and 1970s, directed lending and industrial planning were a disaster. Elements of those methods may have worked in the export-oriented economies of Japan and South Korea, but today India and China are trying to get away from such policies.

The Differences Between India and China

China and India are dissimilar in ways that go much further back into history than their new-found interest in the market economy. China's uniform language, ethnicity, and nonsectarian religious sensibility are polar opposites of India's genetically intermingled and uncountably diverse populace, its twenty major languages, and seven major religions. In China, there is apathy if not outright antipathy to formal religiosity. Chinese religion is largely devotional rather than institutional, ancestral rather than deistic. India's religious devotions assert the power of institutional framework, most notably the family as more important than the clan. In

China, life is more important than the soul; in India, the value of a religion can be more important than the value of life.

Hinduism has a long history of fanaticism, more so than the region's other religions, having vanquished Buddhism in its own birth land by converting doctrinal tenets into idol worship (the human Buddha became an avatar of Rama, the first god). China, in contrast, has its own long tradition: absorbing "barbarian" conquerors and converting them to its own concept of civilization, during which the barbarians' original goals become forgotten.

China is a dictatorship that holds a tight rein on the press. India is a political democracy, although the realities of party politics make it more of a casted college which voters are invited to approve. India's press has such a no-holds-barred approach to the facts that its ability to inflame opinion extends far beyond the mere 50 percent of its population that can read.

China, too, has its fanaticisms, but they come down on matters of public order, not religious beliefs. China has replaced the fanaticism of Maoist doctrine with the fanaticism of money-making, and in so doing has spawned an almost surreal combination of a state autocracy driving a market economy.

In the 50-odd years since India won independence and China had its Communist revolution, the destinies of these two different social elephants have only modestly entangled politically. They fought a border war in the Himalayas in 1962. Their relations are now peaceful and their economic ties are strengthening into a commercial web that joins two very different ideas of the relation between social and economic development. Both want far more from other countries than they want from each other.

As the 1990s proceed to 2000, Indians—especially those who write for the business press there—wonder what values the China-focused economies of East Asia have learned that can benefit India's values. Sometimes this is overt, as in 1991, when economic crisis pushed some Indian economists and politicians into emulating the concept—though not the social thinking—of what East Asia's economies had done. They noticed that India did not have the vulnerability to certain vital links like oil transport and, some say, the climatic hostility that forces people to work hard just to keep warm and fed.

India's strengths are China's weaknesses, and vice versa. China changes from within faster than India but the results are more unstable. China has too little law and bureaucracy; India has too much. China lacks the structure to manage the dynamism of its economic energy. India has a great deal of structure but lacks the dynamism.

Southeast Asian countries have invested in both, although more goes to China than to India. Singapore's Government Inc. has plunged into hard-assets development in China and Singapore's Business Inc. invests heavily in the soft assets of Bangalore. This strategy will probably see Singapore doing better than either, yet even the most boisterous Southeast Asian investors are overlooking China and India as consumer markets. Indeed, it is very difficult to find any but travel guides to India in Singapore and Kuala Lumpur book shops, yet whole shelves abound with books about China.

The Role of Democracy in the India-Versus-China Argument

Many international investors see China losing its luster as an investment site compared with the growing attractiveness of India. China is an avowedly communist country which derives 80 percent of its gross domestic product (GDP) from the state sector. Laws are still poorly defined and arbitrary in execution. Administration is by and large unpredictable and corrupt. There is no sizable stock exchange or domestic private equity. There is no banking system beyond state-owned banks. There is no freedom of the press or media. There are no indigenous entrepreneurs or managers of the type which Western companies look for. English is spoken or understood only by those who have to deal with tourists—even that only recently and to a limited extent. China is regularly in conflict with the United States and even more regularly in conflict with its neighbors.

Hence many investors argue that India is in the long term a better place for investment. India has a democratic system with well-defined laws. There are courts which administer justice. There is a highly educated and intelligent civil service. There are plenty of well-qualified English-speaking managers. There are thousands of private-sector entrepreneurs to collaborate with. The government sector produces far less than 20 percent of the GDP and employs less than 20 million people. There are over twenty stock exchanges. There are several banks owned by the state and the private sector, and all major international banks have commenced operations in the country. There is rampant corruption in India, but it is being exposed relentlessly—an amazingly large number of highly placed officials have recently cooled their heels in jail. On the international political scene, India has no major differences of the type which China has with the United States. All of this should have made India a more attractive destination for foreign investors.

Surprisingly, this line of reasoning cuts little ice with a number of Indian economics analysts. These ask why, despite all the seeming advantages enjoyed by India, has China been more successful in attracting investment? China has sustained a growth rate of 12 percent a year for the last five years, double that of India's average of about 6 percent. China's GDP will likely quadruple between 1980 and 2000 while India will be lucky if its GDP grows by 100 percent. China's GDP is already more than double that of India's, and by 2000 it will probably be three times that of India's. By 2020, the GDP of China may surpass even Japan's. China is on the road to becoming an economic superpower, these analysts say, and the gap between India and China is steadily growing.

What this line of thinking underscores is a fear that India will be geopolitically a subeconomy to China. A number of influential Indians believe that the single major underlying reason for India's relative backwardness compared with China is that immediately after gaining independence India chose to bring its political structure in line with the political systems adopted in the most developed western countries. Western-educated leaders decided to extend voting rights to everybody, irrespective of the person's intellectual or economic stake in the country. In 1991, the government lowered the voting age further to 18, resulting in a government voted into office largely by people who have little understanding of long-term economic policies or their complications. China, in contrast, retained the political structure of a centralized ruling elite backed by the military when economic liberalization started in 1978. China's political leaders are able to think in long terms and take bold steps which they are confident of carrying through.

This line of reasoning reflects the enduring power of India's command-economy, isolationist school of thinking, now laced liberally with anti-democracy views. China has been introduced as the new geopolitical bogey to replace the United States. Dated though it is, this argument still has persuasive power. Even those many Indians who are not quite this protectionist in their frame of mind reluctantly concede that all of the successful Asian tigers—Singapore, South Korea, Malaysia, Thailand, and Indonesia—opted for the liberalization of their economies well ahead of liberalizing their political systems.

The danger to this argument comes when it is wedded to the belief that democracy favors those who are least able to accept its responsibilities. This argument says that India's form of democracy is too heavily based on emotional communalism and casteism, and not enough on reasoned discourse. The argument says that Indian political parties have neglected to assert the need for a strong economic policy. No political party, for example, has set out to double the national wealth in 10 years and then relentlessly pursued that goal. India, they say, will progress only if political leaders have the courage to admit that the democratic basis of society is being thwarted by too much of the wrong kind of democracy.

The foregoing is an elitist argument for limited democracy that has been a part of Indian political thinking from Independence. In its modern context of China-fear, it has several faults. One is that China's domestic savings rate of 35–40 percent is occasioned by China's enforced savings programs—a feature common to other Chinese Asian societies such as Taiwan and Singapore as well. Also ignored is where China's foreign investment comes from. Up until 1995, over 80 percent of foreign investment in China was by overseas Chinese, of whom there were some 50 million versus about 15 million nonresident Indians (NRIs). Overseas Chinese are predominantly in business, compared with Indians, who are predominantly professionals.

Despite these and several other flaws in the limited democracy argument, it draws several conclusions that are believed by many who do not buy the argument itself:

- Leave the policy for foreign investments up to the banks. Foreign shareholding should be permitted in all economic activities, although there can be exceptional industries and services where foreign shareholding may be limited, such as defense-related industries, agriculture, and so on.

- Once an economic policy is formulated, it should not be tampered with for 10 years.

- Eliminate the government's ability to consider investments on a case-by-case approach and let scrutiny be only in exceptional instances.

- Allow exchange control to be administered by commercial banks. At present, exchange control is applicable only on capital transfers by Indian nationals. However, in practice, if a foreigner or an NRI has to invest in India, there is a bureaucratic procedure involving the Reserve Bank of India (RBI), which has to authorize such investments so that repatriation of capital and dividends are possible.

- Allow states to set up their own Special Economic Zones (SEZs). One of China's greatest successes has been the Special Economic

Zones set up in Guangdong and other coastal states. Each of these zones has considerable autonomy in allowing foreign investment in their zones.

Indian business houses have to be reassured about the role of FDI. Every time there is an election looming on the horizon, Indian businessmen and xenophobic parties raise the old specter of foreign domination of the Indian economy. It is time that this is laid to rest by an open and rational debate in the media and in business associations.

In essence, this is a call for the government to play a proactive role in developing Indian companies where India has a competitive advantage, as has been done by South Korea and Japan. The idea is to discourage appeals for protection against foreign investment in India by helping Indian industries capture and dominate their own markets. The industries most likely to be affected would be textiles, garments, leather, diamonds, jewelry, software, engineering, and electronics.

ASEAN and India's "Look East" Policy

Many Indian businesses "Look East" toward ASEAN, the Association of South East Asian Nations. They believe that in the long term the ASEAN countries will offer better opportunities than the West.

Until quite recently ASEAN countries looked askance at India, even though some ASEAN countries have sizable Indian communities. Their doubts were due to India's long embrace of socialism and its stifling bureaucracies. The years since about 1994 have seen substantial changes in attitude, although incidents such as the Indian governments refusal to allow the Tata business empire to forge an alliance with Singapore Airlines still causes heads to shake in Southeast Asia.

In 1992, the ASEAN accorded India the status of Sectoral Dialogue Partner. This basically meant that the two sides could engage each other in trade and investment in specific sectors such as tourism, science, and technology. More formal recognition came in early 1996, when the ASEAN boosted India to Full Dialogue Partner, a status so far conferred only on the United States, Canada, the European Union, Australia, New Zealand, Japan, and South Korea.

India's policy makers have doubts about too close a relationship with the ASEAN. They are worried about the so-called "Flying Geese" development model that has brought the ASEAN so much of its prosperity since 1980. This model proposes that the ASEAN countries became a captive base for first the Japanese and then the South Korean investment and trade, and from these built their own captive bases in countries like Myanmar and Cambodia.

This model is a variant of the Value-Added Ladder model in which the ASEAN economies move into those areas of manufacture that Japan and Korea vacate so that their internal economies can climb the rungs of the technology ladder.

These metaphors being mixed notwithstanding, India's economists debate whether the general idea—technological advances being shed continually downward—is really appropriate for India. The countries that make up the ASEAN are diverse and in different stages of technological and market sophistication. They cannot provide leadership to any but the meekest national entities—hence their ventures into Myanmar and Cambodia. Also, given India's sheer size, depths of poverty, and uneven regional development, Indians believe it unlikely that India can practicably hitch itself to any one particular developmental theory.

The Federation of Indian Chambers of Commerce and Industry (FICCI) secretary-general, Amit Mitra, cites a different model that may be more appropriate for India, the "Cultural Affinity" model. Because of similar social behaviors and cultural attitudes, Europe and America were able to engage in investment and trade with each other to great mutual benefit over an extended period. Mitra believes that the same model holds true of India and Southeast Asia, but not of East Asia.

Moreover, the geographical proximity between India and the ASEAN reduces transportation costs. India's advances in software technology and relatively cheap labor add to its complementarities with the ASEAN. The ASEAN's place in India's trade matrix has improved significantly. The Indian business community shows signs of seeing the opportunities with the ASEAN, initially in trade and investments. The Confederation of Indian Industry (CII) has an office in Singapore discussing deals. The FICCI has an office in Indonesia for the same purpose. In a 1996 FICCI seminar on expanding ties with the ASEAN in Singapore, India's external affairs minister, Pranab Mukherjee, spoke of the need for cooperation in the field of small and medium enterprises. He suggested that Indian enterprises set up two or three major impact projects every year either in India, in one of the ASEAN countries, or in third countries with ASEAN collaboration.

INDIA'S INVESTMENT ATTRACTIONS

India's moves to liberalize its economy and welcome foreign investment have done a lot to reverse its backward image. In foreign affairs India has much improved its relations with China and the United States. The East and Southeast Asians are in general agreement with India's international policies, although their main interest is the size of India's market. They have not made overtures to reconcile the APEC and EAEC (East Asian Economic Caucus) agendas with those of the SAARC.

However, Asian memories are long, and while other Asians are confident about India's finance and manufacturing sector opportunities, they are wary of the consumer-products sector. Four points of caution are (a) product piracy, (b) the potential for recurring squabbles of the KFC and Pizza Hut type, (c) equitable access to politically protected markets, and (d) India's tendency to dominate regional trade. Asian investors want to know what India's reaction will be if they begin to see the potential of Sri Lanka, Bangladesh, and Nepal as cost-efficient manufacturing centers for their own consumer products if those products happen to be exported to India.

India's attraction for overseas investment is a balance between (a) the general trend toward gradually tighter global interest rates to curb inflationary pressures, which would hand India higher debt costs for equity and bond issues, and (b) Moody's recent upgrade of India's debt rating to Baa3 from Ba2.

The rate at which approved FDI is growing is a positive indication of the growing global interest in India. The United States has traditionally been the largest foreign investor, accounting for nearly 40 percent of the FDI approved during the period 1991 to 1993. The global network of expatriate Indians (NRIs) has accounted for the second largest category of investments approved during this period. Other leading investor countries are the United Kingdom, Switzerland, Germany, Japan, and France. An interesting development has been the increasing investor interest from South East Asian countries such as Thailand and Singapore as well as other nontraditional investors such as Oman and Mexico.

The Promise of India's Consumer Market

The sheer size of India's consumer market attracted investors even before the 1991 reforms. Throughout the 1980s, although private consumption expenditure grew at 13 percent per annum, it outpaced inflation by only a few percent. Hence real growths ranged from 4.6 percent in 1991 to 2.1 percent in 1995. On the other hand, real-term private consumption is expected to double from 3 to 6 percent from 1996 to 2000. In today's prices, consumer spending amounted to Rs 3.4 trillion ($97.7 billion) in 1991.

Significantly, state consumption as a percentage of the GDP roughly doubled that of private consumption between 1988 through 1993, but now is predicted to reverse so private consumption exceeds state by roughly 20 to 50 percent from 1996 to 2000.

However, this overall consumer spending growth was (and still is) spotty, with wide differences in growth rates among various sectors. Transport and communication have increased up to 21 percent per annum; consumer electronics reached as much as 30 percent. Consumer spending has moved sharply from primary commodities to manufactured goods and services. This shift accompanies increasingly sophisticated consumers who make sizable portions of their new-product purchases based on magazine and television advertisements.

Consumption also has been fueled by supply. Properly positioned and marketed foreign brands have achieved comfortable market shares in almost all sectors of the consumer market. Most important is the dramatic rise in the market's size and spending power. The critical mass of India's upper middle-class households is considered to be 50 million mostly urban, ad-savvy, quality-hungry consumers; the actual figure is nearer to 100 million. This market is growing 20 percent a year as the overall economy fuels income levels. There is strong evidence that this rapid growth is unlikely to slow:

- sustained economic growth of 5.5 percent per year since the 1980s;

- a decade-long record of annual productivity increases over 7 percent in the manufacturing and service sectors;

- sharp increases in farm incomes due to increases in output and support prices;

- continued increases in urban population to over 300 million in 1994;

- similar increases in the number of households headed by salary earners, professionals, and businessmen to over 200 million in 1994;

- the emergence of multiple-income urban households (a major break with the traditional past);

- increased media awareness from broadcast and satellite television, radio, print, and, above all, the influence of films;

- levels of consumer-durables financing rising from negligible levels in 1980 to Rs 20 billion ($571 million) in 1994.

The evidence is clear: The time to market to consumers rather than state enterprises has arrived.

Medium-Term Outlook

India's medium-term economic prospects are favorable. The reform process has strengthened the economy to the extent that India should be capable of weathering most external shocks for the foreseeable future and should not have to revert to the highly protected regime of previous years.

India has a number of advantages that are not generally present in such abundance in other emerging economies. These include a well-developed private sector, which is becoming increasingly relieved of the burden of regulation; a large and increasingly wealthy middle class; a relatively well-developed financial system and expanding capital market; a large diaspora, which is increasingly influential in developing businesses and providing investment funds; and a broad tradition of democracy, which has proved itself capable of surviving communal upheavals.

Long-Term Outlook

Here, too, India's economic future is more promising than it has been in a long time. Politics is finally catching up with social changes that have been upwelling for more than a decade. A rising middle class, massive exposure to the television of the world, and a collective sigh of relief at the end of a five-decade political mindset that finally ran out of steam—all of these are undercurrents of change more momentous than anyone imagined.

India is entering an era of coalition government after 50 years of political hegemony. Never before have so many diverse and not always agreeable regional groups suddenly acquired so much power in the national arena. To some this raises the fear of instability, chaos, and bankruptcy. Others cite the success of coalition governments in many other places with diverse cultures. They feel that coalitions are the best solution to the demands of India's complex populace.

Indeed, India itself is essentially a coalition and has been since Independence. So was the Congress party in its heyday, when it represented very diverse ideological, economic, and regional interests. Moreover, the voting patterns from the grassroots in the 1996 election may very well instill a greater degree of responsiveness in the various parties.

Those parties are mindful as never before of how much India needs to mend its economic fences if it is to contain its social order. Nearly every state government teeters on the edge of bankruptcy. The government has vowed hands-off on too many unproductive state enterprises and exit regulations that make it virtually impossible to close unprofitable companies or lay off nonproductive workers.

These and other command-economy legacies of the past have not made India a less attractive investment site compared with, say, China or Brazil. They will, however, encourage certain kinds of investments and repel others. The brouhaha over fried chicken gave many people the impression that India was hostile to consumer products in general. In fact it was a rebellion against outside companies encouraging meat consumption in the face of Hindu India's long tradition of vegetarianism.

Other kinds of consumer-related investment have met with a far different reception. Makers of refrigerators and washers have been welcomed when their package includes moving the manufacture of their goods to India. Others who ignored that message have had a less friendly reception and now find themselves bogged down in costly distribution and after-sale service inefficiencies.

On the macro scale, India will remain a strong magnet for power, water, and communications investments for many years. But the government will be far more keen to restructure bad deals, as the Enron case certainly was from the perspective of the Maharashtra state. What India wants from investment of any kind is more manufacture brought onshore, more technology transfer, and more jobs.

Just how positive India can look at overseas money is shown in the way the quite recent entry of global investment banks has been positioned with respect to India's banking industry.

Some firms opt for sleeping partners—either friendly overseas Indians or locals who can be helpful with contacts. This means buying a seat on one of India's stock exchanges ($750,000 in Bombay).

Others acquire minority stakes in joint ventures, leaving the management primarily to their local partners. Merrill Lynch, the American securities house, paid $15 million for a 29 percent stake in DSP Financial Consultants, an Indian investment bank, while Goldman Sachs paid $35 million for a 28 percent stake in the securities and investment-banking arms of Mumbai's Kotak Mahindra. France's Banque Paribas set up shop with Indian partners in much the same way.

A third route was taken by the British firm James Capel, which bought 51 percent of a small Mumbai stockbroking firm, yet put only one of its people in the joint venture as joint chief executive.

By whatever entry route, they want access to several markets. One is fund management for overseas and local investors. Morgan Stanley leads this trend, with almost $2 billion under management in India. Unit Trust of India, a state-owned fund manager, estimates that the $24 billion now managed by some sixteen different firms could grow by as much as 20–30 percent a year between 1995 and 1998.

The foreign banks also want to trade Indian equities. They have helped Indian firms raise $5 billion abroad since 1992 in the form of Global Depository Receipts (GDRs), which are listed on foreign exchanges and backed by shares held on deposit in India. This would also involve them in privatizations, believing these to be inevitable.

To say the least, this is quality investment for a quality purpose. Yet its amounts are likely to be molehills compared with the quantity of investments likely to come from mid-sized companies with clear target markets within India's enormous middle class. Few realize that India has the largest middle class in the world—roughly 100 million in the upper range and 200 million in the lower. Together they are larger than the entire population of Japan and very close to that of Europe and the United States.

In real spending power, India's middle class does not have much wherewithal—yet. But it has been growing inexorably as an economic force and, more important, as a political one. Middle classes all over the world tend to be stability-oriented, financially conservative, educationally minded, and politically middle-of-the-road.

The clear consensus within India—from the government to the press to the average worker with daily mouths to fill—is that right now everyone wants stability and a better future. Given that these were the same signals being sent to most of Southeast and East Asia's governments two and three decades ago, India's wind of change is promising indeed.

NOTES

1. Estimates from several different sources range between 5.0 and 6.0 percent. Hence we will use 5.5 percent as a reasonable average in this book.

2. There is considerable debate in the Indian business press just how accurate this figure is given the extent of India's shadow economy. For our purposes it seems reasonable.

3. India's Parliament consists of two houses—the *Lok Sabha*, the House of the People, and the *Rajya Sabha*, the Council of States. The president is the constitutional head of the government, although the real executive power resides in the

Council of Ministers, with the prime minister as its head. The Council of Ministers (in effect a cabinet) is collectively responsible to the Lok Sabha.

The Lok Sabha is composed of people's representatives. It has a maximum of 552 members. Members serve five year terms, unless the Lok Sabha is dissolved sooner.

The Rajya Sabha has a maximum of 250 members, including 12 members with special knowledge or practical experience in literature, science art, and social science. Members of the Rajya Sabha are elected indirectly. The 12 special members are nominated by the president; the remaining members are elected representatives of states chosen by the elected members of legislative assemblies of the states and union territories.

4. Regionally, the damage wreaked on India by Indira Gandhi was not unique to her alone. In Sri Lanka the government of Sirimavo Bandaranaike also embarked on a path of socialist reform which was first coopted by and then merged into the personality cult of its leader, resulting in a loss of democracy and the ruin of the economy. The two "socialist sistres," as they are sometimes called, did more damage to their respective countries than any other factor in their recent histories.

2

Business Investment and Finance

TODAY'S BUSINESS CLIMATE

Before 1991, administrative controls and licensing requirements of the License Raj sharply restricted economic activities. Private investment was permitted, but only in certain industries, mainly those requiring sophisticated technology or offering export potential. These few companies were governed by a series of regulations embodied in the Foreign Exchange Regulation Act of 1973—hence the use of the term "FERA Companies" to describe Indian firms with foreign holdings and foreign investors with equity holdings in Indian firms. The maximum holdings allowed were 40 percent in most companies and 74 percent in export-oriented companies. Nonresident Indians (NRIs) were allowed equity investments of up to 100 percent in projects they established themselves, although they could not repatriate their profits abroad.

The July 1991 Rao-Singh economic reform program (now generally summed up under the rubric "liberalization") inaugurated a series of measures to improve private-sector participation in the economy and encourage foreign direct investment. India's industrial environment quickly became far more flexible. Except for eight specified industries (as of mid-1996), all licensing requirements have been abolished. The convertibility of the rupee on the trade account has also simplified the procedure for importing raw materials.

In October 1993, further amendments removed most of the remaining restrictions on FERA companies. Indian and foreign businesses are now free to use foreign trade marks, establish branch offices, and act as agents or technical/management advisers. Although the public sector continues to retain a monopoly in defense, atomic energy, rail transport, and five other basic industries, and a certain number are still reserved for the small-scale private sector, liberalization dramatically opened India up for private-sector investment.

Today the most notable conditions on governing foreign investment are as follows:

- The limit for foreign equity participation was raised to 51 percent from 40 percent in thirty-five high-priority industries, including industrial and agricultural machinery, chemicals, and hotels and tourist facilities. This limit also applies to trading companies engaged in export activities.

- Foreign companies may conduct oil exploration, development, and refining.

- Up to 100 percent foreign equity is allowed in the power sector, electronic hardware technology and software technology parks, export-oriented units, and companies located in the export-processing zones.

- The requirement to balance dividends against export earnings for all industries was removed except in the case of industries producing a specified list of consumer goods (mainly food and bakery products, beverages, and wines).

- Importation of capital goods and plant machinery is automatically approved.

- There have been significant reductions in import duties, with most capital goods now attracting tariffs between 20 and 40 percent. An Export Promotion Capital Goods Scheme permits the importation of capital goods at a concessional 15 percent duty.

- The requirement that foreign investment must be accompanied by technology transfer has been abolished. In some thirty-five high-priority industries, automatic clearance is given for foreign technology agreements involving a lump-sum technical know-how payment of up to Rs 10 million ($285,715).[1]

- Foreign technicians may be freely hired to engage in foreign development of indigenous Indian technologies.

- Exporters and other foreign exchange earners may retain up to 25 percent of their foreign exchange income in foreign currencies; this is increased to 50 percent for companies in export-processing zones and 100 percent for export-oriented units.

- India has significantly streamlined the approval process through the Foreign Investment Promotion Board (which operates on the one-stop-shop principle), which was originally set up under the office of the Prime Minister specifically to attract, negotiate, and approve foreign investment, and now moved under the auspices of the Industries Ministry.

India's business climate is now largely conditioned by these main features:

- the third largest pool of technical and scientific personnel in the world (after the United States and the former Soviet Union);
- an English-speaking professional work force;
- a strong entrepreneurial mentality;
- highly attractive wages by international standards;
- a large and diverse manufacturing sector;
- a widespread trade and distribution network;
- sophisticated marketing and informational services;
- a strong, if time-consuming, legal framework;
- well-developed capital markets and a highly regulated securities industry;
- further liberalizing and deregulating of business, trade, and foreign investment.

The economy in which the above sets of conditions operate can be quickly sketched as follows.

As of August 1996, India's was the fifth largest economy in the world and—based on purchasing power parity—the second largest among the developing economies. Private enterprise dominates all but a few industries. Unfortunately, those few industries—an example being the notoriously inefficient Air-India—are considered sacrosanct despite the fact that they represent a considerable drain on the country's resources. The largest infrastructure industries such as the posts, road, rails, and ports are still government-administered, although a phased program of public-sector divestment and restructuring is underway. Telecommunications have been liberalized, although corruption scandals have made an ironic mockery of the term and temporarily thwarted any immediately tangible benefits that overseas investors had anticipated.

Foreign investment is today considered equal to—and as welcome as—domestic investment. Import barriers have dropped radically and are in line for yet more cuts. Capital markets freely court foreign investment. Banking controls have been eased. Private investment—tepidly supported by India's declining personal savings average of 22 percent of the GDP—is strongly encouraged. Much private capital finds its way into shares purchases and unit trusts (India's name for mutual funds). The tax structure has been simplified and its rates reduced—a somewhat moot point given India's enormous levels of undeclared income. The Indian rupee is convertible in both current and capital accounts, resulting in the rupee appreciating steadily in foreign exchange markets.

These reforms were expected to produce social and economic instability. That did not happen, although there is considerable political posturing over the pros and cons of the fact that "things aren't the way they used to be." The real fact is that things are, and are not, the same; exactly which becomes a matter of personal selectivity.

India's restructuring plan was accompanied by a stabilization plan that produced a reasonably smooth transition from a mostly controlled to a mostly free economy. Stabilization has not notably reduced output. Economic growth and exports have picked up. Capital markets are anything but stagnant. Foreign investment has increased quite sharply but is still severely hampered by India's sclerotic bureaucracies.

In sum, India's 1991 reforms largely accomplished their goal of rejuvenating the country's business environment and opening the economy to foreign investment. Most important, they firmly established a sea change in thinking that is unlikely to be shunted aside by India's endlessly parochial political squabbles.

Investment Prospects 1996–2000

The following descriptions and their supporting figures are an amalgam of information available in printed publications and online via Web sites and e-mail. Generally speaking, the numbers in the *Economist Intelligence Unit* publications tend to come closest to averages drawn from data that appear in print, but are somewhat lower than averages of numbers available online from Indian sources. The accuracy of online economic data has not as yet been firmly established, as it tends to reflect near-term assessments and the optimizing effect of changing data online being a lot easier than changing it in ink.

A good Web address for online researchers to start with is the site for the *Monthly Economic Report* of the Department of Economic Affairs, Centre for Monitoring Indian Economy, and the *Economic Survey* of the Ministry of Finance:

http://www.indiaserver.com/biz/dbi/MEA13.html

India's business outlook for the next four years is one of steady growth of approximately 5–6 percent per year. The leading sector will be industrial manufacturing, which will benefit from the gradual process of economic reform and the opening up of the economy to foreign trade and investment. However, growth will not solve the problem of mass poverty, and inflation will continue to be difficult to control. Companies across a broad range of industries benefit from easier access to financing, lower financing costs, and lower customs and excise rates. On the other hand, there are some restraining factors that are likely to operate for some time:

- Higher interest costs will reduce both profit margins and consumer demand.
- Political uncertainties will not go away and will continue to affect investment from abroad.

Most Indian and overseas economists project the country's GDP growth at 5.5 percent for 1996–1998, rising to 5.7 percent by 1999–2000. The GDP per head is expected to increase from an estimated $330 in 1995–1996 to $428 by 2000, still far below the median personal income in the Asia-Pacific region. In real PPP terms this represents an average growth of 3.3 percent per year, since the country's annual population growth of 2 percent per year eats into the GDP growth rate.

Most economists expect that the government will allow its current spending to rise faster through 1996–1997 to fund its populist pre-election largesse, but thereafter government consumption will increase more slowly—some estimate only about 4 percent per year—as the government strives to bring its budget deficit under control and lower inflation.

Private spending is forecast to grow at an average annual rate of 5.1 percent from 1996 to 2000 due to the development of manufacturing and service industries and the gradual opening of the domestic market to imports. Investment growth is expected to increase to about 6 percent per year by 2000. Exports of goods and services, which grew by 17 percent in volume terms in 1993–1994, are projected to increase by 14 percent in 1996–1997, despite the depreciation of the rupee. The volume of exports is expected to grow at a reasonably fast rate through 2000. Imports of goods and services grew by approximately 11.5 percent during 1993–1994, but the growth rate shot up to 21.7 percent during 1994–1995, bolstered by demand growth and industrial recovery. Import growth is expected to exceed the export growth rate by a small margin during most of the forecast period due to the recovery of both public and private investment, which will attract increasing quantities of capital and consumer goods. In 1996–1997, however, import growth may be held back by the slowdown in capital investment.

Inflation and Monetary Policies

Inflation has now become the main focus of monetary policy, and well it should since inflation is perceived by many to be the single most volatile ingredient in India's economic stabilization efforts. The already persistently high rate of inflation means potential political trouble for any government; hence the problem is being given serious attention.

While there was no change in the liquidity ratios prescribed for banks, the Reserve Bank of India has clamped down on credit expansion. This has resulted in a reversal of the earlier trend toward declining interest rates (although it most certainly has not effected the promotional efforts of major credit card providers). Bank deposit rates, which are not yet deregulated, were raised and lending rates have followed suit. Perturbed by the rapid growth in money supply during 1994–1995, the RBI has opted for a tight money policy.

The rupee has held its nominal value against the dollar, supported by large foreign investment inflows and inward remittances from NRIs (Nonresident Indians) overseas. In real terms, this has meant an appreciation of the currency, with the RBI stepping in to prevent nominal appreciation. However, pressure on the rupee is now expected to build up as a result of:

- a slowdown in capital inflows because of political uncertainty and generally increased caution about emerging markets on the part of investors in the developed world;

- a widening of the trade and current-account deficits as the import growth rate outstrips the export growth rate;
- continued high inflation differentials between India and the rest of developed Asia and the United States.

Although a sizable devaluation is unlikely unless political or economic events result in loss of confidence in the economy, the rupee is likely to depreciate by 7 percent in 1996 and 10.6 percent in 1997–1998, and then depreciate more gradually, by an estimated 3 percent per year, through 1999.

Bank lending rates have declined from 20 percent per year at the start of the 1991 reform program to 15 percent per year in 1995–1996. Tight conditions in the money market and increased demand from industry have pushed up bank lending rates to 15.5–16 percent per year. There has been a commensurate increase in overall yields in the market, and the cost of government borrowing has gone up. While lending rates are deregulated, deposit rates continue to be regulated by an RBI-specified ceiling on bank and other deposits.

Interest rates are likely to remain high as long as inflation is a problem and will therefore come down only gradually. Credit availability from the banking sector will also be constrained. India's social welfare programs introduced in the 1994 budget are likely to put a strain on resources. The funds squeeze on the corporate sector will probably continue at least until 1998. Banks can be expected to remain fairly selective in lending because they need to clean up their balance sheets as a result of the imposition of capital sufficiency requirements.

Imports, Exports, and Trade Balances

After a period of sluggish growth, exports began to grow strongly after 1993. Much of this growth has occurred despite an appreciation of the value of the rupee against the dollar (the United States is India's largest market). The government thrust toward exports and incentives such as cheaper and easier financing and tax benefits have helped to provide a boost to exports. Several factors enhance the competitiveness of India's exports:

- lower interest rates;
- cheaper inputs as a result of lower duties and import tariffs;
- easier access to quality inputs with the lowering of trade barriers;
- the rapid expansion of world trade.

Exports are expected to expand steadily no matter what happens in India's unpredictable political picture. They are being helped by structural changes in the economy and by the expected depreciation in the value of the rupee. In current dollar terms, export growth will be faster from 1997 to 2000, when rupee depreciation is expected to be slower. By 1999–2000, the value of merchandise exports is forecast to reach $53 billion.

Import growth, which remained sluggish during the first half of the decade, took off in 1994–1995, pushed up by the demand created by the industrial recovery and facilitated by the further easing of tariff barriers. Growth in oil imports was relatively subdued because of higher domestic production and the continuing softness in oil prices. The overall volume growth rate of imports of goods and services reached 21.5 percent in 1994–1995 as a result of the rise in nonoil imports. The weakening of the rupee will make imports more expensive.

Because of faster import growth there is likely to be a steady expansion of the trade deficit from $4.5 billion in 1995–1996 to $8 billion in 1999–2000. The increase in foreign direct and portfolio investment in India in recent years will generate steadily increasing net outflows of interest, profits, and dividends, rising from nearly $5 billion in 1995–1996 to more than $7 billion by 2000.

Tourism will probably grow more slowly, while expenditure on trade-related services will be boosted by the development of the country's exports. The net inflow of remittances (largely from expatriate Indians) will grow slowly to about $3 billion. On current assumptions, therefore, the current-account deficit will swell to $9.2 billion. However, the GDP should be increasing fast enough to prevent the deficit from representing a greater proportion of national output than it does at present. Inflows of lending and FDI are expected to continue to cover the deficit.

Foreign exchange reserves rose to $20.8 billion at the end of fiscal year 1994–1995. Although the inflow of foreign portfolio investment has slowed considerably, it has been made up to some extent by continuing inward remittances from expatriate Indians investing in the country and a recovery in exports in the last few months of the year. Some erosion of the reserves can be expected during 1996–1997 because of the widening of the current-account deficit. Repayment of the principal on debt is forecast to peak at $5.5 billion by 1996–1997, and to remain high thereafter; hence there will be a steady financing pull by the government. This will probably be funded largely by borrowing from abroad, although foreign investment will also make a contribution.

Foreign direct investment is still relatively low, hindered largely by India's still unresolved disparity between what the Centre claims to need and the state bureaucracies, which takes seemingly forever to grant approvals, and 1996's series of corruption revelations. Total external debt is expected to pass the $100 billion mark in 1996–1997 and exceed $110 billion by 1999–2000. Since the growth of the GDP and exports will outstrip the rise in foreign indebtedness, the debt service ratio is likely to drop from 24.6 to 16 percent.

Hence, the prognosis for growth is generally positive. The positive impact of the reform program—especially on industry—is clearly evident. Released from tight controls, industry has responded well, and investment and demand levels have picked up. Increasing incomes are underpinning demand growth. Several factors support continued expansion in industrial growth over the next ten years:

- adequate supply of labor;
- more and more educated managers;
- a large entrepreneurial class;
- an established banking and financial system;
- an active capital market;
- legal structures—albeit slow and frustrating—are predictable and understood.

Four factors have had a strong influence on India's overall economic position over the last five years:

- Foreign currency reserves are comfortable.
- Food grain stocks have built up.
- Foreign capital inflows are growing.
- Exports have shown a healthy upward trend after being battered by the loss of the USSR markets.

Taken together, these factors indicate sustained economic growth through 2000 and probably beyond.

Multinational Investment

Numerous multinationals have established their presence in the Indian market. Certain sectors—especially infrastructure—that had been government sectors have now been opened to foreign investors. Thus far foreign presence is only moderate in the core and infrastructural sectors of industry and is more pronounced in noncore sectors of consumer goods, intermediates, and services.

A number of global power giants have committed investments of up to $42 billion to generate 38,000 megawatts of power over the next few years. Prominent among them are Enron Power, Cogentrix, and Mission Energy. However, constant thwarting by political pressure groups and turgid state bureaucracies has taken much of the gilt off the power sector's lily.

Liberalization of the mining sector is attracting majors like Amoco and Alcan (who already have an equity stake in an Indian venture). The oil and gas sector has also been liberalized. Enron Oil, Occidental, and various other large oil corporations have known but secretive investment strategies.

The government has unveiled a telecom policy that allows private participation in basic and value-added services. Global telecom players like Motorola, Fujitsu, Alcatel, Ericsson, and AT&T have already established a manufacturing presence in the country and are awaiting normalization of the policy. The 1996 Sukh Ram scandal put a serious crimp on future investment timelines, as many once-granted licenses may now have to go through a more open and time-consuming tender process.

The engineering industry has a sizable multinational presence in certain sectors. Asea Brown Boveri, GEC-Alsthom, and Siemens are large players in the electrical engineering and power equipment industry. The lubricants market has witnessed the entry of Caltex, Shell, Elf, Mobil, and Pennzoil. The heavy machinery, machine tools, and similar sectors are dominated by Indian business houses and the public sector.

The consumer sector has a large multinational presence. Whirlpool, General Electric, and Electrolux are among the major players in white goods. Hoover has also entered the consumer durables market. Whirlpool has acquired controlling stakes in their Indian ventures, and GE has entered the market in an alliance with Godrej, one of India's largest consumer durable companies. Sanyo, Philips, and Goldstar enjoy a major presence in the consumer electronics industry, and have been joined by Sony and Hitachi.

Consumer nondurables involvement is widespread. The Indian soaps and detergent market is one of the largest in the world. For some time it is likely to be dominated by the existing major players, Unilever's Hindustan Lever subsidiary, Procter & Gamble (P&G), and Henkel. Unilever has been in India for several decades and has established many of its international brands like Surf and Lux. P&G has recently entered the market with Camay and Head & Shoulders. Henkel has faltered with a poor start with its Henko detergent introduction.

Hindustan Lever, Nestlé, Cadbury, Schweppes, Agrolimen, and various other global food majors have a large presence in the Indian food processing industry. Pepsi and Coke have made the Indian soft drinks market their latest battlefield. Bata is virtually synonymous with footwear in the country. The Indian garment industry has witnessed the recent entry of Pierre Cardin, Benetton, Levi Strauss, and Wrangler, with leading shirt brands such as Arrow, Louis Phillippe, and Van Heusen available just about everywhere. The array of ads in India's glossies would be perfectly at home in Singapore or Dubai.

A Poor Regulatory Framework Hinders Infrastructure Investment

India's infrastructure represents the country's most substantial and important investment potential, but it is yet to be meaningfully tapped. Most investors (local as well as overseas) are held back by India's poor regulatory framework in infrastructure. The government courts promisingly but fails to carry through administratively. Much of this is due to miscommunication and plain old bureaucratic ponderousness at the level of the various states. The government's mid-1996 make-haste effort to clear some 350 proposals worth $4 billion was impressive, but critics are asking how much of it actually found its way into ports, roads, power generation, and telecoms.

The government has responded by restructuring the Foreign Investment Promotion Board (FIPB) in order to broaden and hasten the automatic approval process. A new Foreign Investment Promotion Council has been formed comprising members of the private sector to launch sectoral and project-specific promotional campaigns for attracting FDI. Now foreign investors are promised an official response to their proposals within six weeks. This cuts little ice with investors who reply that that is what they were promised before.

Most foreign investors maintain that the problem in infrastructural investment is the unaddressed but urgent need for a proper regulatory framework. Over 200 expressions of interest have been registered proposing investments of $85 billion that would add 78,000 megawatts to India's capacity. Of this, fifty-three proposals were from foreigners and were worth $42 billion and 38,000 megawatts. The actual 480 megawatts of new power generating capacity in progress is only 0.6 percent of the amount that the private sector would like to invest. Hence there is a growing prospect for worse and worse shortfalls in power. With demand for electricity growing at 9 percent per annum, India's Ninth Five-Year Plan (1995–2000) would require additional capacity of 57,000 megawatts. The Tenth Plan (2000–2005) requires yet another 65,000 megawatts. The private sector would have to face coming up with $150 billion of investment capital in order to satisfy this demand.

Power shortages are the most serious threat to the industrial expansion of the country. The Reserve Bank of India Annual Report for 1995–1996 bluntly states, "The problem of serious bottlenecks in this area has to be addressed in the near future since they will hinder industrial growth. Investments in infrastructure have to be increased sharply without delay."

So far, foreign investors remain dubious. They point to regulatory problems as the chief cause of their diffidence. Japanese investment is a case in point. Japan's MITI reports cite India's "huge potential market including a middle class population of a few hundreds of millions" and sees India as a geographic bridgehead to Africa and the Middle East. However, MITI sees India's major need as "the government must take steps to ensure an active role in formulating transparent rules with regard to project operation and contractor selection, and see to it that the operations of the state electricity boards are improved."

The Japanese Khaparkheda power project in Maharashtra is an example. Investors are constantly frustrated by delays in decision-making. They were ready to invest, but bureaucratic clearances at the state level continually stonewalled progress. A MITI study group visited seeking clarifications on India's power policy in general and the Maharashtra state policy in particular. Government spokespeople responded with the familiar assertion that $6–8 billion of funds were needed every year for power generating capacity, and of that, $4–6 billion had to come from outside sources. Unfortunately, no one could answer why the Maharashtra project was locked up in a fairly straightforward approval process at the state level.

The situation with roads is even more daunting. According to an Arthur Andersen & Co. report, of India's over 1.4 million miles of road, one-half are not surfaced. National highways stand in the greatest need of attention, as they account for 2 percent of the overall road length but 40 percent of road traffic. Road traffic will boom in the coming years and more need to be built. Only 5 percent of the national highways are four lanes (and 15 percent are single-lane only). Another 32,000 kilometers of road is badly needed as soon as possible. Private-sector participation is imperative since government support is only Rs 30 billion ($857 million) while the country-wide investment requirement is $30 billion.

An intractable problem is how such an investment will be recouped by private investors. Tolls by themselves would have to be prohibitively high if they alone were to repay the debt. The Ministry of Surface Transport has floated the vague idea of "shadow tolling," in which investors might recoup their investment by being paid an agreed amount over a certain period. The Ministry did not further clarify how this was to be done and what recourse investors would have if it was not. Another Ministry idea was to allow private investors to develop motels, fuel stations, and highway inns along the highways and partially recoup their investments through the profits. No one asked the investing contractors whether they had any experience with retail commercial establishments in a market of unknown potential. Nor has anyone asked why Indians should suddenly flock to expensive motels and eateries when cheap food is available everywhere and most overnighters are truckers who sleep in the cabs of their trucks.

The government has amended the National Highways Act to allow a more reliable form of recoupment method via the collection of tolls. A 5-year tax holiday and a 30 percent tax rebate for an additional 5-year period within the first 12 years of the facility becoming operational is now permitted; but, given the risks involved in highway construction, foreign investors have to have an assured return of at least 20 percent before they invest.

The government "also wants to see that superhighways connect all major ports in the country. This is one of the major decisions which we are going to take and also with regard to certain legislation about acquiring the land which will ease the burden on the investor." This again is an example of a government long on desire and short on specifics.

Hence, while actual FDI continues to rise, very little of it is entering the infrastructure sector. In 1995–1996, direct FDI reached $2.13 billion, for the first time in half a decade equaling the inflows of portfolio investments. This was a promising start but still did not really address the fact that administering infrastructure investment is the major weak spot in India's reform program. The government continually reiterates its need for $10 billion in FDI for investments in power, ports, roads, telecoms, and surface transport. Yet the government's inability to develop a smooth regulatory framework has not resulted in major investments of any significance, much less $10 billion worth.

How FDI Fails, Case I: Uncoordination with the State Bureaucracies. Over the past five years, only about one-fifth of foreign investment proposals have translated into actual foreign-currency inflows. One reason is that only in mid-1996 was the Foreign Investment Promotion Board (FIPB) transferred out of the corruption-infested Rao administration Prime Minister's Office to the Industry Ministry, where it should have been in the first place. Over the next few months Industry Minister Murasoli Maran made a considerable dent in the backlog of 424 cases pending with the FIPB—in just three sittings he cleared 113 FDI proposals with a value of Rs 7,000 crore ($2 billion). In order to clear proposals faster, the FIPB has also directed that all administrative ministries reviewing FDI proposals give their comments on a project within 15 days of receiving the proposal.

Even so, the huge gap between the projects that have been cleared and the ones that have actually materialized in the form of cash coming into the country persists. It is a problem that the Industry Ministry is being obliged to tackle without having been given the manpower and funding to suddenly approve outstanding proposals, much less tackle the bureaucratic hurdles throughout India's complex industrial investment infrastructure.

Although the FIPB was originally established in 1992 for the express purpose of helping foreign investors set up their projects and helping them overcome bureaucratic hurdles, this has not actually happened. After obtaining the FIPB's clearance, investors still have to negotiate an obstacle course of other clearances, ranging from the Reserve Bank of India to those of the various state-level departments—each of which in turn scrutinizes the project proposal all over again.

The much-maligned states do have some cause for their demand to re-approve a project already approved by the FIPB. A representative of the Tamil Nadu Industrial Development Corporation explains, "Though the FIPB clears the project, we at the field level are not informed what the potential investor is planning to do in our state. The FIPB proposal does not mention the location, the amount of land required, the range of products to be manufactured, or the likely time-frame for its completion. As a result, we have to verify all these ourselves to ensure that the proposal conforms to the rules laid down by our state laws." An adviser to the West Bengal Industrial Development Corporation (WBIDC) concurs: "It is we state-level agencies which have to sort out issues like land, power, and roads." In effect, getting an FIPB go-ahead has become just the first bureaucratic hurdle to be cleared rather than a definitive go-ahead.

At present, the Industry Ministry is not usually aware why projects are being delayed, for there is no formal means of tracking them. In 1994, the government tried to start an informal tracking process by sending out over 2,000 letters to companies asking then to furnish details of how far their proposals had progressed and how much money had been brought into the country. Only 300 replied. The tracking project was abandoned and has not been renewed. One would have thought at least serving those 300 better would have come to someone's mind.

Now the Industry Ministry "is preparing" a comprehensive set of guidelines that it says will make clearances both faster and more transparent. The new guidelines would increase the list of industries in which foreign collaborations get automatic approval from the present thirty-five to fifty-seven. The Ministry also wants to allow foreign collaborators to increase their equity stakes from the present 51 percent to 75 percent in the expanded list (presently only the current list is eligible for a 75 percent stake). In addition, the Ministry wants to appoint an autonomous body to monitor and report on the status of foreign investment and collaboration proposals cleared by it. It has shortlisted the Mumbai-based Centre for Monitoring Indian Economy (CMIE) and the Delhi-based National Council for Applied Economic Research (NCAER) for the job.

However, investors and state government officials both point out that these steps simply improve efficiency at the Industry Ministry level. Mere "monitoring and reporting" of the reasons for delays in investments do not, in themselves, push other layers of the bureaucracy into eliminating the delays. The Ministry's efforts are a step in the right direction, but much more needs to be done lower down the ladder at the state level. Unfortunately, the moves toward transparency at the Centre level as a result of the last two years of corruption scandals have not made much headway in the opaque halls of state bureaucracies.

How FDI Fails, Case II: Coddled Children Like Air-India. Most analysts believe that India has room for three major carriers. India's domestic air traffic is increasing by about 10 percent each year. Executive-class seats are hard to come by, and during the tourist season the waiting lists are long for economy-class seats as well. Hence, when India announced its version of an open-skies policy in 1992, private carriers were expected to quickly make inroads into the government's monopoly by offering better service. Travelers were fed up with delays and substandard service on Indian Airlines and its international counterpart, Air-India.

Half a dozen startups poured millions into making flying within India cheaper and more pleasant. However, although private carriers took off quickly enough, grabbing 40 percent of India's market in two years, government rules aimed at protecting its monopoly carrier just as quickly began driving the private airlines from the sky.

One of the small fleets' problems were their own optimism. Projected earnings did not materialize to cover the costs of fuel, leased airplanes, spare

parts, and taxes. By mid-1996, two of the biggest carriers, ModiLuft Ltd.
and East West Travel & Trade Links, were grounded with financial problems, and two others were groaning under debt. Only Jet Airways India
Ltd., 40 percent owned by Malaysian Airlines Systems and Kuwait Air, was
thriving.

The reason the Indian government did not help the upstarts was the
government's long-standing obsession with protecting the public sector.
The government intentionally made it difficult for the private carriers by
imposing long bureaucratic delays in getting permission to expand. Modi-
Luft waited more than 18 months for permission to bring four planes to
India. India's powerful Tata Group sought permission for 20 months to sign
a $518 million joint venture with 40 percent equity from Singapore
Airlines. But since that venture would likely become a market leader, the
Civil Aviation Ministry refused to approve the proposal.

Authorities also raised navigation fees, aircraft landing fees, and parking
charges. At the alleged insistence of Indian Airlines, the government also
forced private carriers to fly unprofitable, low-traffic routes as a condition
for operating between major cities. With their limited financial resources,
small carriers needed more time to generate revenue before being forced
into lesser markets.

Indian Airlines officials blame the private companies' financial woes on
bad management. Yet aviation officials have admitted to the press that
politics prevented full opening of the skies. The Hindu-nationalist Bharatiya Janata Party, for example, threatened to fight any new foreign investment in airlines. India's weak ruling coalition decided not to push for
liberalization in this area.

The Manufacturing Sector

The manufacturing sector is broad-based and in some subsectors is
relatively sophisticated compared with other emerging economies. In the
past, this sector has performed poorly. Since the advent of liberalization,
however, this sector has improved rapidly, expanding approximately 8.7
percent in 1994–1995 (the year for which the most recent precise figures
are available), with every prospect of continued rapid growth over the
1996–1998 period. As investment picks up, the sector should be able to
improve efficiency, particularly in high-tech sectors such as electronics,
computers, software manufacture, and pharmaceuticals.

Some industries are likely to remain protected. These are mainly involved in the production of consumer goods and are the domain of the
small-scale or "unorganized" sector. The manufacturing sector in general

will remain burdened by restrictive regulations relating to the shedding of labor.

A Surge In Nonmanufacturing Companies

The mid-1990s have seen a remarkable surge in the number of registrations of nonmanufacturing enterprises such as real estate, finance, trading, and investment. This somewhat offsets the significant drop in the number of manufacturing companies during the same period.

The number of manufacturing companies as a ratio of total company registrations has declined from 54 percent in 1987–1988 to 28 percent in 1994–1995. The number of trading and finance companies as a ratio of total company registrations climbed from 41 percent in 1990–1991 to 57 percent in 1995–1996. In 1994–1995, finance or finance-related companies alone accounted for 35 percent of all the companies registered.

This is a highly regionalized phenomenon. In West Bengal, 85 percent of the companies registered in 1994–1995 were classified as investment, trading, or construction-related. In Delhi, the number was 65 percent, as was the figure for Maharashtra. Of the 7,900–odd companies registered in West Bengal in 1994–1995, only 10 percent were manufacturing enterprises.

Private companies form the majority of the companies registered: just twenty-one government companies were registered in 1989–1990, and twelve in 1994–1995. Most of the new companies registered were small—those with an authorized capital of up to Rs 5 lakh ($14,285) accounted for one-third of all non-government private limited companies registered in 1994–1995. If authorized capital of up to Rs 10 lakh ($28,570) is considered, the percentage leaps to 87 percent. Since subscribed capital is usually much smaller than the authorized capital, the tinyness of these companies is noteworthy. It seems that the small sector and individual entrepreneurship flourish the most in a liberal economic environment—and in the regions where the bulk of financial activity is concentrated. There has also been exponential growth in the sheer number of companies registered. In the first nine months of 1996, 41,000 companies were registered, compared with 1994–1995's 30,000. This number is almost equal to the entire corporate population during the 1970s.

Five states accounted for 70 percent of the total companies at work in 1994–1995: Maharashtra (22 percent), Delhi (18 percent), West Bengal (14 percent), Tamil Nadu (9 percent), and Gujarat (7 percent). At the other end of the spectrum, Tripura, Manipur, Nagaland, Arunachal Pradesh, Meghalaya, Dadra, and Daman & Diu attracted less than 100 companies—again reinforcing the compartmentalization factor.

Most of these companies are concentrated in just a few districts within most states, usually close to or at urban centers. Three-fourths of the companies in Andhra Pradesh registered their offices in Hyderabad, Secunderabad, and the nearby Ranga Reddy districts. In Maharashtra, Greater Bombay, and Thane, 85 percent of all firms are registered in the state of Pune.

State governments have not really begun to grasp the consequences of so much regional compartmentalization of finance.

Two Detailed Looks at Actual Investment Today

Information such as the above tends to be fairly meaningless within the context of India's immensity and diversity. Below are two case examples that help give a sharper focus to the overall picture. It would be quite possible for the overseas investor interested in India to use Internet sources to assemble the type of information given below for any region in India. This book must be more abstemious with the detail work, for it would quickly become another book in its own right. The following Internet addresses are a good place to start looking at what investment in India is really like these days:

The Hindu (a daily newspaper):
   http://www.webpage.com/hindu/

India World business directory:
   http://www.indiaworld.com/open/biz/index.html

India Government Business Directory:
   http://www.webindia.com/india.html

Software Technology Parks of India:
   http://www.stph.net

Gov't of India NYC Office business facts:
   http://www.indiaserver.com/biz/dbi/MEA2.0.html

How to Invest info:
   http://www.indiaserver.com/biz/dbi/MEA3.0.html

Doing Business with India:
   http://www.indiaserver.com/biz/dbi/dbi.html

Insider News:
   http://www.globalindia.com/index.htm

General Info:
   http://www.indiacomm.com/

Economic Times (daily news):
   http://www.economictimes.com/today/pagehome.htm
   (E-mail: times@giasdl01.vsnl.net.in)

Business Services Syndicate consultants:
   http://www.indiagate.com/commerce/busi.html

Indian Economy:
   http://www.webcom.com/percent7Eprakash/ECONOMY/
   ECONOMY.HTML

Case I: The Data Entry Industry and India's New Business Thinking. The global growth in data entry and processing has added a new dimension to India's software industry. India thus far has been somewhat slow to pick up on the opportunity. However, that tardiness is quickly being overcome.

In 1996, U.S. companies outsourced over $1 billion worth of data entry work. Most was done by companies within the United States, but the arrival of the combination of cheap satellite communications and efficient imaging technologies have quickly changed the market. Now only the scanning of original documents is done in the United States. Data extraction and entry are telelinked to cheaper sites. India can deliver data at about one-third the prevailing U.S. costs.

All of this is largely due to the growth of "Programmers' Plateau" in Bangalore. (For awhile Bangalore was called "Silicon Plateau" because of its location on the Deccan Plateau, but the fiercely independent Indian software community was not about to tag along in the wake of *any*one's silicon nomenclature when "software" impresses people as much more brainy.) India's share of the world's exports of software content has grown from 50 to 80 percent annually in the last few years. This has inspired new business opportunities, notably in data processing. Reliable communication links have opened up yet another segment, transcription services, software customer support, and back office operations. Some of the client industries are very large: global finance, travel, insurance claims, legal and medical transcription, existing printed materials that must be reformatted for CD-ROM, and so on. There is also seasonal demand from sources such as Yellow Pages, electoral rolls, share transfer records, public issues, and so on. Moreover, as India's telecom policy moves toward allowing international 800 numbers, much 800-based customer support can feasibly shift to India.

The enormous potential in data entry has not been fully exploited in India. China produces 2 billion characters (keystrokes) a month, the Philippines 1 billion, and Trinidad (the earliest offshore base to enter the field) 7 billion. Only 60 million characters come from India, yet the country has the potential for 5 to 10 billion.

Small though it may be, India's performance has been competitive. In 1994, data processing generated Rs 88 crore ($25.1 million); in 1995–1996, this rose to Rs 136 crore ($38.9 million). In 1996–1997, data processing was projected to grow by about 100 percent.

The same factors that positioned India to do well in the software market work with data processing too—a large pool of English-educated computer literates, the country's vastly improved telecommunications and VSAT facilities, the U.S./India time differential, which has helped develop 24-hour nonstop virtual offices separated only by half the globe, and, above all, a growing breed of entrepreneurs who see the potential of the market. An American transcriptionist is paid about 7–8 cents per 80-character line of data. In India they are paid only 4 cents. The cost saving in outsourcing 700,000 lines is $25,000–$35,000. Data processing has similar margins. The cost in the United States is approximately $15–$20 an hour, whereas Indian companies can do it at $4–$5 an hour.

At present, the three strongest production centers in India are Chennai, Bangalore, and Thiruvananthapuram. The typical business is a one-stop-shop that combines systems integration and electronic media services; the data entry part is usually only one of the services offered. Others offer "software product suites" including CD-ROM publishing, Internet publishing, consultancy, development of services for digital imaging, and document capture.

Most of India's services have targeted the United States, which is still a paper-driven society in which the penetration of image transmission technology is still relatively rare. According to the American Association for Information Management, American business produces 1.3 billion pieces of paper every *day*, of which over 800 million is printouts and photocopies.

Indian companies see their niche as the remote back offices for U.S. companies. They see their remoteness as an attraction: rather than courier sensitive papers around from office to office in the United States, their content can be imaged, sent by satellite, processed, and sent back the next day.

However, in this bright picture Indians see some work to be done on their part. The best technologies cannot fulfill contracts if India does not increase overall productivity to levels on par with international standards. Indians see their principle flaw as not being sufficiently market-driven— they go for price and then consider quality and dependable delivery.

Case II: The Pattern of Overseas Investment in Tamil Nadu. After Tamil Nadu's corrupt comic-opera Jayalalitha Jayaram regime was thrown out of office in 1996, Tamil Nadu saw a sharp surge in domestic and foreign direct investment. Between July 1995 and March 1996, Tamil Nadu totted up Industrial Entrepreneur Memorandums (IEMs) worth Rs 5,859 crore ($1.67 billion). This compares with Gujarat's Rs 21,712 crore ($6.2 billion) and Maharashtra's Rs 13,037 crore ($3.7 billion). It also compares well with Tamil Nadu's prior performance between January 1992 and December 1995 at Rs 3,027 crore ($865 million).

According to local officials, the state government will likely approve investments worth over Rs 10,000 crore ($2.87 billion) during 1996–1997. International investors planning to set up shop in the state include Schlumberger, BMW, and Grundig. Auto manufacturers top the list. Hindustan Motors has invested Rs 250 crore ($71 million) to make 20,000 Mitsubishi Lancer autos. Ashok Leyland has recently built a Rs 400 crore ($114 million) truck plant at Hosur. Other large investments include Rs 1,500 crore ($429 million) by Mahindra Ford India (a 50:50 joint venture between Mahindra & Mahindra and Ford) to produce 100,000 vehicles a year, and Rs 2,450 crore ($700 million) by Hyundai Motor India to make another 100,000 vehicles. Hyundai Motor India plans to add another investment of another Rs 1,400 crore ($400 million) to raise its production capacity to 200,000 vehicles per year. These projects will generate downstream investments of perhaps Rs 300 crore ($85.7 million) in ancillaries. Tamil Nadu has attracted so much vehicle-related investment because of its already well-developed auto component industry. Some 47 percent of India's domestic auto components' total output and 35 percent of its total component exports come from the state.

Thapar Du Pont's 50:45 joint venture between the Thapar group's flagship Ballarpur Industries and U.S. chemicals giant Du Pont (the remaining 5 percent is held by Japanese engineering major Mitsui) was attracted mainly by the presence of several large tire companies such as MRF, Dunlop, and TVS Tyres. This prompted Thapar Du Pont to shift its Rs 625 crore ($179 million) project to manufacture nylon 6,6 fabric to Tamil Nadu in June 1995 following a pullout from Goa. Almost 95 percent of the fabric will be sold to the tire industry.

Tamil Nadu has adopted several initiatives to encourage such investment. In 1995, the state announced that all megaprojects with an investment of over Rs 1,500 crore ($429 million) would receive special concessions, the most important of which was a sales tax waiver for 14 years, compared with the 5 to 10 percent offered by other states. Mahindra Ford India and the Hyundai Motor India projects came in largely because of this concession.

To eliminate the transportation bottleneck for high-volume exporters, Tamil Nadu plans to develop a port at Ennore as a satellite to its existing port at Chennai. The 1995–1996 Union Budget provided Rs 78 crore ($22 million) to develop a port at Tuticorin that would facilitate the flow of goods to and from the state. Given the promise of these facilities, Hyundai Motor India agreed to export autos worth Rs 935 crore ($267 million) by 2003, and Thapar Du Pont agreed to import 99.7 percent of its raw materials.

The Tamil Nadu state government has set up a standing committee on industrial development to look into the other demands of industry; Chief Minister Karunanidhi is its chair. Tamil Nadu has removed several obstacles such as its high sales tax. Until recently, the sales tax on raw materials was 5.6 percent, compared to 2 percent in Andhra Pradesh and 1.5 percent in Karnataka. Tamil Nadu was losing Rs 150 crore ($43 million) in annual revenues because auto component and computer industries were doing their purchasing in the neighboring union territory of Pondicherry. Karunanidhi's 1995–1996 budget responded by replacing the state's hodgepodge sales tax structure (general sales tax, surcharge, additional surcharge, and additional sales tax) with a single-point tariff. The tariff has been lowered on raw materials from 5.6 to 3 percent, and on capital goods from 12 to 3 percent.

However, some major obstacles still remain, notably power. In the period April to July 1996, power supply fell short of demand by 16.2 percent compared with the national average of 11.3 percent. In 1995, the Tamil Nadu Industrial Development Corp. (TIDCO) invited tenders for fifteen power plants of 100-megawatt capacity. By November 1996 they had been opened but no licenses had yet been granted. One reason for the delays was that Tidco asked the companies to quote a fixed tariff for the first 15 years with their tender documents. The state government became indecisive because different companies gave different tariff estimates based on different sets of assumptions, which made it difficult to compare them.

Another problem is environmental activism. There was opposition to the Thapar Du Pont project on the grounds that the plant's high water consumption would draw down the water table at Gummidipoondi, near Chennai, where the plant is located. Nonetheless, work on the project is going on and production is expected to commence by early 1998. Given the Tamil Nadu government's efforts to adapt to investor needs, it seems unlikely that controversies such as this will reverse the flow of investment into the state.

The Agriculture Sector

A happy agricultural sector is vital to India's general economic development. It is the largest employer of labor. This labor guarantees India virtual self-sufficiency in foodstuffs. Growth is likely to be steady over the forecast period at around 2.5 percent a year (assuming that favorable weather prevails). There is great potential in areas such as food-processing, where significant value-addition can be achieved. However, the sector as a whole remains tightly regulated and needs liberalized internal controls.

These projections are based on the assumption that agriculture will continue to expand steadily. However, the agricultural sector remains weather-vulnerable. While the ability of the economy to withstand a bad harvest is much improved as a result of substantial food grain stocks and an ability to import in time of need, any setback in agricultural production would affect a large section of the economy and would impact industry through its effect on demand.

Almost 75 percent of India's people live in rural areas. Agricultural development and the virtual absence of agricultural income tax have led to increasing disposable incomes. Together with the integration of rural areas and urban centers brought about by modern communications and job mobility, consumption patterns in rural India have changed dramatically.

So have income expectations. In 1992–1993, rural markets accounted for over 70 percent of the sales of portable radio receivers, mechanical wristwatches, bicycles—in fact just about every popular consumer item except condoms: between 60 and 70 percent of sales of quartz watches, sewing machines, and table fans; 40 to 60 percent of black-and-white televisions, motorcycles, pressure cookers, ceiling fans, and cassette recorders; and 20 to 40 percent of small color televisions, mixer-blenders, and electric irons. Rural expenditure on packaged goods is growing at 23 percent per year starting from the rather impecunious baseline of 1992.

Indian companies and multinationals alike have set rural marketing as the key to their overall market strategy. Some companies have successfully used innovative techniques to capture the rural market share. For example, ITC—a highly diversified conglomerate that goes well beyond consumer products—has initiated various support programs for tobacco and sunflower planters, giving itself (and the growers) a clear edge in the cigarette and cooking oil markets. PepsiCo has similarly involved potato and tomato growers in its bid to capture the snack-food market. Indeed, PepsiCo pays more for both than the government, which has caused considerable ink to flow onto the pages of the virulently anti-subsidy business magazines. Unilever's Indian ventures—Hindustan Lever, Lipton, and Brooke Bond—have extremely well-developed distribution networks in rural areas.

Marketers have devised some innovative, even quite striking, ways to reach rural customers. They would not dare miss any one of the 5,000 rural fairs and festivals held annually all over the country. These fairs attract about 100 million people—almost the entire rural middle class—an audience that is a marketer's dream. Many multinationals have designed products or changed their brand names to give them a rural flavor.

Investing in the Agricultural Sector. The foregoing is based on a continuation of the agricultural sector's productivity. That can only happen with some very substantial reforms, which will prove to be a major investment challenge within India and abroad.

Agricultural reform is a major priority for the government. Its policy is to reinvigorate the sector by encouraging private investment in every agricultural activity, emphasizing food-processing and marketing new products. According to analysts at the McKinsey & Co. in Delhi, developing India's agricultural sector between 1996 and 2001 would require the investment of well over Rs 100,000 crore ($285.7 billion) just to address the sector's existing problems. These problems cover the entire length of the food production chain, from farm to distributor to retailer.

Agriculture accounts for more than 30 percent of India's GDP and employs more than 60 percent of its labor force. In 1993, the total value of agricultural production was more than Rs 165,000 crore ($471 billion). This, surprisingly to many outsiders, exceeded the production value of the combined chemical, metal, and petroleum industries. On the other hand, farm productivity is still very low. The value added per agricultural worker is only 10 percent of China's, 5 percent of Thailand's, and less than 0.2 percent of the United Kingdom's or the United States's. Despite significant improvements in recent years, agricultural yields remain low. In rice, for example, India's yield is less than one-half of China's. Large-scale crop waste in harvesting, storage, and transportation worsens the situation. More than 15 percent of wheat and 20 percent of fruit and vegetable production is lost before it reaches the consumer.

Increasing agricultural productivity is a potentially significant growth engine for the Indian economy. Productivity increases would result, among other things, in substantially increased large-scale agricultural exports. At present, domestic consumption absorbs practically all of the agricultural production. Even though India accounts for 10 percent of the world's wheat production, its share of the 1993 world trade in cereals was only 1 percent.

The food-processing industry is significantly underdeveloped. One reason is that it is dominated by unorganized players. India's value addition by food-processing is only 7 percent; in China it is 25 percent and in Thailand 40 percent. In basic operations such as sugar-cane crushing, rice dehusking, and flour milling, only 23 percent of food in India is processed on a commercial basis. More than 70 percent of this occurs in small unorganized companies. Less than 5 percent of all agricultural produce is processed by professional companies. Except for the relatively few leading players, food companies have limited marketing skills and a poor appreciation of customer satisfaction. Most food products are a poor value for consumers.

The underdevelopment of the agricultural industry is not necessarily the result of poor industry economics. In recent years, food-processing has been one of the more profitable industries in India. Between 1985 and 1994, food companies significantly outperformed the average Sensex stock market index. This good performance is likely to continue as the market develops further and access to processing technology improves.

The outlook is that as incomes increase, people will start spending significantly larger amounts on food. Initially, as income increases, people will first respond by spending more on basic-quality, hygienic, unadulterated, packaged foods. Volumes will primarily be in staple products such as packaged flour, spices, rice, and oils. Per-capita incomes of Rs 30,000 ($857) adjusted in terms of purchasing power parity are generally agreed to be a critical threshold, after which expenditure on food grows very quickly. Generally, marginally affluent people do not buy more food but rather more expensive foods, reflecting higher value-addition through processing.

India is rapidly approaching the per-capita Rs 30,000 threshold. The next few years should see the food-processing industry experience sharply rising consumer demand for high-quality and innovative products. All segments of the food market indicate good prospects for growth, from fairly basic but better-processed foods to high-value items such as breakfast cereals and pre-prepared meals.

Indian processors will likely profit most by capitalizing on these opportunities. Although global players may dominate specific product segments (breakfast foods being a good example), they will likely garner a relatively small share of the overall market, leaving most of the opportunities open to local players.

All this said, the agricultural industry is plagued by two other problems: inefficient distribution and the dominance of *kirana* (corner-shop) retailing. The highly regulated system of private distribution via middlemen is notoriously inefficient. It also creates quality problems for food-processing companies as well. Manufacturers of baked goods find it difficult to impossible to systematically buy wheat of a particular specification. The mills have no choice but to take what the *mandis* (wholesale markets) offer, which is usually a mixture of several different types of wheat.

Retailing is fragmented, highly individualistic, usually inefficient, and mostly confined to *kirana* shops. More than 3 million retail outlets operate in India, ten times the number in Indonesia, the only other Asian country with such sharply defined distribution territories and reliance on tiny shops mostly selling the same goods. Collectively, India's retailers generate retail sales of more than Rs 150,000 crore ($428.6 billion). Yet the average retail outlet generates less than Rs 5 lakh ($14,286) in sales in a year, less than 25 percent of the Indonesian average and 2.5 percent of the U.K. average.

Most marketing specialists believe that these low-cost *kirana* operations will continue to dominate for quite some time. This will hamper the entrance of new players hankering after a major mass-market penetration. A different sector likely to be affected by mass-market production will be center-city supermarkets, whose rentals and distribution costs are making it difficult for them to reduce their overheads to the competitive levels now being offered by suburban superstores. The latter are so efficient that they have driven down the cost of retailing to unprecedented levels. These superstores are likely to be powerful industry catalysts. To fill their long rows of shelves with new and increasingly upscale quality products, they will encourage innovation in the food-processing industry, which will in turn push up prices at the producer level.

All of this is very promising, but it masks the quite formidable barriers to increasing agricultural productivity and a stronger food-processing industry. These barriers are (1) structural disincentives remaining in the current government regulations, (2) inadequate infrastructure development, and (3) the high levels of investment required throughout the industry chain.

Archaic (but still very powerful) ceilings on land holdings have resulted in millions of tiny subscale farms with low productivity. These lack the financial resources and local road and irrigation infrastructure to install productivity-enhancing measures. The limited-holding policy prevents corporate farming, which would bring technological advances. Worse, it drives farmers straight into the hands of the local moneylender/thug enforcer/politician nexus, which is the prime cause of India's rural economic woes.

Higher up the agricultural economic ladder, food subsidies and levy prices effectively transfer wealth out of the hands of the farmer by diminishing his real profit. The farmer finds it more and more difficult to justify investments in productivity-enhancing tools and techniques.

Infrastructure in India requires major upgrading on all fronts, and has a negative effect even at levels remote from the countryside. The main infrastructure needs are increased port capacity, better bulk-handling facilities, improved road quality and true national highways linking the major cities, quality warehousing and transport hubs close to major production centers, and more cold storage facilities.

Hence improved agricultural productivity implies very large investments in many areas of the economy. Most economists consider the minimum target investment to be Rs 20,000 crore ($57 billion) for tractors, harvesters, threshers, and irrigation systems. Another Rs 20,000 crore *per annum* in increased expenditure would be required to bring up fertilizer, pesticide, and hybrid seed usage.

McKinsey & Co. estimates that investment in upgrading India's food-processing capability needs to target a similar level. To raise the level of fruit and vegetable processing from its present level of less than 1 percent up to 15 percent, for instance, investment of another Rs 20,000 crore is needed. The development of retail outlets to serve growing demand requires additional investments of thousands of crores.

This adds up to an investment of over Rs 100,000 crore ($285.7 billion) over 5 years. The Indian agricultural community and food-processing industry cannot generate this level of finance. Hence the government looks to Indian business houses not presently involved in the agricultural sector and foreign investors to transform the Indian food-processing industry. Unfortunately, the action plans that have been proposed run long on ambitions, but short on details.

Distribution

There are three levels of retail markets in India:

- independent small retailers with only one or a few outlets that they run themselves and offer local convenience but few discounts;

- mass merchandisers with huge professionally run department stores, in which choice is very broad and discounts are moderate;

- large warehouse high-discount operations, which trade off zero service for the widest selection and cheapest prices.

Today's consumer boom has focused attention on the distribution end as manufacturers and retailers both innovate a variety of tactics designed to gain them some kind of control over the market.

Broadly speaking, India's retailing world has only recently developed from an independent-dominated market to one in which independents are a dwindling minority and mass merchandisers and discount houses divide up the rest of the market in roughly equal portions.

Buying a television or a refrigerator or a mixer used to be quite simple. You knew that there were three or four brands on the market and that each had two or three models from which to choose. Where you bought them from depended on the product and how expensive it was. Similar technology and lower priced products, like radios, two-in-ones, mixers, and black-and-white televisions were generally available in small consumer-durables retail outlets, several of which could be found in a city. For more high-end items one had to go to the showroom run by a company's exclusive distributor, who sold both to the trade and to customers. There would be just one or two per manufacturer in each city, and their showrooms were usually in the swankier parts of town.

Such a list of options reflects a revolution in the distribution and retailing of consumer durables. Despite the durables sector boom, the number and type of channels to the consumer have not been growing commensurately. The myriad new brands and models, both Indian and foreign, are jostling for limited space at the retail end. The dynamism of product innovators has not been matched by retailers. As a result, distribution channels have become the most sought-after media in the durables market.

India has a massive and complex sales and distribution network. Over a million market intermediaries—wholesalers, stockists, transporters, and retailers—distribute an enormous variety of goods all over the country. The consumer-goods network directly accesses approximately 3,800 cities and towns and over a half-million villages. Indian trade is largely fragmented, with centralized purchasing for chain stores and supermarkets only a recent phenomenon.

The distribution network in India is predominantly family-owned proprietary concerns. Urban areas have a range of distribution outlets ranging from large supermarkets and superstores to the smaller neighborhood retail store. Virtually every village in India possesses small shops supplied by the local network.

With distribution channels being largely independently-owned and catering to multiple brands, dealer development is of prime importance. The recent strategic alliance between Coke Inc. and Parle—India's leading soft-drink manufacturer, hinged on the latter's distribution strengths. Other similar alliances that have been recently forged are Procter & Gamble with Godrej for soaps and detergents, Hewlett Packard with HCL for computers, and Black & Decker with Bajaj for home appliances. Distribution in India is facilitated by a rapidly expanding infrastructure and service industry.

The Consumer Market

International consumer-goods producers see the Indian market as a billion-strong populace just now achieving the income levels enabling them to make consumer-durable purchases on a large scale. Refrigerator sales, for example, went from 750,000 in 1992 to 1.8 million in 1995. Washing machine sales grew from 325,000 in 1994 to 500,000 in 1995 and were projected to be 850,000 by the end of 1996. Air conditioners shot up 24 percent to 235,000 in 1995 and another 28 percent in 1996.

The story is much the same for cars, color televisions, rice cookers, electric irons, liquefied petroleum gas stoves, and a myriad of nondurable products such as cleansers, toiletries, fashion, study aids, entertainment, greeting cards, giftware—on and on. Hence it is no surprise that considerable thought is being given by marketing people in India and abroad to the purchasing patterns and motivations of India's diverse demographic profiles.

Some look to India's upper income households whose annual incomes are above Rs 70,000 ($2,000) per year. Though modest by Southeast Asian and Western terms, this income level buys a quite comfortable lifestyle in India given the effects of purchasing power parity. This upper income class numbered about 50 million households (150–180 million people) in 1996 and is growing roughly 20 percent per year. Much of the spending potential of this group has yet to be tapped.

Rural areas where rents and other living costs are far lower than in the cities are India's second largest consumer market. Rural Indian purchasing power is expected to be some two-thirds of the country's total by 1997–1998.

The spending pattern of India's high-income group interests sociologists as much as it does consumer-goods marketers. There is real concern about the social effects of the sharp increase of labor-saving household goods and prestige or luxury items. The displacement of domestic service workers, the lengths to which many families might go to keep up with the new consumption trends, and the age-old envy of the have-nots are but a few of their concerns. India's traditional customs are already being warped by the desire for goods rather than cash—there has been an alarming rise in the abuse and murder of young brides as their in-laws use the dowry system to obtain consumer goods through threats and extortion.

India's 1991 economic reforms sparked a sharp movement away from the country's socialist ideals and its License Raj of regulations and restrictions. The movement followed the lead of other Asian countries in the direction of improved competition and efficiency. The climate for foreign manufacturing investment has never been more cordial, yet there is small-scale but high-pitched resistance to "Western pollution" which achieves a certain national recognition over seemingly silly issues such as whether Western fried chicken contains too much MSG. The Southeast Asian and Western attitude that consumers should be able to decide for themselves has not caught on among certain Indian politicians whose traditional background is based on telling others what is good for them while lining their pockets with socialist taxes.

India's change to a consumer economy can be said to have had its roots not on the 1992–1993 budget, which focused on economic stabilization, but on the 1993–1994 budget, which moved sharply in the direction of economic growth. In that year, spending on infrastructure increased 26 percent and excise taxes were cut 10–15 percent—largely on consumer durables. Domestic demand for consumer products—and the industries that make them—raised the value of imports to almost $26 billion, against an export performance of $22 billion. The government has accordingly placed a strong emphasis on attracting export manufacturers.

These two economic facts in India's future are unlikely to change. Consumer demand is likely to be more predictable than the outbursts of politicians. Consumers indicate a clear desire not merely for more useful but for better-made products. Everyone prefers to see them made in India, but there is a diminishing phobia especially among politicians for consumer imports provided that they do not seriously skew India's economy.

However, adequately serving India's consumer market implies a transportation and communications infrastructure superior to the one that exists now, not to mention relaxed governmental regulation. That in turn implies a receptivity in governmental and financial circles to the kinds of social and economic stresses that economic take-off produces, since many Indians' expectation of government is a motherly protectress rather than protagonist of economic or cultural ideology.

India already possesses important prerequisites: a well-trained class of technicians and managers, an uninhibited entrepreneurial mentality, competitive wages compared with Asia's other export manufactories, a growing sense of financial steadiness, and what appears to be firmer and firmer political stability. It seems safe to say that no matter which government holds the political reins, the Indian consumer has decided that economic reforms will proceed.

Advertising

Advertisers in India reach about 75 percent of the population through television, and almost the entire population through radio. The most popular television programs (often love-story films) enjoy a viewership of more than 100 million. There are an estimated 33 million television sets in India, with the largest number in the west and the smallest in the south. Most television advertising in India continues to be on state-owned Doordarshan, which reaches viewers across the country. More than 3 million sets are linked to cable or satellite and are exposed to pan-Asian advertising on the Hong Kong-based satellite channel Star TV (which has recently begun to penetrate the Hindi-language market in direct competition with India's drab state-owned Doordarshan).

Upscale Indian advertising is focused on cable and satellite viewers who are considered to be a more sophisticated, high-income group. Exposure to foreign products is high among wealthy urban Indians, usually through friends or relatives living abroad. The products of foreign multinationals continue to be regarded as being of higher quality than Indian-made ones.

Doordarshan estimates that its signals cover 63 percent of India's territory and 82 percent of the population, broken down into three major segments:

- the national network, which is beamed all over the country and is broadcast usually in Hindi and English;

- the regional networks, which broadcast in the regional languages; these networks exist in most major states outside the north Indian Hindi-speaking belt;

- the metro channels, which broadcast in the four megacities—Bombay, Calcutta, Delhi, and Madras.

Hong Kong's Star TV was introduced in 1992 and reached a viewership of 3.3 million households in less than a year. This gave a considerable boost to advertisers by exposing Indian audiences to foreign products and services. It also laid the seeds for profound changes in social and political undercurrents which cannot be measured but certainly showed up in the public's general attitude that the old politics was no longer serving anyone except the politicians.

India's advertising activity is sustained by a host of top-quality local agencies now being joined by major international firms. These include Young & Rubicam, Lintas, BBDO, J. W. Thompson, McCann Ericsson, Leo Burnett, Bozell, and the French firm Publicis. These leading agencies brought their major Western accounts with them, leaving India's smaller agencies to cater to local and smaller international clients. Many Indian companies have in-house advertising agencies that cut costs and circumvent high agency fees, but at some cost in up-to-the-minute imagery for their products. There is a very active, rural, smaller metropolitan ad circuit, often one-person or husband–wife teams who get and deliver their copy on bicycles!

Advertising-Related Issues

Languages. The Indian constitution recognizes sixteen official languages, with Hindi being the national tongue. In addition, the census lists thirty-three other languages that are each the mother tongue of more than 100,000 people. Besides these languages, there are about 1,600 other languages listed in the 1981 census as mother tongues (the corresponding data for 1991 are not yet available).

All major languages spoken in the north, east, and west derive their roots from Sanskrit and share many common characteristics. These Indo-Aryan languages are spoken by about three-quarters of the population. The four major languages spoken in the southern states are Dravidian languages and are entirely different from those spoken in the rest of the country.

Hindi. While Hindi is the national language of India, it is the mother tongue of fewer than 40 percent of the population. The states of India were reorganized on a linguistic basis in 1956. The medium of instruction in the vast majority of schools is the local language (which is Hindi in a number of cases). However, even where Hindi is not the local language, it has to be studied at the school level; an exception is the southern state of Tamil Nadu, where Hindi is not taught in schools at all.

English. The teaching of English is voluntary and almost nonexistent in rural areas. However, English is the medium of instruction in elite schools, most leading universities, and institutes of technology or management. While no official data are available, it is estimated that 5–6 percent of the population of India is English-literate. Because it is in a sense an elitist language, English speakers generally belong to the middle and upper income groups. This is important to keep in mind when marketing consumer goods.

However, literacy in the Indian languages is spreading much faster than it is in English. The absence of a clearly understood national language and relatively low literacy levels make it difficult for a consumer-goods marketer to communicate a message to a target audience. Two factors have come to the marketer's aid, however:

- The popularity of Hindi cinema, which transgresses linguistic boundaries, has made the language relatively well understood even in the southern states.

- Doordarshan telecasts movies, religious epics, and other programs in Hindi during prime time. These attract audiences in all states and add to the knowledge of Hindi, as well as ensure high viewership of commercials.

Customs. While the vast majority of Indians are Hindu (82 percent), Muslims constitute about 100 million (12 percent) of the population. In addition, there are more than 15 million Christians and more than 10 million Sikhs. However, the differences in religion have had no significant impact on the marketing of consumer goods because the vast majority of the population is Hindu and vegetarian. Hindu vegetarianism may initially have been practiced for economic reasons, but now seems to have acquired the force of tradition. It is perhaps only in the West Bengal and Kerala states that the bulk of the population is nonvegetarian.

The people inhabiting most of the northern, western, and eastern regions are believed to be of Aryan stock, while the inhabitants of the southern region are Dravidian. In general, non-south Indians are fairer, taller, and better built than their southern counterparts.

Their smaller stature has meant that south Indians are much more likely to partake of additional products of high nutritional value. For example, the south accounts for more than 50 percent of the market for milk-food drinks (such as Horlicks and Bournvita). Their relatively darker complexion has resulted in a wider use of "whitening" products than elsewhere in the country. For example, Fair and Lovely, a fairness cream made by Hindustan Lever (a Unilever subsidiary) sells much better in the south.

Also, the north and west of India are more Westernized than the east and south, perhaps because the regions have had greater contact with the West, and there has been greater emigration from these regions to the West. Historically, almost all of the invaders entered from the northwest; the inhabitants of those areas, therefore, were subjected to many influences and were forced to adapt in order to survive.

On the other hand, the inhabitants of the south, which experienced few major invasions, tended to be more resistant to change. As a result, new products in India are often launched first in the north—Punjab, Haryana, and Delhi are believed to be the most "experimentative" areas of the country.

There are also differences in food habits. For example, the north Indian staple is wheat, although rice is occasionally eaten. In the south, the staple is rice. The cooking oils used are also different—groundnut oil in the west, mustard oil in the east, and coconut oil in parts of the south.

Market Research

Market research is fairly well developed. Several leading companies provide some of the best market intelligence services to be found in Asia. One reason is India's uninhibited democracy, which enables marketers to ask questions that other Asians would shy from for fear of their names appearing on some political black list.

The National Council for Applied Economic Research (NCAER) is India's leading survey-based economic research institution on consumer demographics. the NCAER surveys approximately 500,000 people regularly as it seeks marketing statistics for its client base of mainly Indian industries. Several other players, notably Marketing and Research Group (MARG) and Indian Market Research Bureau (IMRB), also provide high-quality primary market research. The Operations Research Group (ORG) conducts detailed audits of India's retail outlets. (One reason for ORG's authenticity is its resolute refusal to provide its raw data to the Indian tax authorities.)

A number of smaller agencies such as Francis Kanoi Marketing Research perform industry-specific studies for syndicated clients. Management consultancies are also well established, with Arthur Andersen, McKinsey, and KPMG providing market feasibility studies and product entry strategies.

The low price–high volume segment is the major market for consumer durables. While the poor may not be getting richer, they continue to buy more and more durables, and comprise the mainstay for most such products. According to a late 1995 All-India survey of 280,000 households by the National Council of Applied Economic Research (NCAER), the lowest income group family share of purchasers of consumer durables increased more rapidly in 1995 after two years of erratic behavior followed by two years of lightly increasing buying behavior.

While the late 1980s saw a significant decline in the proportion of households in the lowest income segments—those with an annual family income below Rs 20,000 ($571)—this decline apparently has been reversing since 1993–1994. None of the income segments has revisited the dramatic changes of the late 1980s. In the lowest income segment, a sharp rise in consumerism in the 1980s slowed to a more moderate pace in the early 1990s and then picked up again somewhat dramatically starting in 1994.

Some studies have suggested that poverty, after declining in the 1980s from 46.5 percent in 1983 to 35.5 percent in 1990–1991, rose again in the initial years of reforms, and began to decline again after 1994. Consumer spending data point to the fact that this may not be quite accurate. Poverty, in fact, may actually have declined all through the period. This view is given credibility by the steady increase in both real wages and procurement prices in the agriculture sector during the reform period.

In 1993–1994, for example, families in the lowest income group owned 47 percent of all bicycles, 17 percent of mopeds, 9 percent of scooters, 11 percent of motorcycles, and 28 percent of quartz wristwatches. The number of new households buying these products in this income category also continued to increase steadily over 1991–1995. Some sections of those who are believed to be below the poverty line are actually buying durables, although in small amounts.

In terms of growth as well as potential, this segment offers the largest scope. While 45 households out of every 1,000 in this income category owned black-and-white televisions in 1989–1990, this number more than doubled to 97 in 1993–1994. For both color televisions and mopeds the growth was around 50 percent while the number of households buying motorcycles doubled. The low penetration levels—less than 50 households out of every 1,000 in the country are owners of most other durables—imply a large scope for farther purchases.

For marketers of both consumer durables and nondurables, the extremely low levels of ownership, in both urban as well as rural markets, can only be good news in the post-1996 election economic picture. However, as the survey illustrates, the market still remains essentially a low-priced one. With the high-income categories still not growing very rapidly, the numbers of very rich are too small to make a substantive consumer base for luxury manufacturers.

The super-rich market is somewhat of a vapor market. The super-rich market segment is not encouraging for the rather over-broad range of expensive automobiles and consumer durables being launched in the country. The number of "very rich" in the country is quite low in real numbers—roughly 600,000 households have an annual income of over Rs 10 lakh ($28,570)—and of these, approximately 74,000 households earned more than Rs 50 lakh annually ($142,850).

These numbers must be considered conservative in light of the unquantifiable amount of unrecorded income among the upper middle and high classes. How conservative is an open question. While a large parallel economy is the traditional explanation for the existence of a huge untapped potential for luxury goods, the NCAER tries to adjust its figures for the readily evident levels of the black-income economy. Since the poor do not have much hidden income, an additional 20 percent or thereabouts has been added to the income of households who earn more than Rs 62,000 ($1,770) annually.

Hence it can be reasonably assumed that the undeclared income is negligible in rural areas and is generated mostly in cities. Based on this, it is estimated that approximately 1.4 million families in the country earn more than Rs 5 lakh ($14,285) annually, while approximately 74,000 families have an annual income upwards of Rs 50 lakh ($142,850). Any upward revision of the share of black income to these income groups will increase the number of the rich, but it is unlikely that these numbers will change significantly.

The Legal Profession

India's legal profession is dominated by a handful of conventionally run firms established generations ago. Run by an old guard, until recently they saw little change prior to liberalization. New partners were rarely appointed. Firms barely expanded. Young lawyers worked years for a meager salary and a glimmer of hope that they would eventually share management responsibility.

Liberalization has forced some, but not landmark, changes. One is related to the large influx of overseas clients over the last few years.

Multinationals seeking to take advantage of emerging business opportunities seek legal expertise in the areas of joint ventures, mergers and acquisitions, offshore and domestic funds, institutional investment, international tax, project finance, and so on. Indian companies seek to establish foreign collaborations, invest in infrastructure projects, and raise money overseas. Both of these sets of needs are fairly new territory for Indian lawyers, and both demand more from them than they have been accustomed to. They are being asked to draft documents and structure deals in areas to which they had little or no prior exposure. For example, until the boom in foreign power plant building began 5 years ago, few attorneys were familiar with international power purchase agreements.

No longer does legal work center on property agreements and disputes. The ability to grasp complex financial concepts has become essential. One consequence has been a shift away from litigation to advisory work. As a consequence of this, the capacity of the general practice lawyer is under threat. Twenty years ago, a lawyer was expected to be a generalist, to know a bit about everything. Now up to 80 percent of legal work involving overseas business involvement is done by experts—a typical case might include detailed knowledge of SEBI regulations, the U.S. tax code, world infrastructure investment practices, and India's excise laws. A number of firms deal almost exclusively in areas such as intellectual and industrial property law and international tax law.

Consequently, Indian lawyers often take recourse to the expertise of foreign lawyers who are more specialized. Indian clients are saying previously inconceivable things like, "Why don't you speak to an international lawyer and get back to us."

Although some Indian firms have developed relationships with foreign firms and foreign firms refer multinational clients to their Indian counterparts, few of these relationships have developed into a formal joint venture. Unlike the international "Big Six" accounting firms of Ernst & Young and Price-Waterhouse, no law firm has acquired a significant market share of Indian international business law. The U.S. firm White & Case established a representative office in Mumbai in 1994, and Chadbourne & Parke Associates of the United States and Ashurst Morris Crisp of the United Kingdom have opened offices in Delhi.

Such informal arrangements have brought problems. In July 1995, the Lawyers Collective, a Mumbai-based public-interest law society, filed a writ petition accusing these firms of engaging in "the unauthorized practice of law in India." The Collective alleged that these firms, which only had approval to act as a communication channel between their head offices and existing multinational clients in India, were in fact doing much more than just that. Their writ petition stated that the overseas firms had not restricted themselves to foreign clients and were in fact doing legal work of a purely Indian character such as negotiating transactions and drafting agreements, and therefore were violating the 1961 Advocates Acts, which permits only those who are enrolled as advocates on the rolls of the Bar Council in India to practice the profession of law in the country. As of November 1996, the case was still pending in the high court.

Until it is resolved, no law firm will put its foot forward in the matter of collaborative practices. Multinationals will continue to use the services of Indian firms. These, in turn, will continue to face sharp pressure to step up the quality of their service. One result has been faster presentation and response times. Lawyers no longer take weeks to respond to a client's query and months to draft a document. Lawyers have to work in response to global time zones and requests for overnight opinions or documents.

Tight deadlines and international standards have forced many law firms into computerization, an area where the absence of India-specific software is proving a burden. Most firms are still using what would be considered primitive word-processing skills and programs that are far behind their counterparts in Southeast Asia and the West. Only a very few firms regularly use e-mail and voice recognition software or maintain databases of global legal events.

Pressuring firms to upgrade are multinationals who are willing to pay high fees for quality and service. These are being charged hourly fees of anywhere between $100 to $300. Indian clients, on the other hand, want international service but not international fees. They prefer (even demand) predetermined fees for a particular matter, and prices much lower than what multinationals would pay. There are no profession-wide norms governing fees. Even within a firm partners are at liberty to quote whatever they think appropriate.

Not surprisingly, acquiring appropriately trained staff is not easy. The few recent graduates who demonstrate potential are recruited at high prices, sometimes by firms other than law firms. In 1996, Arthur Andersen recruited graduates of the National Law School of India University in Bangalore for salaries starting at Rs 18,500 ($529) per month—very high for a young graduate by Indian standards. It is not unusual for recent graduates to command anywhere over Rs 7,000 ($200) per month, which is a bit high but not spectacular.

All of these changes are forcing some firm managements to recognize that it is necessary to train talent within the firm in order to successfully meet the challenge of globalization. After years of molasses-like advancement policies, some firms have appointed new partners and promoted good attorneys through the "associates glass ceiling" into partners. The Partnership Act does not permit firms to have more than twenty partners, yet few firms ever reached that ceiling. Where in the past a young attorney had to have a father or grandfather in the profession to get anywhere, now there are many more opportunities available. The results have made for what amounts to banner headlines in India's legal circles. Gagrat & Co. appointed three partners after only 12 years with the firm. Amarchand Mangaldas opened its partnership to non-family members for the first time. Wadia Ghandy even promoted partners in their early thirties.

The potential for growth is now attracting more people to the profession. In the past, law was the last resort for those who could not get into medical, engineering, or management. Now attitudes are changing. However, liberalization has not trickled down far enough. Only the top dozen or so firms doing international work are changing their ways; for the rest, little has changed. Liberalization has yet to benefit the great majority of the nearly 600,000 individual lawyers practicing in different parts of the country. Most of the country's firms continue to lack the skill and infrastructure needed to support an international practice.

Even given these cosmetic cases, the management style of most firms has not changed. There is a need to introduce new systems for everything ranging from billing to filing. But Indian lawyers are loath to change their ways. The only Indian firm that has reached the legal twenty-partner limit has not appointed a new partner in the last 19 years. Some of the newer firms established over the last 10 years are sole proprietorships with no opportunity for expansion at all. Some younger attorneys who have concluded that they will never be made an equal partner in a firm have invented new styles or organization such as profit sharing plans. However, these are not easy to implement because the Income Tax Act requires the share of each partner to be specified in the partnership deed. Other firms put their junior lawyers on a fixed salary plus a commission on any business they bring in. Still others conduct regular programs to update employees on how to effectively manage clients, negotiate fees, and draft new forms of documents.

Many academics and business people who watch the legal profession in India believe that it is these innovative firms and their ideas which will end up at the top of the legal profession in the coming century. As in so many areas of Indian business, liberalization and competition will eventually move past the obstacles presented by older firms and will end up the biggest successes in the long run.

FINANCIAL-SECTOR PROSPECTS

The progress of financial-sector reform is mixed and likely to remain so. Reform of the banking sector has slowed down in some respects. Debt provisioning and capital adequacy requirements have been established. Priority-sector lending requirements continue, and the reliance on banks to fund government programs is likely to increase. Lending rates have been deregulated, but deposit rates have been only partly deregulated. The banking sector continues to be tightly regulated and public-sector–dominated. It is likely to remain so, although the role of private-sector banks is gradually expanding.

Nor is much progress likely to be made in liberalization of the insurance sector. Direct foreign investment in this sector will meet resistance from entrenched state-sector bureaucracies who fear job losses.

Reform of the capital market will continue to receive attention. Since the beginning of the government's economic reform program in 1991, the Securities and Exchange Board of India (SEBI) has been given increasing powers to regulate the capital market. It has formulated laws for investor protection, covering company takeovers, disclosure requirements, and insider trading. Compliance with these rules in the past has been poor, but greater emphasis is being placed on enforcement and self-regulation. The role of the capital market in the overall economy is now twofold: It is an important provider of finance for growth and investment, and more recently it has assumed an important role in attracting foreign investment flows. Capital-market reform is therefore being taken seriously. Trading procedures and capital adequacy requirements for brokers and other capital-market participants are likely to receive increasing attention, although, given the changes required, the process is likely to take several years.

India's Stock Exchanges

India has twenty-two stock exchanges. The two largest are the venerable 111–year-old Bombay Stock Exchange (BSE) and the fledgling National Stock Exchange (NSE). For decades, the BSE (which has not changed its name, even though the city is now known as Mumbai) has not had to worry about a serious competitor. The upstart NSE has now garnered a sizable market share with policies quite different than the BSE.

The NSE's progress since its birth in 1993 has been striking. Its average daily turnover overtook that of the BSE and has since soared. In June 1996, the average daily turnover on the NSE was almost 15 billion rupees ($428 million), compared with just 5.9 billion on the BSE. The two exchanges each cover over 90 percent of India's market capitalization because the shares of the country's biggest firms are quoted on both. The BSE provides quotes for a total of 6,000 companies (3,500 of which are actively traded), whereas the NSE provides quotes for only 1,500 of the largest ones.

The two rivals are different in several respects. While the BSE is owned and run by its broker members, the NSE is owned by state-owned financial institutions such as the State Bank of India and the Industrial Development Bank of India (IDBI), and it is run by professional managers. Brokers pay fees for using the NSE's services, rather than buying seats on the exchange, as they do at the BSE. And while the BSE still uses brokers and jobbers to quote prices (albeit, since late 1996, via an electronic system), the NSE has an electronic order-matching mechanism that marries buy and sell orders automatically.

The BSE has a long but spotty history. It has a reputation for opacity and not strictly enforcing its rules. A 1995 government report referred to "malpractices and abuses with speculative excesses, price rigging, market manipulation, non-reporting of transactions, evasion of margins, and neglect of the interests of small investors."

It was this reputation, reinforced by a scandal in 1992, that led the Indian authorities to encourage the creation of the NSE as an alternative, in the hope that this would force the BSE to clean up its act. The NSE is often compared with NASDAQ, the American electronic stock market that grew rapidly in the 1980s, forcing the country's traditional stock exchanges to revamp themselves. The NSE exercised a similar catalytic effect on its big Indian rival. Today the BSE seems determined to clean up the Indian bourse's practices. When Reliance Industries, India's biggest company, was accused of issuing duplicate shares to investors, both exchanges quickly imposed a three-day suspension on trading. Their willingness to publicly punish such a powerful firm took many in Mumbai by surprise.

Both companies have expansionist ambitions. The NSE now has over 900 computer links to Indian brokers in 40 cities around the country, connected by the exchange's own satellite link. The BSE plans to plug regional exchanges directly into the BSE's trading system.

The two exchanges compete in other areas. Both plan depository systems that will shift share settlement gradually from chaotic paper-based systems (source of much of the exchanges' fraud) to electronic book-entry ones. The NSE is also developing equity futures and options.

The real winners from all of this are India's investors, who now have access to a modern capital market with competing points of entry.

The SEBI Rules on Takeovers

India's rules on hostile buyouts have changed dramatically since 1996. As a result, corporate India is facing some dramatic challenges. The closely controlled, inefficient managements that survived by taking advantage of laws making it difficult to be taken over are now much more vulnerable. The Securities and Exchange Board of India (SEBI) has established the following new takeover requirements:

- Once 10 percent of a company's equity is bought by a raider, or if management control changes, the takeover code is activated.
- An open public offer is required to buy 20 percent shares.
- Ten percent of the amount must be put in an escrow account as a guarantee.
- Payments must be made within 30 days of close of offer.
- The minimum offer price is to be based on an average of six-month closing highs and lows, or on a negotiated price for acquiring the target company; the higher one will be the offer price.
- Financial institutions can invite takeover bids if one-half the company's net worth has been eroded.
- Competitive offers must be made within 21 days of the original public offer.

While the code is a step in what many analysts consider to be the right direction, it fails to take into consideration the interests of good managements threatened by a takeover. Companies that are family-owned with low equity stakes, small firms with low market capitalization but a strong asset base, or those involved in infrastructure projects are especially vulnerable.

The strongest instrument that such companies had to ward off threats was Section 22A of the Securities and Contract Regulation Act, which allowed companies the right to refuse transfer shares if they felt that a change in management would affect the shareholders. The Depositories Act neutralized this section, and so has left companies open to attack.

Companies are still free to refuse to transfer shares under Section 111 of the Companies Act, but, unlike Section 22A, this can be challenged in the Company Law Board.

The takeover code is activated once a raider acquires 10 percent of the equity of a company. Already some have sought to bypass this rule by acquiring small percentages in the names of family members. Once the raider makes an open offer to buy 20 percent of the shares from the public, under the new code he will have to deposit 10 percent of this amount in an escrow account that is forfeitable in the event of default. Some merchant bankers believe that this amount may be too small in the case of companies whose share prices are low.

The rider in the trigger clause that includes a change in management control tends to benefit shareholders. Since an open offer will have to be made as soon as the company's management changes, shareholders will be in a position to gain from the resultant increase in share prices. Companies cannot gain management control without paying the market price for the acquisition.

FUNDAMENTAL SHIFTS IN INDIA'S BUSINESS WORLD

The Changing Character of Corporate Governance

The pattern of board oversight that grew during India's pre-liberalization days was one of board members investing little and bossing much. Companies were often run like private fiefdoms, flouting norms of disclosure and transparency. Company directors were known to sleep through crucial meetings, awakening to rubber-stamp their acquiescence on sensitive issues. They often sat on the boards of competing companies. Chairmen and CEO's were often the same person. Many of both were recruited through old-school and cocktail-circuit networks. Other board members' main contribution was their celebrityhood. Production figures were disclosed but profit figures were not. The performance of individual divisions was never broken out from overall performance. Managers regarded their job as safeguarding their job. There was no attitude that operational responsibilities should protect stakeholder interests. Boards did not examine auditing practices. The government avoided any responsibility of ensuring good corporate governance.

Post-1991 liberalization brought a closer look at other methods of board oversight. Today Indian business people are familiar with, and hotly debating, two broad types of corporate governance:

- The market-driven Anglo-American model, which raises capital from the markets, and the stock price acts as an approval rating. If the management performs below expectations, shareholders do the "Wall Street Walk" by selling and exiting. If the management consistently fails, an outsider can take over the company by acquiring majority shares.

- The German and Japanese model, which relegates the importance of the markets to second place beneath the interests of shareholders, who rely on banks, insurance companies, and institutional investors to monitor companies on their behalf.

There is no argument that one of these will eventually prevail. The debate in India is which one is more suited to Indian conditions. This debate hinges on the way capital is raised in India.

In the past, international development agencies provided most of India's growth capital. This vehicle has been largely replaced by a capital market. A theory of corporate governance is evolving which tries to reconcile the distinct demands of capital-market and foreign direct investment. The main issue is how directors themselves are to be governed, not how the consequences of their decisions are to be managed.

The public company has come in for the sharpest scrutiny. Most Indian investors and economists readily agree that something is wrong with the way Indian public companies are directed. Directors still control companies through relatively small stakes and adopt strong management but weak oversight roles in their companies. Their power is not counterbalanced by India's institutional investors, who in the main dislike wielding their voting power; when they do so it is usually at the invitation of the government. Most public-company shareholders still remain ignorant of their rights— the main issue they tend to raise at annual meetings is higher dividends.

The private sector, however, has seen several developments come along that are substantially changing the way this sector is being governed. Company managements are slowly becoming more accountable to the stakeholders of the company, which in India means employees, consumers, and suppliers as well as investors. Among these developments are:

- Financial institutions (FIs) are taking a more activist role in response to the Finance Ministry's encouragement to protect shareholder interests and discipline management. FIs have responded with a surprising readiness to use their power.

- Important sections of the corporate sector are searching for a better directorial system than the pastiches that exist now. The Confederation of Indian Industry (CII) has inaugurated a think tank named the CII Task Force on Corporate Governance, which analyzes issues related to the roles of company boards and the function FIs have in modernizing boardrooms.

- Mutual funds, which with the FIs own the largest portfolios of Indian companies, have been given the right to vote on company affairs. Company managements now have a vigilant and knowledgeable shareholder voice that they have to listen to.

- The Securities and Exchange Board of India (SEBI) has drafted a new takeover code that makes it easier for an acquirer to take over a company. The previous code—written only in 1994—took major steps to protect ordinary shareholders during takeovers. The revised code set up a share depository system to help make takeovers more transparent.

- Some corporate boards have tried to circumvent threats to their independence by issuing nonvoting shares; the markets have responded very negatively to nonvoting shares.

- Foreign institutional investors (FIIs) originated a trend toward investor influence over management quality. Local investors were not long in seeing advantages for themselves. Quality of management emerged as a primary consideration in selecting stocks. Financial markets have pounded companies felt to be ignoring investors.

- FIIs are likely to be the largest controllers of large blocks of company stock when the global depository receipts (GDRs) of these companies are converted into domestic equity. While the GDRs carry no voting rights and their holders have little direct say in the affairs of the issuing companies, when they are converted to domestic equity, FIIs acquire a strong oversight voice. Documentation of GDR issues (mainly subscribed to by overseas investors) are far more detailed than the documentation of domestic offers.

- Mutual funds must declare their net asset values every week. Hence they put pressure on companies in which they invest to keep posting high returns. They are also more watchful over management.

These point up how quickly investor power is growing compared with the power of lenders.

India's lenders are primarily concerned with whether a company is generating enough cash flow to repay its loans. Although most FIs nominate representatives to company boards, there is often no correlation between the experience of the nominee and the needs of the company. Moreover, FIs use board nominations as a pool for favors. Typically an FI has a hundred or more nominee directors on their shopping list. Of these, about one-half will be officials in other companies (sometimes competitors), and the rest are retired executives. Governance by favored friends is how most boards become rubber stamps. Today FIs are trying to formulate guidelines that define what nominee directors are expected to demand from company management.

FIIs, on the other hand, are not as concerned with cash flows as they are with capital appreciation. The net effect has been to convince Indian investors to become more concerned with portfolio yield. A tainted company will not be able to raise money from the markets for very long, and its managers know that. Most takeovers begin in the capital markets when predator hopefuls, often working with unhappy shareholders, start cornering shares of a company in trouble. The threat of a takeover is very frightening to most management because it represents ignominious loss of face in addition to income.

They are just as frightened of investor flight, but in this case for purely financial reasons. FIIs are used to high levels of corporate governance and disclosure, and expect the same from Indian companies. They also have the ability to move their money quickly and are restrained by no geographic or cultural compulsions to invest only in India.

One result is more transparency and disclosure. Indian accounting practices can help management hide as much as it reveals in its annual books. For example, data are rarely given on divisional turnover. How can investors judge whether a decision to commit more money to a company is sustainable unless the comparative performance of its division is known?

In response, Indian managers have devised their own takeover defenses. De-subsidiarizing divisions needs only board-level clearance, not shareholder approval; hence management can transfer its most profitable divisions into a separate company. Brands also can be similarly moved around. These really are not poison pills as much as asset gutting, but they have the same effect.

The upshot of all of this is that forces far more fundamental than India's political imbroglios like the Enron, Cogentrix, and telecommunications license debacles are transforming India into an international corporate player using mostly the same rules as everyone else.

Fading Family Dominance

India's family empires are in the throes of the same revolution that is changing the thinking of the country's smaller businesses. When the Rao/Singh reforms began to liberalize the economy they exposed local businesses to market forces for the first time since the country's independence. At first these favored the big empires, since it was they who foreign companies sought as joint-venture partners.

The Gowda/Chidambaram government made more subtle but far-reaching changes. A case in point is the takeover code finalized by the Securities and Exchange Board of India (SEBI). It contains several landmark changes; one is that the SEBI wants to make takeovers—including hostile bids—much easier. Among other things, the SEBI will no longer have to approve a bidder's price.

Much more important is the SEBI's intent to protect the rights of minority shareholders. Any investor who takes a stake of 10 percent in a company must make an offer for a further 20 percent; after that, any substantial increase has to be by an open offer to all shareholders.

In many countries it is uneventful to oblige an investor with 20–30 percent of a company to bid on the open market if he or she wants to acquire the whole thing. In India, however, the new takeover code is a subtle means to replace the families that control most Indian businesses with more widely held companies. The SEBI measures are in reality a vehicle to de-fang India's powerful family dynasties such as the Tatas, Birlas, Singhanias, and Thapars. The SEBI's tactic is to force them into restructuring their businesses if they are to survive.

In the past, the big families could count on the support of India's financial institutions, which own approximately 40 percent of most big companies. However, financiers such as the Industrial Credit and Investment Corporation of India (ICICI) are now trying hard to prune nonperforming assets. They have told families such as the Modis that they must sort out their run-down businesses, close them (which is difficult under

India's restrictive labor laws), or sell. Before, families were often benign investors. Now they are likely to be told to bow out if they do not perform.

This does not mean that family empires are being thrown to the wolves, but it does mean that they are being pushed out of nonproductive enterprises. In India's biggest 250 private-sector companies, family businesses account for about 70 percent of the total sales and net profits. Big families have long walled off major industrial sectors for themselves. The Tatas make trucks, the Birlas make cars (those venerable Ambassadors), the Bajaj family makes two- and three-wheelers, and the Mahindras make Jeeps. Until recently, such family empires faced little competition, and they diversified into any business they wanted. Financing from public-sector institutions was assured, and corporate law codes made it easy to control subsidiaries via small share holdings. The Tata empire, for example, comprises some seventy companies that produce everything from trucks to tea, yet the parent company's average stake in any one rarely exceeds 15 percent.

The old family empires are increasingly vulnerable on other fronts as well. Their most immediate problem is raising capital in India's more open financial markets. With profits dropping in the face of overseas competition, credit that is harder to come by in more scrutiny-conscious international money markets, and a too-small local equity market, many family firms are being forced to weed unprofitable investments they rushed into in more protected times.

The Mahindra family withdrew from oil drilling and instrumentation to concentrate on autos. The Thapars trimmed Ballarpur Industries back to its core paper and chemicals products. A branch of the Modi family pulled out of a joint venture in television with Britain's Carlton Communications because it could not raise the required $20 million. General Electric, which now has sales of nearly $500 million in India, recently bought out its partner in a three-year-old lighting venture because the partner needed its thinly stretched resources elsewhere. Daewoo raised its stake in its auto-building joint venture with DCM, a Shriram family business, from 51 to 75 percent, buying the extra shares when DCM could not raise the $70 million it needed for expansion. Soft-drink bottlers are selling out as their market is transformed by Coca-Cola and PepsiCo. In telecoms, various families are either having to sell their shares in joint ventures or borrow the cash for their equity stakes from foreign partners.

Hence the government's relaxation of the rules requiring bidding for shares on the open market makes it easier for better financed foreign companies to plot takeovers. In the early stages, a foreign firm needs a local partner's contacts and distribution, but once established, foreign firms notice that local partners contribute little in the way of technology or capital. Today there is an established network of consultancies and banks to guide foreign firms, so an Indian partner seems less essential. McKinsey & Co., for example, argues that joint ventures are "hidden takeovers" that can be designed from the outset to move the Indian partner out after a few years. This is most likely to affect the consumer sector as foreign brands move in and sometimes take over.

India's businessmen sit in two camps about these changes. On one hand, many younger members of the leading families have been trained in Western business schools and are quite at home with ideas such as focusing on core competencies and courting non-shareholding stakeholders. The Federation of Indian Chambers of Commerce and Industry (FICCI) says that it sees the point of badly run companies becoming takeover targets, but it does not like healthy companies competing to take over each other. That, it says, is destabilizing just when stability is needed.

A more problematic attitude toward change comes from the twenty or so foreign merchant banks and stockbrokers who have set up in Mumbai and Delhi. With relatively little to excite them in the IPO and shares markets, many are keen to generate corporate-finance businesses. One joint venture was involved in a controversial takeover battle for Ahmedabad Electricity, which was made over by the popular media into a tale of a foreigner manipulating an aggressive local family firm into becoming a surrogate corporate raider. "The predators have been let loose to pounce on the unwary and the big fish will now swallow the minnows," goes the FICCI's vivid but inexact image.

Given India's talent for defying reform, the real worry is that reform will yet again fail to change. On the other hand, it looks as if family dominance will gradually become a thing of the past.

This has some clear downsides in a country as protectively volatile as India. Foreign companies may blunder severely with full control, seeing it as a chance to impose their own business standards—which in India will hit the newspapers and political back rooms as imposing cultural standards. Families are not families in India, they are gods. Look at the gods in the Hindu temple, each with its visages, vehicles, manifestations, and aspects: families.

FINANCE AND BANKING

There are over 61,000 private-sector bank branches in the country, 55 percent of them in rural areas. The State Bank of India—the major public-sector bank—has more than 8,700 branches. These link even remote rural areas with large cities—a great asset to businesses in the consumer-products sector that require in-field marketers and distributors. India's home-market banking services have been strengthened rather than threatened by the entry of multinational banks which have launched competition-fueling services that facilitate monetary transactions across the country.

Consumer financing is a critical—and highly popular—form of consumer-goods marketing. Many nonbanking financial companies provide leasing and hire-purchase services. These have worked very well, especially at the high-end consumer-goods market.

The credit card market has enjoyed a tremendous growth in recent years, commensurate with the increasing affluence of the Indian consumer. The number of cardholders shows signs of doubling every 2.5 to 3 years; in 1996, the number was over 1.5 million. The logos for Diners Club, Visa International, Master Card, and American Express are almost as ubiquitous as Coca-Cola signs, joining the fifteen-odd cards offered by domestic banks.

Changes in the Public Bank Sector

In 1993, the Reserve Bank of India (RBI) instituted new and much more exacting accounting standards. The public banking sector's response was favorable. Its 1994–1995 results seemed to indicate that many had successfully cleaned up their balance sheets, even though red ink from nonperforming assets flowed far more freely than the other kind.

By 1995–1996, four banks—Syndicate, Allahabad, Bank of Maharashtra, and Andhra Bank—had moved from the net loss to the net profit category. However, that cheerful news was attenuated by the fact that three profit-making banks had slid into net losses—Indian Bank, Vijaya Bank, and Punjab National Bank. Central Bank, joining United Commercial Bank, Punjab and Sind Bank, and United Bank of India, continued their existing record of net. Chennai-based Indian Bank made headlines no one wants to see with the announcement of a Rs 1,336 crore ($381 million) net loss, the biggest loss of any Indian bank ever, while former high performer Punjab National Bank reported a loss for the first time in its history, at Rs 95.9 crore ($27 million).

Bankers hastened to assert that these ills are not systemic, claiming, for example, that Indian Bank was going through the process of revealing its true position, which all of the others went through in 1994–1995. To a degree this was true. Indian Bank's disguised nonperforming assets were being acknowledged and the clean-up begun. That may not be as overoptimistic as it looks, given the precedent of the Bank of India, which is held up by many public bankers of what the industry can do. The Bank of India cleaned up in one massive bloodletting. It wrote down Rs 1,089 crore ($311 million) in 1993–1994, with gross nonperforming assets of 43 percent. It curtailed credit expansion and intensified recovery to make a strong 1994–1995 showing with a net profit of Rs 276 crore ($78.9 million).

The RBI is giving banks a much shorter leash than they have been accustomed to in the past. This has caused no end of chairman hand-wringing in the press, but has also removed a lot of red ink. For example, the RBI has adopted a stringent definition of nonperforming assets. It also has mandated that if one bank in a consortium classifies an account as a nonperforming asset, then all of the other consortium members are bound to do the same. (Earlier, they were bound only by the decision of the lead bank.) This meant that a number of accounts which would not otherwise have been classified as nonperforming now had to be provided for. The net effect was higher provisioning. According to the Indian Banks Association (IBA), the provisions and taxes of nationalized banks as a whole rose to Rs 4,775 crore ($1.36 billion) in 1995, against Rs 2,667 crore ($762 million) the previous year.

Bankers expect the RBI to tighten up further following a debacle at Indian Bank but say this case does not indicate a deficiency in the central bank's monitoring systems. The RBI was aware of the Indian Bank's irregularities and had tried to regulate the former chairman's excesses, but political pressure won out.

The 1995–1996 results indicate that, in the years ahead, banks are going to need more ability to change strategies in response to their perception of the market. The financial markets in India are in a state of considerable flux after the new RBI rules. The year 1995–1996 was a challenging one; banks saw the market go from a bounty of liquidity to very tight conditions, they had to cope with volatile call money and foreign exchange markets, and they had to deal with perennially constrained resources. Moreover, for 1995–1996, the banking industry showed a deposit growth of only 11.8 percent, as compared to 19.5 percent the previous year.

More pertinent, however, is the fact that banks have been under continuous pressure to reduce their nonperforming assets. All banks report ongoing recovery attempts, but problems still persist since bankers report that the recovery tribunals that were set up to hasten the process are not working well. Banks still need to launch a massive recovery program, because recovery is slowing down. The RBI is concerned that fresh accounts will continue to go bad. India's capital market still is fairly weak and multinational banks are coming in. With corporate margins falling, corporate accounts could result in an influx of unforeseen NPAs. Banks are being confronted with a number of new sectors, such as hi-tech agriculture and telecommunications, with which they have little experience. For everyone, not least public banks, these are experimental and therefore high-risk areas.

The RBI intends to continue its tightening of bank accounting norms. Bankers are divided on whether this is desirable. Some agree with the principle effect, the shift from the security backing of an asset to its performance, which requires banks to err on the side of caution in accounting.

Others argue that the risk assessment for credit requires a larger view than financial analysis alone. They call for evaluation based in part on management insight and experience. This might sound like letting the fox guard the henhouse, but what this argument really asserts is the fear of a culture of managers who keep a clean record by avoiding decisions.

Another controversial issue is occasioned by the fact that most banks hold security portfolios in excess of their statutory requirements. They would like to sell these in the secondary market and reinvest the proceeds in higher yielding new securities. Unfortunately, a secondary market for government securities has yet to develop. Canara Bank started retailing government securities, but met with only modest success; it has now applied to start a money market mutual fund as a better option.

Another concern is the pressure on margins. While deposit growth is expected to pick up over the next few years, in parallel with the transition to a market economy, if advances (loans) do not grow strongly, lending rates might fall. Advances for the nationalized sector grew by 19.2 percent in 1995–1996, compared with 26.8 percent the previous year. With competition heating up and resources increasing, public banks cannot push lending rates up; hence margins are likely to fall. This elevates efficiency to a level of importance that it did not have before.

Efficiency in fact is a major stated concern for banks today, although it is hard to determine what is statement and what is reality. Most everyone agrees that public banks have to upgrade the quality of their management, information systems, and computerization. Some banks link only a few percent of their total branch system on a computer network. Bank managers agree—in principle, anyway—that better MIS is crucial in that it allows head offices to analyze the consolidated information available to it and communicate to the branches by e-mail, which improves supervision. Here the bogey of India's telecommunications sector debacle is often held up as the culprit.

The emphasis on efficiency is also hitting the ranks of management. The public banks are reworking their strategies to increase productivity and achieve larger business volumes on existing personnel power. One technique has been to adopt the profit-center approach. Central Bank chairman S. Doreswamy points out that his bank has focused on 833 of its 3,080 branches, of which 660 have been turned into profit-makers—in 1995–1996, they contributed 40 percent of the total profits and their own profit growth was 35 percent. Says Doreswamy, "We want more ground-level participation. The bank is extending the profit-center concept to the branch level, to encourage grass-roots consciousness of issues like profitability spreads, costs, and cash management."

At the Bank of India the emphasis is on marketing rather than selling, meaning better market research and the introduction of new customer incentives such as concessions in service charges. Branches handling advances above Rs 10 crore ($2,86 million) will report directly to the head office. Rural branches now are to be responsible to area officers; the head office will be responsible only for broad policy. Lending will follow the cluster approach, with a computer center for 20–30 branches. The Bank of India will also concentrate more on its nineteen foreign branches, which contribute 25 percent of its profits.

Branch location is getting almost as much attention as branch management. After several years of consolidating their networks and dropping money-losing branches, some banks are opening new branches in more market-astute locations. Union Bank requested ninety-five new branch licenses from the RBI last year to continue its strategy of opening specialized branches for small-scale, agriculture, and special corporate clients. Of its anticipated 2,500 branches by the year 2000, 500 will be specialized branches that are expected to account for 80 percent of the bank's business. This is in effect niche banking that is not directed at high-value business but at location potential. The Dena Bank similarly plans to expand its network by 130 branches by 2000.

In all this it appears that banks are refocusing from growth with profit to profit with growth. This is a major shift in strategy. Not surprisingly, public banks have turned to consultants for help. McKinsey & Co. in particular is targeting the banking market, since most of the India's bank profits come from 200–odd top corporate accounts—the sector most strongly being courted by private and foreign banks.

Until two years ago nationalized banks were thought of as part of a single banking entity, with little to differentiate between them. Loss-making banks saw no client-driven drop in deposits or advances. Now they realize that depositors and borrowers will eventually exercise their discretion. While it will take awhile for market awareness to change much at the domestic depositor and borrower level, overseas correspondent banks and importers are much more attuned to the efficiency of a bank. Government institutions also have guidelines about capital adequacy, minimum capital norms, and ratings.

India's public banks are so poorly differentiated because of their 100 percent government ownership. Some believe that as the government divests more and more of its stake, banks will receive more autonomy, starting with matters like recruitment and compensation. Nonbanking subsidiaries of banks are already free to set their own salaries and recruit talent on college campuses. Others say that so long as the government holds a majority stake, going public will not mean more autonomy, although there certainly will be greater pressure on profit, dividend, and earnings per share.

Competition is certain on a variety of fronts. A growing number of private and foreign banks are nibbling away at the public banks' market share. Deposit market share of public banks fell from 62.6 percent in 1991 to 57 percent in 1996. In advances, their share fell from 57.2 percent in 1991 to 51 percent in 1996. Moreover, nonbank finance companies (NBFCs) have the freedom to set high deposit rates—a freedom to which a good number are offering interest rates of 25 percent and above, based on high-risk profit projections tied to real-estate speculation.

The public bank response to foreign banks and NBFCs is tepid. Some say that since private and foreign banks compete for urban and big-ticket business, their small network will keep them out of the India-wide market. Others dismiss the NBFCs out of hand, pointing out their small resource raising networks, urban concentration, and dubious asset base. On the other hand, they keep a wary eye on the rural-based Private Local Area Banks (PLABs) that are promising to bring low costs and high technology to the countryside. PLABs will be a formidable challenge to the public banks' rural base.

Hence the near-term outlook is for the differences between strong and weak banks to become even more apparent, and the outlook through 2001 predicts some shakeout but much better customer and profit awareness.

The Private Bank Sector

In 1994, IndusInd Bank was India's first privately held bank to start operations. It had a single branch and equity capital of Rs 100 crore ($28.7 million). By late 1996, IndusInd boasted a deposit base of over Rs 2,000 crore ($571 million) and a branch network of eleven. Close on its heels is Global Trust Bank, with deposits of Rs 1,870 crore ($523 million), and ICICI and UTI Bank, both of which have crossed the Rs 1,000 crore ($285 million) level.

These and five others (as of late 1996) constitute India's new breed of private banks. They are still no match for the long-established and government-owned public banks in terms of size, but their growth rates are making them a force to reckon with.

In profit terms, these private banks have been impressive. Global Trust reported a Rs 24 crore ($6.96 million) net profit for the six months ending 30 September 1996. IndusInd was expected to report a net of somewhere around Rs 35–40 crore ($10–$11.4 million) for the same period, compared with Rs 45.6 crore ($13 million) for all of 1995. Profit estimates divulged by most of the other banks show a similar upward trend.

Private banks are in a deposits race, trying to attract merchant and retail banking customers in order to raise cash. With their multibranch access, automatic teller machines, various incentive packages, lower minimum balances, and branch networks several times larger than those of an average foreign bank, the private banks are trying to position themselves against the foreign banks, not India's public-sector banks.

Corporate deposits constitute a good chunk of the total deposits of most private banks. Since their reach is still fairly limited, some 80 percent of their deposits are presently wholesale in character. However, corporate deposits are expensive. The average cost of Global Trust Bank's deposits rose to 11.32 percent in 1995–1996 from 9.35 percent in 1994–1995. The high cost of certificates of deposits (about 17 percent in 1995) has brought several to replace them with retail deposits.

On the assets side, private banks specialize in companies after short-term working capital finance. Depending on their parentage, history, and the thinking of their management teams, each has a distinct business strategy. While IndusInd and Global Trust are perceived to be aggressive, others like HDFC Bank and ICICI Bank are considered more conservative. Over 50 percent of Global Trust's lending is devoted to export financing, which helps it refinance the debt. IndusInd focuses on international banking and domestic corporate banking. NRI (Nonresident Indian) services and international banking are their key areas—the bank has an NRI shareholding of 40 percent. IndusInd wants to develop greater strengths in investment banking as part of its strategy.

In contrast, HDFC Bank is more staid in its approach, avoiding trying to cater to large companies that are being courted by the larger banking consortia. Although HDFC Bank's ability to meet the funding needs of large companies is modest at the moment, it sees an opportunity in fee-based services such as forex management. HDFC Bank's high capital adequacy ratio of 23.5 (on 31 March 1996) reflects its caution and consequent underutilization of resources.

ICICI Bank's executive vice-president, P.H. Ravikumar, says that his bank is "heavily into core banking and focuses on working capital and short-term funding needs."

IDBI Bank has a different client profile. They believe that larger companies are already served well by the large commercial banks, but that cannot be said for mid-sized companies. The average corporate client of IDBI Bank has a turnover between Rs 50 and 80 crore ($14.3–$22.8 million). As IDBI grows and acquires more branches in metros, it expects to be in a better position to target larger corporations.

Times Bank is the envy of the market for its ability to indulge in a much higher adspend, being part of the Times of India publishing group. Times Bank launched operations only in August 1995 and quickly built a deposit base of Rs 700 crore ($200 million) and advances of Rs 535 crore ($153 million).

Not surprisingly, most private banks give rosy projections for their futures. IndusInd hopes to grow by at least 65 percent every year for the next five years. It is expected to be looking at a balance-sheet size of Rs 3,000 crore ($857 million) by March 1997. Since it was able to raise equity shares at a price of Rs 50 ($1.43) each from private placements with its shareholders, IndusInd hopes to go public by issuing shares at a premium some time during the middle of next year.

Three banks, HDFC Bank, Global Trust, and Bank of Punjab, have now gone public. Most of the other private banks that have not yet gone public are waiting for the capital market to revive from its 1996 doldrums before attempting to do so. They also feel that a three-year dividend track record will enable them to raise money at a premium, knowing that if they fail they will have to issue shares at par. From the shareholders point of view, it is preferable that the issues are delayed so that investors have a track record to go by. Even though the business strategies of these new private banks sound impressive, only their numbers after three full years of business will really paint a reliable picture.

A Closer Look: ICICI as an Example of Indian Private Banking

India's banks are not renowned for their fascination with new technology. The Industrial Credit and Investment Corporation of India (ICICI),

India's second-biggest development bank with $7 billion of assets, is a notable exception. Indians using the Internet can open an account with the group's commercial bank by visiting its Web site (http.://www.india-world.com/icicibank).

ICICI has always been a somewhat unusual animal, straddling the public and private sectors. Conceived in 1955 by the Indian government and the World Bank, it was originally a private-sector lender to big industrial projects. Its founding and largest shareholders were three Indian unit-trust (mutual-fund) and insurance companies. When these were nationalized in the 1970s, the bank's status as a "public finance institution" meant that it had to conform to government policy. In return, it received tax breaks and easy access to the corridors of power.

In recent years, a clutch of foreign institutional investors, including America's Fidelity and Britain's Schroders, have bought up 9 percent of ICICI's voting shares. In August 1996, they acquired another 24 percent in the form of a $220 million issue of global depository receipts (GDRs) that do not carry voting rights until they are transformed into ordinary shares. Their willingness to invest in ICICI testifies to its reputation for dynamism compared with its bigger but more lethargic rival, the $12.7 billion Industrial Development Bank of India.

ICICI still bears the legacy of the era when it concentrated more on building its assets than on boosting its profits because it had little incentive to do otherwise. Only when the Indian government decided in 1991 to cut off cheap funding for development banks was ICICI shaken out of its complacency. Forced to tap into the international capital markets, it quickly became more choosy about who it lent to and at what rates. Bad loans still account for 6.7 percent of the bank's overall loan portfolio, down from 8.8 percent in 1991.

The bank has moved faster than its rivals to reinvent itself. Naryanan Vaghul, its managing director until April 1996, split the bank into thirteen separate profit centers, set up a new commercial bank (ICICI Bank), and formed two joint ventures, in securities and asset management, with J. P. Morgan. He also built up an influential investment advisory service for firms and the government.

In April, ICICI made another break with the past by choosing not to replace Mr. Vaghul (who has retired as managing director but remains chairman) with a long-serving insider. The new managing director is Kundapur Kamath, who at 48 is young for this position. Mr. Kamath's foreign experience also sets him apart in Indian financial circles. He has spent eight years abroad, first with the Asian Development Bank in the Philippines and then with Bakrie, an Indonesian financial-services group.

One of Mr. Kamath's aims is to accelerate the change in the bank's culture. It developed, he says, during a time when "the amount of your profit was dictated by administrators, not by what you did."

Another of his objectives is to turn ICICI into a "universal bank," by diversifying into areas such as consumer leasing and insurance. He wants to develop the bank's fee-earning business, especially by becoming a syndicator of loans rather than just a lender. Even so, lending will still account for most of the development bank's business as the demand for new credit in India is expected to grow quickly.

Given the eruption of foreign competition in India's banking markets, ICICI has little choice but to adapt. Mr. Kamath promises to shun businesses with poor returns, such as the share depositories currently being set up in Mumbai. Providing the bank does not overreach itself, its willingness to change combined with its political contacts should make it even more of a force to be reckoned with.

Islamic Banking

Muslims comprise more than 100 million of India's peoples. According to Islam usury or interest is forbidden (*haram*) but profits are not. Hence Muslim banks have certain special requirements and banking terms that outside banks should know about. These are briefly summarized here, and any Islamic bank can provide more exact details.

Where in a conventional bank the depositor and the bank normally share a contractual relationship, Islamic banks call this profit sharing and charge a fee on expenses. The bank's administrative costs have to be met and are not fixed. The *Qur'an* (Koran) only lays down strictures against interest, while giving profit sharing (*mudrabaha*) and leasing (*ijara*), and sale of goods at a specified profit margin (*murabaha*), are not. Interpretation and application of these principles is something that has to be worked out, and some amount of compromise is to be expected. (The commonly used terms of Islamic banking are defined below.)

Some banks have worked out innovative interest-free deposit schemes that are linked with interest-free loans, for example *Iqra* (education) deposit, *Aqad* (marriage), and *Haj Umra* savings programs (which save up for the Muslim's *hajj* or pilgrimage to Mecca). Savings under these schemes entitle savers to an interest-free loan of up to 25 percent of matured deposits.

The NBFC format allows much freedom to experiment. Since reserve requirements are lighter and the rate of interest or rate of return can be variable, or even linked to profits, it allows interest-free organizations the freedom to tailor their deposit mobilization and deployment in a manner suited to their individual needs.

The balance sheets of most Islamic banks abroad reveal that their favored route for mobilizing working funds is by means of *mudarabahs*—agreements in which one or more partners provides finance while the others contribute management. The profits are shared in an agreed proportion while losses are borne by financiers alone in proportion to their share capital. All of these funds except *amanah* (current deposits) do not give any guarantee of either repayment of the principal or assurance of a rate of return. In keeping with Islamic principles, the rate of return is variable and linked to the return earned from the deployment of the funds. The bank also gets a share of the profits (losses are not shared) or a fixed fee for managing funds.

These funds are also allowed to be invested jointly by the bank, usually in real estate, construction projects, equity, or other productive assets, and are not subject to taxation as a composite entity.

Even though the handful of those involved in Islamic finance is growing fast, there have been compromises along the way. The Indian Islamic bank Bait-un-Nas'r was set up to mobilize deposits on a no-profit–no-loss basis. It has 100 percent current deposits and no assured rate of return apart from repaying the principal. Deployment of funds are generally in interest-free secured loans. Since the organization was not allowed to profit from this activity it has devised a method of working out its administrative costs on a quarterly basis and charging these to its borrowers as a service charge. This service charge, which is in the range of 12 percent per year and similar to that charged by other banks, is a cause for some embarrassment to proponents of interest-free finance. Similar service charges are recovered from borrowers by most credit cooperative societies and are in the range of 5 to 12 percent.

Key Islamic Banking Terms

Riba: interest, which is forbidden (*haram* or the prohibition of usury is the cornerstone of Islamic economic thinking).

Kard-i-hasan: an interest-free loan.

Sahib-al-maal: the financier as distinct from the *mudarib* or individual or institution that provides the entrepreneurship and management.

Shirkah: a partnership in which two or more people share the financing and management of a venture.

Ijara: refers to leasing activity and recognizes the legitimacy of rental income since the leasor is partaking of the full loss of the business activity.

Mudarabah: one of the most favored Islamic formats; it refers to an agreement in which one or more of the partners provides finance while the others contribute management. Profits are shared in an agreed proportion and losses are borne by the financiers alone in proportion to their share of total capital.

Murabaha: sale of goods at a specified profit margin. The term is used for describing a sale agreement where the seller buys the goods for the buyer and sells them on at a fixed price that includes a markup. The payment has to be settled within an agreed period either in installments or as a lump sum.

THE BUSINESS COMMUNITY'S PROBLEM AREAS

Labor

Labor in India is divided into two broad categories:

- The 30 million-plus who work in the organized sector and constitute high-wage islands in a sea of poverty. These organized workers are virtually unsackable and are often led by irresponsible leaders who are politically well connected.

- The 300 million people working in small sweatshops, farms, and so on. For them, there is no job protection, no living wage, and no security. The Indian work force is considered to be easy to train and fairly stable. English is widely spoken by managerial and supervisory personnel, and to some degree by the unskilled. The literacy rate is 48 percent (roughly twice as high for men as for women).

The labor force, about 330 million as of 1995, has grown faster than employment, which has risen at an average annual rate of 2 percent. Underemployment remains significantly higher. With many well-educated individuals within the ranks of the unemployed, competent staff, including technicians and engineers, can be found without much difficulty. Unskilled labor is easy to find and is the source of much abuse.

India's labor force is growing at an estimated 2.5 percent per annum due to longer life expectancy. This will exacerbate unemployment. A 1992 study by the International Labor Organization estimated that there will be 20 million unemployed in 1993–1994. The work force was 333–million strong in 1992; it will grow to 374 million in 1997 and 425 million in 2002.

India is a member of the International Labor Organization and complies with conventions that it has ratified. It has enacted comprehensive legislation to provide a good working environment for labor and protect their interests. The following are the key labor law provisions:

- Industrial relations are regulated by the Industrial Disputes Act, which provides for just and equitable settlement of disputes through negotiations, conciliation, arbitration, or adjudication.

- The Factories Act, 1948, regulates working conditions in factories. The Act prescribes minimum standards for working conditions and facilities related to manufacturing processes, handling and storage of materials, discharge of effluents, fire precautions, working hours, and health facilities.

- The Minimum Wages Act, 1948, empowers the appropriate governments to fix and revise the minimum wages and allowances payable to workers and also to regulate the conditions of work such as hours of work, overtime, and so on, for workers in the notified employment under their respective jurisdiction.

- The Payment of Bonus Act, 1965, requires payment of bonuses to certain categories of workers whose wages do not exceed Rs 2,500 per month. The Act ensures payment of minimum bonus of 8.33 percent per year, with the maximum bonus not to exceed 20 percent of the salary or wage earned during the accounting year.

- The Payment of Gratuity Act requires the employer to pay gratuity to certain categories of workers on termination of service. This Act applies to all workers, without any wage limit.

- The Employees' Provident Fund Act applies to workers whose wages do not exceed Rs 3,500 per month in some industries and establishments. The employer and the employee are required to make matching contributions of 8.33 to 10 percent of the employee's salary to the fund.

- The Employees' State Insurance Act covers sickness, maternity, and employment-related injuries. The Act applies to workers whose wages do not exceed Rs 3,000 per month.
- In addition to the above Acts, several states have enacted Shops and Establishment Acts that regulate working hours, prescribe minimum standards of working conditions, and provide for overtime and leave salary payments to workers in certain categories of shops and other establishments.

India's labor laws still make it next to impossible to change the costly and inefficient public sector. Nor have India's cumbersome exit regulations simplified the process of plant closures in loss-making enterprises. Most important, the government has ignored the need to liberalize the "unorganized" sector of consumer-goods industries that presently benefit from substantial protection. The principal victim, of course, is the Indian consumer, and this influential populace is beginning to tire of mediocre products and inflated prices compared to what they see during their travels and on television.

Vested Interests

In contrast to much of Asia, India has a vibrant democracy, and changes of government are regular and generally orderly. Nonetheless, patronage is a powerful electoral tool, much coveted by MPs, and the best intentions of the central government can often be thwarted at the state and local levels. Vested interests, the natural corollary of patronage, exert considerable and often conflicting sway over politicians. The most influential of these interests include the following:

- **Farmers.** Approximately 70 percent of the electorate live in rural areas and have become accustomed to generous state handouts for fertilizer, equipment, irrigation, and electrical power.
- **Bureaucrats.** Decades of central planning have bred an entrenched bureaucracy that is proving extremely difficult to wean away from the perks of public office. So far, the government has avoided laying off civil servants and is unlikely to do so despite the 1996 general election.
- **Trade unions.** Overly protective unions oppose any relaxation of India's restrictive labor laws and the modernization or privatization

of state industries. The unions are strong and closely linked to politicians, giving them a powerful voice in parliament.

- **Big business.** Although big business has generally welcomed the process of economic liberalization, not all businessmen are keen to see tariff barriers come down quickly, given their companies' inefficiency and lack of competitiveness. Industrialists will remain a powerful lobby, not least by virtue of their substantial contributions to the Congress party.

- **The middle class.** This group is growing rapidly and is estimated at approximately 200 million. In general, the middle class remains a force for change, having acquired their growing wealth through economic liberalization. Many sympathize with the Bharatiya Janata Party (BJP) as an alternative party of government. They will remain the key battleground between Congress and the BJP in the next election, underlining the need for the government to press ahead with economic reform.

Monopolies

Economic reforms are changing Indian industry slowly but surely. For the first time, India's big business houses are facing increasing competition in key market segments from foreign firms. The influence of fresh and possibly keener competition has forced Indian companies to rethink corporate strategies with significant consequences for foreign entrants. More and more, local firms are:

- forging strategic alliances with foreign multinationals;
- selling off peripheral businesses to concentrate on core areas;
- relinquishing control of joint-venture firms to foreign partners;
- becoming production bases for large multinationals;
- launching new products and brands.

In a bid to protect their turf, several Indian market leaders, in sectors ranging from consumer products to drugs to telecommunications, have entered into joint ventures with foreign firms. This is particularly the case in sectors and products where technology is key and competition is intense. For foreign firms, the willingness to tie up opens up new avenues for entry into India.

Unable to compete with established foreign brands, several Indian companies have decided to become production bases for multinationals, thus widening the scope for foreign companies looking to enter the country. However, not all Indian firms are capitulating to multinationals. Some are planning to combat them with strategies based on ethnic brands, lower pricing, and/or superior distribution. Ethnic brands have been used successfully for hair-care products, toothpaste, health tonics, and baby-care products.

Other companies are hoping to preempt competition from new entrants into the market by creating new products and models. Hero Cycles launched three different bicycle models—one for the city, one for cross-country, and one for children. Godrej Soaps introduced a premium-quality soap called Evita. Since marketing costs are climbing, however, generous budgets to launch products are becoming extremely unlikely. It is considered wiser to draft marketing plans every three to six months. There is also a shift away from lavish advertisements to plug a product; more manufacturers are now relying on direct marketing or trade promotions to get their message across.

Monopolies and market dominance per se are not illegal—only unfair trading practices are. Trading practices that still fall under the MRTP Act include:

- maintaining prices at unreasonably high levels;
- inhibiting competition in the production and distribution of goods;
- promulgating false information about products.

In January 1992, the government ended the 1973 Foreign Exchange Regulation Act's ban on trading (i.e., buying goods from other firms for resale) by foreign-owned corporations. Most restrictions on a company's freedom to sell are found in the MRTP act, which defines a restrictive trade practice as "any action that obstructs or distorts competition in any manner, manipulates prices or affects market supplies of goods in order to impose unjustifiable costs or restrictions on consumers." Arrangements relating to such practices must be recorded with the Registrar of restrictive trade agreements. Parties to unregistered arrangements are subject to prosecution.

The government generally regards the following practices as objectionable:

- insistence on resale-price maintenance;
- prohibition of the sale of competitors' products;

- making supplies of one product contingent on the sales of another;
- any restriction on the class of persons to whom goods may be supplied;
- imposition of territorial restrictions and allocation of markets;
- provision of rebates, discounts, and commissions;
- establishment of an exclusive dealership;
- awarding of incentive bonuses.

The MRTPC may investigate any trade practice:

- on receiving a complaint from a consumer or a voluntary consumer organization;
- at the request of the central or state governments;
- on receiving an application from the registrar of restrictive trade agreements;
- on the basis of its own information.

Education

While about one-half of the population of India is illiterate, enrollment in primary, secondary, and higher secondary education has increased considerably over the past two decades. India has nearly 200 universities and more than 6,000 general and professional colleges. In addition, about 1 million Indians are enrolled in engineering, technical, and medical colleges. The country is estimated to have the second- or third-highest number of engineers and scientists in the world.

The reason is that the government spends much more generously on higher education than on the primary and secondary levels. Consequently, India has a well-educated work force that is frequently too skilled for blue-collar work. By contrast, those who fill the blue-collar ranks are relatively ill-educated and therefore difficult to train in operating state-of-the-art machinery.

International investors will mainly be interested in the quality of education they can expect from India's universities and private schools. The story is promising, but mixed.

University-Educated Talent. India's government-funded university system is under intense pressure brought by the country's transition from socialism to free markets. Several established schools, such as the University of Delhi, are poised for a radical—and controversial—change of course in the battle for resources and relevance.

The universities want to bring employment-anxious students home to better facilities funded by the private sector and to professional courses tailored to the needs of industry. Says one university president, "Every society needs philosophers and poets, but we have overdone it."

India suffers no dearth of accredited universities. Since 1947, the number has leaped to 204 from 20, and the student body has grown twenty-five–fold to 6.1 million. The government predicts that it will swell to 8.4 million by the turn of the century.

India's success in producing world-class graduates has been a mixed blessing. For years, the economy could not absorb so many talented engineers, scientists, and business managers, prompting a considerable brain-drain. A 1996 study by the Indian Institute of Technology in New Delhi revealed that nearly 25 percent of its graduates between 1980 and 1990 emigrated. More than one-half of the school's computer-science graduates did the same.

Since 1991, the technical job market has improved, but there are still mismatches of supply and demand. Of the 5,000 graduates who received doctorate degrees in the sciences and engineering in 1993, only 20 percent found jobs in their field. In the highly literate southern state of Kerala, jobs are so scarce that many graduates work jobs far beneath their capabilities.

Disillusionment with job prospects for university graduates has popularized a parallel education system of unaccredited technical, engineering, and management schools purporting to teach the practical skills needed in the workplace. There are no accurate estimates of the size of this sector. Educators in Kerala estimate that there are 2 lakh (200,000) students enrolled at professional schools in that state alone—as many as are studying in conventional universities there.

Testimony to the same reliance on non-university training is seen in empty University of Delhi classrooms—students are off taking backup courses elsewhere. Even the university's formerly prestigious St. Stephen's College is no longer at the top of every high-school student's wish list. The 1,100–student St. Stephen's still ranks as India's foremost and is renowned for long having produced India's government service and private sector elite. Yet in 1996 St. Stephen's had to accept 100 applicants to its physics department in order to fill the class of 40—the remainder opted for private engineering schools or the top-flight Indian Institutes of Technology (IIT) because they have better job opportunities with practical technical degrees than degrees in pure science.

Elite St. Stephen's wants to exploit the demand for other professional courses such as management and computer science that are currently not on offer. The motive is partly financial. Like many colleges at the University of Delhi, St. Stephen's can hardly cover expenses. The college relies on government grants for 95 percent of its budget. The rest comes from regulated fees. Basic tuition is set by the university at Rs 15 (43 cents) per student per month—a pittance even by Indian standards—and it has not been raised for decades for fear of political repercussions. However, the university allows individual colleges to set their own fees for professional courses, and these could exceed Rs 30,000 ($857) per student per year.

The College has persuaded the Delhi University board to accept corporate research grants for the first time. Some of the grants would go into a general fund to subsidize liberal-arts departments. The rest would be used to establish self-financing professional schools within the university, covering business, communications, and computer technology, in collaboration with private industry.

These ideas arouse strong passions in India, where the political left fears the influence corporate interests would wield over admissions and curricula. Leftists heavily criticized a 1995 bill proposed in Parliament to allow private universities. Other pressure groups have challenged private medical-school fees all the way to the Supreme Court. All this said, the direction is clearly toward more market force thinking in India's higher education.

Management School Talent. In mid-1996, *Business India* magazine commissioned a study by the market research organization ORG of 234 students of management institutes in Ahmedabad, Bangalore, Delhi, Mumbai, and Pune. Among the questions asked was the criteria they expected recruiters to apply during the course of selection. Thirty-nine percent felt that personality would be perceived most crucial, followed by 21 percent with communication skills and 15 percent on work experience. They were also asked about choice of jobs. As many as 30 percent of them would prefer the financial services/banking sector, while management consultancies and consumer-product marketing (MNCs) were the choice of 23 percent each. Interestingly, 36 percent each reported that growth prospects and learning experience were the prime reasons for choice of company; compensation package was preferred by a far distant 14 percent.

There seems to be a very strong middle-class salaried bias among management-school graduates. Only about 5 percent of the India Institute of Management (IIM—India's premier management training institution) graduates come from business backgrounds. An overwhelming 70 percent come from the children of civil servants, public-sector executives, and defense personnel. There seems to be a strong urge among the children of these government-sector parents to join the corporate sector, with its visibly glamorous lifestyle. It also could point toward the changing emphasis of desirable professions among the elite in Indian society. For example, among the students coming from homes in the non-government sector, there are five times the number of children of university teachers as there are of doctors.

The India Institute of Management graduate has been filtered through a selection process that spans almost a decade of the student's life. The stereotypical graduate was usually at the top of his (most are males) class in school and highly achievement-oriented. He usually was also an engineer, which meant that he had been through some of the toughest post-high school entrance examinations. To enter an institution like the IIM also meant that the student had again been through a filtering process. These kids were usually among the best available talent in the country. The IIM course also encourages strong communication, and these students combine a high degree of native intelligence with strong logical processing strengths and good communication ability.

While multinational employers tend to like IIM graduates for their sense of competitiveness, they are often viewed in India as brash and mercenary. Some of this is normal family-business antagonism to college graduates of any kind, but even former Hindustan Lever chairman T. Thomas has stated that the IIM should only admit students who have been working in industry for some years. This observation becomes increasingly important because current placements out of the IIM show that a large number of them are entering some of the world's largest industrial and strategic consulting companies setting up shop in the country. IIM placements have also been moving into the hitherto booming financial-services sector rather than conventional fast-moving consumer-product marketing or finance.

CONTINUED REFORMS MAY BRING PROBLEMS FOR FOREIGN BUSINESSES

Two events forced Prime Minister Rao's reforms in 1991: an ideological shift among elite sections of Indian society and a crisis that demonstrated the consequences if reforms were not pushed through. During the 1980s, many Indian economists, bureaucrats, politicians, and journalists began to call for an overhaul of India's command economy. The collapse of the Soviet Union pointedly hinted that socialism was unlikely to solve history's economic woes.

In 1991, India's government had been expanding more or less continuously since Independence. It taxed as much as it could. It borrowed as much as it could. By 1991, the point had come where India could well have to default on its international obligations. Foreign exchange reserves were next to zero. The budget deficit had soared. Inflation was rising.

When the Rao reforms began, many people realized that it would not be enough to reform the central government alone. Much economic activity in India came under the jurisdiction of the states. Some were ruled by parties espousing command-economy or socialist rhetoric. Yet these also saw the need to reform. One reason was that their own finances were as bad as the Centre's. Some states began privatizing industries under their jurisdiction, which even Manmohan Singh did not dare to suggest.

However, political pressures ensured that subsidies in many sensitive areas were maintained. The result today is that India's liberal consensus is intact but muddled, operating but sclerotic. Presently, all three of India's major parties are now united behind three propositions that they presently see as politically inviolable:

- Liberalization must continue in order to attract private and foreign investment; without it, the state and the public sector will no longer be able to control the economy.

- To survive politically, India must continue subsidizing the causes of influential lobbies, acknowledging that it could bankrupt the exchequer.

- India cannot significantly liberalize its labor policies, allow firms to lay off unneeded workers, or close loss-making firms.

Unhelpful as this mix is likely to be in turning India into an economic tiger, there is a political (if not economic) logic binding all three elements to the near future.

However, these political accommodations mean that almost all of India's states will not have enough revenue to invest in education, health, and nutrition. As the East-Asian tigers have shown, this trinity is as vital for growth as the above trinity is vital for political stability. Without expanded education, India cannot create a more productive work force; without rural investment, agriculture will not flourish. Public investment in roads, power, bridges, water supply, and irrigation has also suffered, cramping industrial development.

Normally these would be considered areas of opportunity for the private sector. Indeed, the private sector is stepping in with power plants and telecoms. However, there are many areas like rural roads, new classrooms, and books for which it is much more difficult to secure private finance.

In terms of India's ability to rebound economically given larger infusions of foreign FDI, it is the third point in the consensus—no sackings—that poses the biggest problem. An enormous amount of capital is tied up in unprofitable factories. Most are in the public sector. In most burgeoning market economies these would be liquidated and their assets, labor included, redeployed more productively. However, the government is terrified of antagonizing trade unions, who are voluble, volatile, media savvy, and wise in the intricacies of the blind emotions that undergird so much of India's public activity. Hence the government has done nothing to liberalize labor laws or speed up exit procedures.

Presently India's public sector ties up more than one-half of the country's industrial capital. Ironically, the competition brought in by reform will drive more of them toward insolvency—raising the very likely prospect that "foreigners" will be blamed for India's social ills. While the 1991 reforms made the private sector more dynamic and efficient, they also revealed the comparative inefficiency of the public sector. The implication for foreign investors is that they are likely to be blamed for India's social problems, yet not likely to be given due credit for its improved economy.

Listening to the Locals

It is extremely important for business people coming to India to do their homework on the mistakes made by Western powers during the Colonial era and to devise ways to not repeat them. Although this subject is briefly sketched in Chapter 7, readers should thoroughly read Barbara Crossette's *India—Facing the Twenty-First Century* (Indiana University Press) and some of the other titles in Appendix B: Additional Readings to get a better picture of the India they are about to enter.

Too many business people by far are convinced that the globalized market economy is the key to the betterment of the world. Anyone who believes that has not done their homework. India mastered these ideas some 2,000 years ago and indeed for nearly five centuries was the greatest unified business and trading empire the world ever knew, until today. Virtually every theme of today's globalized market economy was invented in India—a fact that has largely escaped the syllabuses of the MBA programs in the West. Nor has the brash West in its business theorizing experienced the same type of comeuppance that India did in the fifth century A.C., when age-old Hindu religious values reasserted themselves yet again and religion became India's supreme social force for centuries. Nor has modern business experienced the kind of destruction that India lived through in the thirteenth century, when tribal hordes invaded from over the Himalayas, or in the fifteenth and sixteenth centuries, when the political society was of one religious mind and economic society of another.

Yet, of all the horrors in India's history, their experience with the colonizing mentality of the West is far and away the worst. The Raj era, which makes for such spectacular epic films, in fact was one of the most mindlessly exploitative and smugly ignorant regimes in the history of economic development anywhere on the globe. To read the dispatches home from British governors and private colonials is a glimpse into appallingly self-satisfied minds who had so little understanding of the Indians and their immense span of culture that all India might as well have been a giant kennel. To think or act like the colonials is a guaranteed formula for disaster in India.

There is indeed great benefit to investing in India. But not if the idea behind it is that India is but a marketplace and Indians are so yesteryear that they need the wise services of the investor more than anything else in the world. If business people arriving in India today return to the smug behavior patterns of the past—no matter how updated and internetted their appearance—they will end up on the same dust heap of ignominy as the British. If they listen to Indians as equals and learn to absorb the wisdom and ideas of Indians as partners in progress, then they will have done a great service to their home countries and the image of business itself. The real opportunity in India isn't the profits to be made. It isn't helping replace the past with a future that on balance doesn't look a whole lot different. The opportunity in India is learning from the Indians.

NOTE

1. Throughout this text the rupee-to-US dollar rate has been calculated at the November 1996 rate of $1 = Rs 35.

3

Management Matters

I recall one instance where a business venture sought to draw down on an already approved credit line. They first had to submit 32 separate approvals. Then each of these had to be resubmitted to the original official to verify them.

G. Sabarinathan of Technology Development
and Information Company of India

For all of its cultural magnificence, street-scene exoticism, and business opportunity, India can be an irritating, exhausting, and exasperating place in which to live and do work.

One reason is that many visitors arrive wearing blinders. The psychology of doing business in India is a very different proposition than anywhere else in the world. Many people remain persistently blind to the fact it is their thinking, not India's, that needs to change.

There are three macro conditions that affect business operations in India. These lie beneath caste, religion, and history. These macros can strongly affect a business's economic chances, especially in the conduct of daily business.

THREE MANAGEMENT MACROS

The Psychology of the Indian Male

It is easy to overdo it when applying Western child-rearing and family models to interpret other peoples' behavior. The fundamental myths are not the same, and neither is the psychology. In India, forget Freud. Entirely different patterns exist in Indians—especially in males—that explain why business associates and employees think so differently about authority, job security, responsibility, and candor.

The Indian baby is typically indulged, nurtured, and constantly handled. Every whimper brings a caring response from the whole family. Infants quickly learn that the surest way to get attention is to cry.

The technical term for the result is *narcissism*—the feeling that there must be an immediate gratifying response to every wish. Male children in India are led to feel that they are the center of the universe and deserve their role. The mother-figure is all-nurturing and all-attending. Indian men term their country "Mother India" and symbolize her with the sacred cow. They also expect their women to act like cows.

There is considerable separation shock upon the arrival of the next baby. This typically happens about the age of three (most Indian mothers breast-feed until that age). Being abandoned in favor of a younger brother or sister is exacerbated by the fact that the child is simultaneously thrust out among the community so the mother can devote her full time to the new one. The child finds his specialness lost. Suddenly, crying as a bid for attention gets nowhere.

The most common reaction is withdrawal into being alone, which is more satisfying than the disappointments imposed by others. This habit is reinforced by India's primordial religious beliefs in which life's cravings produce nothing but suffering; hence the only worthy goal is to somehow escape existence altogether. The forest hermit and wandering ascetic are in part childhood rejection response reinvented as "enlightenment."

However, the gratifying self-containment achieved in withdrawal competes with the need to be gregarious if one is to get one's fair share. A behavioral pattern develops in which being aloof coexists with gregariousness. For foreigners, the result is difficulty divining the true feelings of Indian associates, especially the intrusion of sudden uncommunicative remoteness into easygoing friendship.

If the relationship with the mother represents bliss and disappointment, relations with the father are even less satisfying. Indian fathers—and Indian men in general—tend to be demanding, not easily satisfied, critical rather than supportive, aloof, authoritarian, and self-centered. The negative consequences of not yielding completely to fatherly authority result in unquestioning acceptance of the father's word. Youngsters learn to cry excessively to mothers but not assert any unhappiness to fathers because of the likelihood of an unpleasant response. Authority conflicts with narcissism, and neither wins.

India's historical solution has been to devise escape hatches from reality. If the parental—and later the material world—is a cycle of disappointments, it must be the spiritual world where supreme bliss resides. Indians grow up yearning for a guide who is nurturing, sympathetic, and harmonious. Historically, that person has not come in the form of a savior, but in the form of the *guru*, the wise and kindly teacher who has himself escaped from the world's turmoils but lingers on to reveal how others can find the longed-for sense of perfect inner calm.

Mental Organization and Business Organization

Most Westerners consider logical reasoning to be the only valid way to draw conclusions. Indians view rational thinking as but one of four kinds of conclusionary methods, all of which are equally valid:

- **Reason** is deduction or induction applied to information supplied by the senses.

- **Intuition** arrives at conclusions by nondeductive emotional feelings and does not use sense information; typical intuition begins where logic leaves off.

- **Insight** reaches out beyond both mind and senses to the direct illumination of natural law (for example, the Buddha's Enlightenment).

- **Mystic**, which is the direct experience of God, the gods, or the One (the unity of all existence), cannot be explained to another human by any of the above.

These four kinds of thinking go a long way toward explaining historical behavior patterns in India—the extraordinarily complex cosmologies of India's religions, the Hindo-Buddhist view of *samsara* or the endless rounds of existence, the labyrinthine psychology in the sculpture of Hindu temples, the game of chess (invented by early Indians), and the modern bureaucratic maze in which decisions come about without any particular person apparently doing the deciding.

Unfortunately for the newcomer to India, so many different and simultaneously valid methods for arriving at a decision can result in decisions that seem—and are—very illogical. This explains why Hinduism is so unconcernedly self-contradictory. It is important to realize that whether a decision is logical is not the point. The point is whether the decision is valid from the Indian point of view.

To make matters more confusing, while India's institutional memory may be long (the durability of the caste system is an example), many Indians have an exceptionally short conclusionary memory. They often cannot recall which conclusionary method they used to arrive at a belief. Indians will hold a truism to be perfectly valid even though they cannot recall how they arrived at it—it might have been logic, intuition, or a leap of faith—hence bizarre beliefs such as that U.S. satellites stop in orbit to shield Pakistani spies from detection as they cross into India, or the conviction that "Killer Carbide" deliberately caused the Bhopal environmental disaster to satiate Western India Hate. A person using deductive reasoning would conclude these to be unsupported by the evidence. A psychiatrist might say that they are witch hysteria in modern dress. A sociologist might talk of scapegoat tactics used to deny personal responsibility. Some Indians, on the other hand, might call these explanations examples of how outsiders invent pretexts to hide the way they are corrupting India. Others might say that these are examples of how Indians invent enemies because they cannot face the one in the mirror. The foreigner really has only one effective response to the illogic of India: acceptance.

Contracts

Most Indians view written contracts as essential to a business relationship. They should be very detailed and adhered to scrupulously. To put contracts less elegantly, you can safely assume the formula, "No Contract = No Money."

Verbal agreements are not considered binding and never should be used to infer financial commitment. Memorandums of Understandings (MOUs) are common tools used to document initial interest, but are not usually formally binding. However, an MOU that is not formalized into a written contract can eventually be held to be a de facto written contract; some key factors can be money transfer or acquiring employees.

It is not uncommon for an Indian business executive rather than a lawyer to negotiate and approve contracts with overseas companies. Lawyers are not used that much in contract negotiations—they are usually the ones you go to when things go wrong. Senior business people can legally commit a firm without (and sometimes in spite of) an attorney's review. India's extraordinarily old legalistic mentality (reflected in its religious and caste minutia) indicate the detailed and binding character with which they view a contract. Indian business people have been tough negotiators since childhood and have had to bargain for every improvement in life.

Do not assume that Western-educated Indians are wholly Western in attitudes and practices. They tend to combine the best virtues of East and West, especially when it comes to combining entrepreneurial flair with the tight contract.

Wherever possible, insert precise payment terms into your contracts. Some Indians have been known to delay or ignore payments once the ink is dry. Clauses requiring payment up-front or at specific stages in the completion of a transaction reinforce the contract's validity.

Management and Mismanagement

From the foregoing it should be clear that it is unwise to presume that Western management theories will work in India just as they do in, say, South America or Eastern Europe.

In India two management models coexist. The private company is usually hierarchical, while the public company and government bureaucracy are usually concentric.

The Indian private-sector business structure is usually a hierarchy manned by many layers of fairly toothless functionaries. Indian management thinking pushes power toward the top, just as in Indian families. Individual managers usually have a fairly broad latitude in which to make decisions, but the real power in those decisions is limited. You might liken Indian management authority to unfunded mandates.

The public-sector management model is usually the Concentric Circles model, in which various satellite hierarchies relate to a core leadership, not in a vertical order, but surrounding a center of power.

The roots of this double system lie in the tradition that most of India's early clans were loosely associating republics which merged both management styles. Largely autonomous families or tribes related to a regional clan that, often as not, was not based on power but prestige (often symbolized in clan totems). Within each clan, families operated on the hierarchical system.

Hence, when dealing with a private business you will find it very clear who makes the decisions. Indian businesses can be intensely hierarchical, with a great deal of micromanaging done by a single authoritative person, beneath whom middle managers are little more than implementors.

When dealing with a government bureaucracy, on the other hand, you will often find that the titular decision-maker is often but a spokesperson for a collective process in which it is hard to pin down exactly how or why a decision is made. One result is a great deal of ad-hoc decision-making by the contact person at the front desk whose signature on a piece of paper is all you really need. The diffuse, ad-hoc character of Indian bureaucracy is one reason why India's bribery system is so ineradicable.

Day-to-Day Working Relationships

Employer-employee relationships often manifest remnants of the colonial system in which workers were considered part of a large family, treated with genuine regard, and given fairly autonomous responsibility. One result is an intense preoccupation with job security. Another is high-profiling the visible perks of position. A third is indifference to the quality of the actual work performed. A fourth is the primacy of personal over company needs.

An enthusiastic application of the latest theory from Harvard is unlikely to do much more than dig in already well-planted heels. The astute thing to do is to work around unproductive behavior rather than confront it.

The most common difficulties in day-to-day labor-management relations are:

- Management does not understand Indian "face."
- Foreign managers do not understand the Indian's deep psychological need for validation.
- Management does not understand the primacy of family in workers' values.
- Foreigners do not understand the Indian sense of work ethics.
- People are often afraid to admit their failings, particularly when it comes to mastering a particular technology or equipment.

Face

In India, as in much of Asia, face is a complex phenomenon rooted in anxiety over self-esteem. In general it can probably be said that highly pampered childhoods terminated with sharp obedience demands create a conflict between an idealized self-image and the harsh discomforts of the world. The result is an overwhelming fear of criticism and a correspondingly overwhelming reaction against criticism when it does occur.

Face is mostly concerned with external dignity—how a person thinks he or she is seen in the eyes of others. Few things cause Indians loss of face more quickly than being unappreciated (or underappreciated) for what they perceive as their true worth. Not being promoted when the time is due, not getting due recognition for good work, excessive criticism, and, above all, public rebuke—these are face-losers no manager should indulge in.

Throughout Asia the concept of face is also associated with denial and false belittlement.

Denial. Denial is simply pretending that things are not so. You will find it very difficult to get the true facts from anyone—especially if those facts are negative. This is a powerful response throughout all of Asia and is behind the phenomenon of advocates of "Asian values" ignoring that their societies do exactly the same things they despise in the West.

Denial has important consequences for the manager in India whose company funds the business he or she manages. Indian denial quickly takes the view that the company merits this infusion of foreign capital, and having so merited it, the money really belongs to the Indian managers to do with whatever they like. This can produce some otherwise inexplicable behavior. A German manager assigned to a newly-purchased resort hotel in Kerala arrived to find that his staff had moved their families in, occupying more than one-half of the rooms. The managers said the hotel would earn so much from the other rooms that they really deserved them for their families as a perk in lieu of higher pay.

Mistakes. Indians rarely take responsibility for mistakes. Accountability is often weak. Errors and oversights are blamed on subordinates or simply passed over. Some Indians are not good at carry-through or meeting deadlines. Procrastination is common, especially in the public sector.

False belittlement is a refinement of "we're really just simple and humble folk here" when in fact they are quite devious and thieving folk. In India this takes the form of belittling technological ability when in fact Indians are very capable technologically—their complex four-part thinking process is a hint. False belittlement of the "we're just not very good at these advanced things" is not the bid for attention it might be elsewhere. Rather, it is pretending the inability to fathom a situation in order to buy time so that you can truly master it and then you can be safely edged out of the picture. You can take it as a given that everyone directly under you wants your job (or rather, its salary). False humility will tell you whom to watch the most.

Face-Saving in Typical Management Situations

There are three areas where the above observations affect management-employee relations.

Criticism. The most effective Indian managers compliment in front of others and criticize behind closed doors. Replace "criticize" with "critique" and you are halfway there. The other steps are simple:

- Critique in privacy, in a quiet voice, and with respect.
- Do not begin with what is wrong with an employee. Ask the employee what he or she considers their better and poorer points. Quite often you will find the employee self-critiquing the very behavior you have in mind. This gives the employee the "good face" quality of having been honest with you.
- Acknowledge each of the employee's good qualities as seen by him- or herself, adding a few of your own.
- Critique the particular issue you have in mind. *Keep it single-issue oriented!* Ask whether there are mitigating factors you do not know about. Quite often there are.
- Suggest ways *both of you* can improve the situation.
- End your critique by acknowledging how valuable you find the employee.
- Make certain thar the employee knows that the critique is strictly confidential.

In addition to the above procedure for a one-on-one critique, there are other more generalized rules:

- Delegating a critique sends the signal that the employee is not worth your time—a slap in addition to a rebuke.
- Never demean employees behind their backs—it *will* get back to them.
- Avoid favorites and whipping boys.
- Never play one employee or group of employees off against an-other—"divide and conquer" was a ferociously hated practice during colonial days.

Praise. "Public praise results in praiseworthy employees" may sound trite, but morale in India is demonstrably better when managers have praise for everyone, even though it may be only a particular person or team that is being acknowledged on a specific occasion. The three rules of praise are: "Praise Often, Praise Accurately, and Don't Overdo It."

- Praise publicly and even-handedly.
- When praising a particular employee, praise the work group as well.
- Always have a few words of praise for everyone, even if it is a particular team that is being especially praised on a specific occasion.

Protecting Bosses. Much of Indian management style derives from the British colonial legacy, when the colonial decided and the local administered. Most decisions were made at the high level and natives were not encouraged to participate. This approach unwittingly reinforced the already strong Indian psychological attitude that authority is arbitrary and often wrong, but it is authority nonetheless.

Today, boss-protection is part of the denial mechanism. The result is that bosses are shielded from the consequences of bad decisions in order to save the face of the establishment as a whole. Lower level employees are reluctant to make decisions. They fear loss of face if they are wrong, yet also loss of face if they make a good decision that was someone else's duty to make. It is common to find decisions that can easily be made at a lower level referred up the chain of command to management levels far superior to the actual matter at hand.

As a boss you will be told the truth about things only with reluctance and after much prodding. This is especially true if you ask an employee to critique your own style or one of your decisions. As a boss you are a combination of the all-nurturing mother and the all-expecting father.

The Primacy of Personal Needs over Productivity

In India, personal needs and family come first. Work is the necessity that produces the money that supports the family. Work has little socially redeeming value in and of itself. There is no "work ethic" as such, but there are definitely "work ethics"—the do's and don'ts associated with one's work.

Foreign managers often chafe at the amount of time spent on personal and family life in the office versus the time spent on work. One chronic complaint is "India time," which often runs on a different schedule than "time-clock" time.

You can expect numerous disruptions to the productivity of your business day. There really isn't much you can do about them, as labor unions, politicians, and the legal establishment tend to support placing personal over business values. You can expect some or all of the following:

- Roads and public transport are especially congested in the mornings and in the evenings. People traveling by public transport tend to leave home at a time they *predict* will get them to work on time. Showing up early for work is quite unusual, but being late is common. The idea of making up tardiness by working late or during lunch has not caught on.

- Certain services such as school buses for smaller children are not well established in India. Hence a parent who has to go to work anyway takes the child to school on the way. Someone who takes a child to school will arrive late on the job without feeling any need to explain why.

- Government and many public-enterprise bureaucracies such as electrical or telephone companies insist that individuals present themselves in person—a married person cannot act on a spouse's behalf, and your maid or driver probably will not even be allowed in the door. Many private businesses such as banks have the same rules. Many offices have a rule that receipts for payment transactions have to be affixed with a postage stamp that is then signed over, which can be done only by the person involved.

- Transacting personal and social business on company time is quite acceptable practice. This practice is called "short leave"; it usually occurs two or three times a month and consumes anywhere from two hours to the rest of the day.

- There is very little tradition for doing ordinary transactions over the phone. A bank manager who has known someone for years still expects to see them in person rather than talk to them by telephone.

- Most offices close earlier than the normal 5:00 P.M. so that people can do their grocery shopping. The Indian custom is to buy food for each meal rather than for the day or week.

- In areas where telephones are not common, there are occasions when an employee does not report for work and does not call to tell you—with no telephone it is difficult to contact one's office.

- Personal business appointments on office time are normal practice—employees expect the right to "drop in" to see a business associate whenever they want.

- Long waits in line are common in India; it is not unusual to wait two or three hours to see someone. This is especially the case with public health care. An employee who wants to see a doctor will take the day off (unannounced if the malady has arrived overnight), expecting not to actually see the doctor until late in the day.

- Religious duties also affect the day-to-day running of a business. Some of these are the ceremony to mark embarkations or new beginnings. Chanting special prayers on an auspicious occasion will temporarily stop all work and usually result in the rest of the day off. Muslim employees have a weekly special prayer time that falls between noon and 3.00 P.M. on Fridays; normally Muslims work half-days on Saturdays to make this up.

Trust-Building

Indians tend to trust only when convenient. This is more likely to occur in the internal relationships between your working partners, who may not have worked together until you came along. It is relatively easy for you as a foreigner to become accepted and trusted, assuming that you do not ask anyone to do something unscrupulous. In India, mistrust is easily acquired and almost impossible to eradicate. It never hurts to quietly ask your colleagues what is the *pukka*, or proper thing to do, in a situation that is unfamiliar to you.

It is very helpful to socialize fairly often with your Indian counterpart and their families. To Indians trust is a personal bond that spills over into business life. Your colleagues will go out of their way to entertain and take care of your family. Introducing your own spouse and children to your colleagues goes a long way toward cementing a relationship via the all-important Indian sense for the value of the family. Lucky you if you have teenagers with a good pop music collection—the selection may drive you crazy but the word will soon be around about how "cool" you are.

Most Indian professionals perceive it an honor to conduct business with foreigners. However, be wary of some types who talk a good deal but never sign one—some people relish the prestige of appearing familiar with foreigners and love to "talk deal."

When Decisions Go Wrong

Decisions are often intuition supported by inadequate research. Most are made by one person at the top of the organization. Younger managers take to research avidly—to the point where they get bogged down in it. Group consensus is not the priority it is in other Asian countries. Decision-making is accomplished quickly and with finality.

These are almost perfect preconditions for disastrous decisions. Once it happens, a bad decision involves massive loss of face in a society that finds personal error almost impossible to accept. Denial is the first—but often not the worst—problem you will have to deal with.

Evidence that the decision is wrong will be suppressed—you often cannot get vital evidence, it will be delayed, or often it will be doctored. Poorly explained delays and "can't seem to locate that file just now" are warning hints that something is seriously wrong.

However, Indians have subtle ways of publicly identifying who is responsible for a bad decision. Tamil Naduans "beat the dog in front of the lion"—a middle manager uncharacteristically sharply berates an underling in the presence of the manager's boss. The remarks are really directed at the boss. West Bengalis subtly accuse with "the mouse with the long tail"—so vigorously denying that their boss has made a mistake that everyone knows the boss is guilty as hell.

Often you will find that accepting blame yourself goes a long way toward mitigating a bad decision's effect on morale. Everyone knows that you do not have to abide by the rules of Indian psychology, so unless there is serious risk to your own position, it is sometimes best to gracefully self-sacrifice.

Thinking Plan B

Correcting a bad decision involves careful face-saving. A decision should never be "wrong." Rather, "the circumstances changed unexpectedly" and "it appears we must make some minor modifications." The "modification" may really mean scrapping the project, but don't put it that way.

"Plan B" is preemptive damage control—foreseeing disaster before it happens and prethinking options to put into effect if it does. The "Plan B" strategy has not really caught on in India. Since hardly anyone admits to making a mistake, there isn't any need to plan for one, is there?

If you introduce Plan B thinking with an officious name like "strategic contingency effectuation," it will sound like the latest advance in management art. Using words as cosmetics, your counterparts are likely to embrace it avidly. The most useful thing you can insert into any Plan B strategy is a face-saving mechanism for re-allocating the onus of a decision gone wrong.

If you really want to excel at the art of Plan B strategy in India, find an English translation of Kautilya's *Artha Shastra* (The Science of Governance). Kautilya has often been called India's Machiavelli. This slights him. In fact he was one of history's most perceptive observers of the failings of the powerful, and his *Artha Shastra* is one of the world's greatest studies in spin-doctoring disaster.

"No" = "Not At This Time But We Will Carefully Leave That Option Open"

Generally Indians dislike "No." They also dislike "I." They may drop negative hints, delay, talk in grand circumlocutions, or simply ignore an issue to death. Underlings are very good—almost poetic—at telling you what they think you want to hear. Younger and more professional Indians are more willing to be forthright, but in general any reluctance to state things definitively can be taken as a sign that something negative is being hidden or avoided.

Indians use subtle body language. Some grasp both ears to indicate that they really don't want to hear this. Others indicate agreement by wobbling their head from side to side in a kind of flat figure-eight. Do not automatically assume that a nod of the head means approval; all it really means is "I hear you."

There are dozens of such gestures. They vary from region to region and often from caste to caste. To a Muslim, holding the hands out palms upward while looking at the sky means "Allahu Akbar" ("God is Great"), which is an affirmation. A Hindu may use it to signify, "May I be reborn in a higher state," which is a negative affirmation of his present existence. It is a good idea to get a verbal response rather than hope that you've got the local body signs down pat.

When you do say "No," couch it as gracefully as you can, try to use "we," and always insert an option that you may later change your mind.

In India there is an exception (often many of them) for every rule. For every minus in India there is a plus. Try to take notice of the things that work well in India—the power of positive observation can be just as important as the power of positive thinking.

MANAGING EXTERNAL PROBLEMS

There are unexpected and sometimes costly hidden realities associated with startups and daily operations in India, but the *India Means Business* kit distributed by India's Ministry of External Affairs does not mention them. You will find the complete picture hard to extract from the representatives of Price-Waterhouse, Ernst & Young, and other accounting and consulting firms that advise on Indian business investment. Consultants, after all, want you to retain their services, at which time they will *then* tell you what they know.

The only people who will say anything truly candid are expatriates already in India. But interviews with them tend to paint an overly negative image, largely because your queries are likely to focus on the ruts in their experiences, not the byways they have found to success. India can focus one's attention almost maddeningly on petty details, since there are so many of them.

There are two types of problems related to business in India. Some are external to daily operations, such as the overall legal and business conditions that affect one's business no matter where it is located. These are dealt with in this chapter. Others are internal, such as personnel management and working with other business people; these are the subject of the next chapter. Since most problems can be avoided by properly planning, Ernst & Young and Price-Waterhouse can provide a detailed checklist that you should complete before you buy an airline ticket.

The Big Picture

In dealing with India you will usually be dealing with a business mindset of a very different order: monopolistic rather than entrepreneurial, exclusionary rather than free-market, preoccupied more with politics than production, abusive to its management, terrified of its workers, and fearful of technology.

Indian denial of self-responsibility is in such a state that India is the only country left in the world where you will hear of the use of English commonly referred to not as "the language of international communication" or "business's *lingua franca*," but as "the legacy of arrogant Western Imperialism." It is one of the few places in the world where the Cold War mentality hangs on, only now rephrased as "North—South imperialism." It is always tempting at this point to bring up India's treatment of its own minorities in the Northeast, Kashmir, and the Deccan, not to mention India's economic bossing around of Sri Lanka, Nepal, Sikkim, and Bangladesh. Don't. Self-righteous hypocrisy absolving one's own behavior is at the core of any denial system. As *India Today* magazine put it in an editorial, "It is an Indian trait to look for scapegoats wherever there is a need for self-criticism."

Hence, when you hear virulent criticism of the shortcomings of Western business practices, what you are really hearing is unhappiness over India's own shortcomings. Many of them emanate from the skewed socialism of the Indira Gandhi years. Underpinning these is the legacy of 3,000 years of the trader mentality, which considers the most advantageous form of business to be the monopoly holding the customer hostage. This applies as aptly to the business of labor relations as it does to customer relations.

With the exception of the software community, the Indian business and finance communities in general are poorly prepared for high-energy, high-speed, high-stakes East Asian/Western-style business. Unions and bureaucrats have next to no grasp of the consequences of the realities of the global business community. Most companies that you are likely to deal with will be suppliers, services, and distributors. These industries have endemic problems that you will not be able to change. Indeed, the very idea of change is viewed with fear—India's early religions all had a component of fear of change prompting withdrawal from reality.

Attitudes About Finance

Although your business may not involve finance, it is useful to have a perspective on Indian behavior patterns in this key area, since they will reflect on attitudes toward *your* finances.

Many businesses enthusiastically court export orders from overseas but fail to organize themselves financially to fulfill them on time. A large proportion of temporarily unused capital goes into property or shares speculation rather than interest-bearing accounts. Middle-tier companies approaching the equity market often seek to list only a small portion of their equity, intending to keep as much as 80 percent under family control. Short-term finance is far easier than long-term finance. Borrowers often pay less attention to the business intricacies surrounding their loan proposal than the size of the cash pool it makes available. Lenders often pay less attention to the business plan than the political connections of the people presenting it. Business plans (when they exist) are so Pollyanna that they often predict first-year equity growth greater than the GDP growth.

These imply a pattern of short-sightedness that carries over into operational management. Most of your vendor businesses will habitually focus on short-term goals and give low priority to strategic planning. On the labor productivity front, you can put into one statistical table (Table 3.1) the kernel of India's core problem for the overseas business person.

Table 3.1

	Factory Worker Average Monthly Wage (US$)	Value Added per Manufacturing Worker (US$)	Multiple
Indonesia	39	320	8.2
Sri Lanka	42	296	7.0
Philippines	83	500	6.0
Bangladesh	40	168	4.2
India	66	212	3.2

Although the figures in Table 3.1 are from 1994 and have changed somewhat, the proportions have not. What they say is that India gives you the least Asian value for what you pay. The major saving grace is that you do not have to pay much.

Starting Up

Most business people report a fairly arduous transition from arrival to the commencement of operations. This is the time you will be dealing with the fullest, slowest, and sleaziest impact of India's entrenched bureaucracy. Long before you buy a plane ticket, you need to establish networks with other business people who have been through India's startup blues. Most countries have affiliated in-country Chambers of Commerce geared toward mutual self-help. This is the best place to start, as contacts here will lead you directly into the Internet business community of India. This in turn will save you huge amounts of time and grief. (See "Business Addresses in the United States" for initial contacts.)

Given half a dozen Indian e-mail and Web site addresses, you can rapidly expand them through referrals and today's commercial search engines into a reference bank that was unimaginable even a year before this book was written. This writer's Yahoo search and subsequent follow-ups on November 14, 1996 yielded 1,434 references to industry in India and 771 to business finance. (These were only the published references. Due diligence would have yielded many more e-mail addresses.)

First the Bad News

The author's November 1996 search zeroed in on problems with India's bureaucracy. Most complaints went on to say that unions and fearful Indian competitors can add their own share of headaches for the newcomer.

Here is a sampler of direct quotes culled from personal and e-mail interviews with American expatriates doing business in India:

- Government legislation usually sets no clear boundaries, no clear line of implementation from policy to practice. I call them "directionless mandates."

- Projects are hard to authorize because no one person has been given the authority.

- Most bureaus do not show an organization chart of who's who and their functions. Most cannot even tell you who to call if you need information.

- The local government Official Telephone Directory lists a Board of Investment, an Industrial Development Ministry, an Industrial Development Board, a State Development Bank, a Small Industries Development Board, a Small Industries Development Department, and an Export Development Board—but it does not tell you where they are, who runs them, or what they do.

- When you call a government bureau and the people there cannot help you, they also cannot tell you the name of the organization that can.

- Nobody knows what anybody else does.

- The third through fifth levels of government are where the corruption is. That is where corruption is truly endemic because those are the jobs that change the least and where you find the entrenched incompetents.

- I never had a policeman ask for a payoff, never had a car mechanic charge exorbitant prices, but the state governments employ the most dishonest people in the world.

- The business environment changes from day to day but no one in government keeps track of it. I don't think they know how.

- Government people do not decide, will not commit, and cannot respond.

- Opposition parties say that they will shake things up and reform the government. But when they get in power they turn to those same bureaucrats for help keeping them in power.

- The surest way to lose an employee is to promote him. They turn promotion into an automatic double raise by going somewhere else and getting a hiring bonus above their current pay.

- Most people who respond to the appointments ads want any job, not necessarily the job you have.

- Employment agencies are even more incompetent than the people they send over. The skills of their "registered" employees are never what either one of them claims.

- Telephone, power, and water are the worst bureaucracies.

- Never use the postal system; use couriers and faxes.

- It takes two weeks to get a container unloaded and turned around.

- I could not eliminate my absenteeism and "personal leave" problems. So I added 20 percent to my labor force and pay everybody 20 percent less than I could.

- Union leaders do not know technology; hence they do not know what job perks to demand. So they demand that you give their family members management positions.

- Union leaders do not seem to know that there is a place called India; the only geography they know is their union hall.

Dealing with Labor

India's labor picture is complex and changing. Most new businesses opt to build in so-called "greenfield" regions where land is cheap and where there has been little history of union involvement. Ford and Hyundai, for example, are building plants in the enthusiastically free-market state of Tamil Nadu, well away from the fiery socialist militants of Mumbai and West Bengal. Others employ contract workers or keep their work forces below thresholds for compulsory union recognition.

"Labor" must be carefully distinguished into its union and nonunion components. Nonunionized private-sector labor "can be among the most efficient people in the world, if properly guided." (K. Gopalkrishnan from Motorola Inc., India, in 1995). Adds Scott Bayman, CEO of General Electric (India), "Indian labor has enabled GE to become a low-cost global manufacturer with world-class production" and "the technological capabilities of Indian labor are quite high."

This will also be immediately obvious to the newly arriving visitor surveying what he sees from the taxi on the way into town. It is difficult to imagine a community more busily at work than the streets and shops of India. The old myth of the lazy Indian worker is a lie that should have been dust-heaped years ago. The amount of physical and mental labor Indians put into daily survival is extraordinary. It is the Indian government's choice of economies and the unions' choice of tactics that have let India's labor down, not the other way around.

A Case Study in Labor Relations Gone Wrong

When labor relations go awry the result can be horrendous. It is worth stepping aside for a moment to examine the 1996 case of Peugeot, France's second largest auto-maker, and its labor troubles at a Mumbai factory. This dispute has sparked a labor clash that goes to the root of the role of labor in India's economic changes.

Peugeot's and Fiat's Indian partner is Premier Auto, a farsighted family business empire trying to break away from the stifling monopolistic thinking of family-owned manufacturing companies during India's controlled economy era. During its 1996 contract renegotiations, Premier wanted to trade high-wage increases and production-related bonuses for control of production and wages that would bring Premier into competitive alignment with other Indian auto-makers.

Union troubles began when Peugeot insisted on enforcing long-ignored safety rules mandating that sheet-metal presses should be operated with both hands. Some workers objected on the grounds that the rule enforcement was not tied to lower productivity concessions. The union leader involved was Dr. Datta Samant, who led a 1983 strike in Mumbai that lost over 100,000 textile plant jobs there. Dr. Samant built up his union in the 1970s with a series of often violent disputes that won high wage increases. He defends violence with, "Labor issues cannot be settled in a peaceful manner."

The Peugeot dispute delayed parts being sent to the Uno factory, which in turn led to production and bonus disputes and eventually lockouts at both plants. Dr. Samant then tried to dictate output and pay. Some workers crossed picket lines and returned to work, but production stopped for several weeks.

Samant states that he sees union disputes as a lever against foreign investment, arguing that overseas investment will only lead to lower pay and layoffs. (The fact that it creates jobs escapes him.) The Indian business press counters that Samant is trying to use the Premier dispute rebuild his (and indeed all of old-line labor's) dwindling reputation in the face of new thinking from outside.

This dispute became a *cause celebre* because it was the first big labor conflict to hit the hundreds of joint ventures set up since economic liberalization began in 1991. Premier had opted to use its existing plants in Mumbai for both Fiat and Uno cars instead of moving to a greenfield location, calculating that the projected investment of $165 million is far lower than the cost of a new site. Maitreya Doshi, Premiere's 34-year-old managing director, says that union leaders "have to wake up to the new reality." He reckons that it is "better to take a hit and cure the system" now while Premier's production is low, rather than wait until it reaches its intended production of 120,000 autos a year.

The lesson to overseas business people is clear: Look as carefully at the management style of local union leaders as you do at the style of the management where you plan to invest.

This again is a case where e-mail can discover things that were impossible to predict a few years ago. An investor in the United States who wants to know if he or she should "go greenfield or buy plant" in India can find out in hours what the union style or political atmosphere is in, say, Maharashtra or Uttar Pradesh.

Strike Risk: Feared Versus Real

Most workers in the public sector and the older industrialized private sector belong to a union. Despite the fact that fewer than 0.5 percent of all private-sector workers go on strike in any given year, Indian employers rank labor regulations third (after high taxes and interest rates) on a list of thirty-three constraints to expanding or diversifying their operations.

Public-sector strikes exert indirect effects: unreliable deliveries, power outages, and communications failures. These can be as debilitating as if your own plant is being struck. Public enterprise strikes in the next state over can affect your suppliers and distributors even if you happen to be a state line away.

Private businesses, especially manufacturers in Export Processing Zones (EPZs), do not report significant problems with labor strikes. In EPZs, labor problems rank twenty-sixth on the list of thirty-three constraints.

When overseas-owned firms are closed due to labor problems, in most cases it results from heavy handling by the company's Indian management.

Overheating works on both sides, and unrest can rapidly escalate into "us versus them" confrontations involving very real threats of violence. Overseas managers must be selected for their ability to be even-handed, bland in public utterances, and their ability to remain unruffled in the face of in-your-face (literally!) hostility.

Strike Psychology and the Wildfire Effect

When the Maharashtra state government shut down Enron's operation in Dabhol in 1995, the venture came to an end with a highly symbolic act: The doors to the football-field-sized air-inflated tent that sheltered the administrative center were opened to let out the air pressure. A large crowd of people danced and shouted "Jai Hind" ("Hindu Victory!") and "Bharat Mata ki jai" ("Victory to Mother India!") as they watched what the press gleefully described as "American Imperialism deflating to the joy of the masses."

The only problem was that the dancers were freshly out of a job. They were Enron employees cheering the end of their employment even though it meant a bleak future for them all. There is no Workers' Comp or unemployment benefits in India.

Indian stoppage psychology can be self-contradictory. Most strikes last a week or less, but their emotional fury can be unnerving to the outsider. There is a strong component of "drawing conclusions from conclusions" in Indian anger. The effect is similar to "crowning" in a forest fire. Remember that this heat will cool when everyone is back to work, so never respond to emotion with an emotional reply—it will be long remembered.

Management Talent

India has an overall unemployment problem (up to 25 percent in some areas and sectors), but a manpower shortage in the management and software/computer areas. India's educational institutions train about 5,000 new managers a year, against a demand for about 30,000 from industries fueled by foreign investments. There is a perennial shortage of qualified management personnel at all levels, beginning with shop-floor supervisors, ascending through production and general managers, and into the ranks of upper level professionals in research and development, planning, finance, and marketing.

Although wage and salary numbers will change upward over the next few years, as of late 1996 some representative numbers were as follows:

- Minimum wage in large industrial enterprises: Rs 225/day ($6.42);
- Junior manager, consumer products: Rs 6,800–7,000/mo ($195–$200);
- Senior manager, consumer products: Rs 12,750–23,000/mo ($365–$657);
- Top executive, consumer products: Rs 28,000–42,000/mo ($800–$1,200);
- Junior engineer: Rs 2,700–2,800/mo ($77–$80);
- Senior engineer: Rs 7,700–13,700/mo ($220–$390);
- Executive/consulting engineer: Rs 16,250–24,250/mo ($465–$693)
- Junior manager, financial services: Rs 3,900–4,000/mo ($111–$114);
- Senior manager, financial services: Rs 9,500–17,500/mo ($271–$500);
- Top executive, financial services: Rs 25,000–40,000/mo ($715–$1,143);
- Junior software engineer: Rs 4,250–4,500/mo ($121–$129);
- Senior software engineer: Rs 9,000–16,000/mo ($257–$457);
- Top executive, software company: Rs 21,000–32,000/mo ($600–$915).

Job-Hopping

Western ways, and television especially, have brought changes to India's offices. One is that business life comes to a halt during critical cricket matches. As a Texas Instruments manager put it, "If it's India versus Pakistan and you manage a fab lab, you're better off letting everyone go for the day. Otherwise your reject rate will be astronomical."

On a more mundane level, attitude differences are showing up in the form of a generation gap. Young business people behave according to the Western models of business life they see on television and in the movies, and from counterparts they meet in the course of their internationalized occupations. This goes against the grain of older business, people who value company loyalty more than personal ambition (conveniently forgetting that it was their personal ambition that started the company in the first place).

Many young people have little company loyalty. The microreason is reaction against the "silk ceiling"—India's term for occupational limits in a family company where promotions are nominally based on ability but family scions have pre-abilities nearer to the top rungs of the ladder. (These progeny often lack the drive of their fathers and are pejoratively known as "the sons of their fathers.")

The macro reason, however, is that the younger generation is acutely aware that today's business world has suddenly begun to provide opportunities for a fast rise that did not exist a few years ago. They are eager to ascend and simultaneously aware that today's economic boom is sensitive to politic machinations in New Delhi. They fear that if the wrong set of politicians worms into power, India's mid-1990's boom could crash just as quickly and business will return to its tried-and-true formulas, one of which is that you can neither fire nor promote people. Hence they job-hop with the idea that if things crash, they will be higher up the ladder than if they had stayed loyal aspirants.

The early-1990's tactic of poaching from other industries and public-service units has backfired. The result is a now-ingrained tradition of job-hopping, job-hostaging, and salary expectations near overseas levels.

You will be faced with job-hostaging ("pay me higher than your competition or I'll go there with everything I know about you") and the almost certain likelihood of a high turnover of employees—especially youthful ones in the financial professions. A raise can be an incentive to "double job-hop it"—going to another company with the news of the raise and then extracting a similar one as a signing incentive.

Most large firms have responded by providing in-house management training. Some financial-profession bodies such as the Institute of Chartered Accountants, the Institute of Management Accountants, the Institute of Chartered Secretaries, and the Institute of Financial Analysis have been training middle managers through their professional accreditation process. Their management syllabuses often reflect a blend of Western and Indian management thinking that is well worth looking into when you start your own human resources training program.

Damage-Controlling Disaster

While India's business press publishes some of the best in-depth writing anywhere in the world, the same cannot be said for the popular press. Written mostly in Hindi and local languages, the foreign visitor will rarely have an inkling about what lies behind those jagged-looking headlines scattered in loose heaps on the tea-shop tables. In this case ignorance is bliss, because India's tabloids make the British and American ones seem like models of restraint.

The mix of populism and the press emotionalizes India's denial mechanism to the benefit of culpable local officials and the detriment, and even danger, of overseas managers. An example worth retelling is what happened to Union Carbide during and after the 1984 Bhopal incident.

Union Carbide officials working with Indian lawyers and international experts have concluded that on the night of December 2, 1984 a disgruntled employee passed over for promotion to a supervisory job pumped about 2,500 pounds of water into a methyl isocyanate tank through a hose connected to a pressure gauge. This set off a fatal chain reaction. This evidence comes from the suspect himself and was corroborated by others on duty at the plant that night.

Over 2,500 people were killed overnight and later through secondary illnesses. At the news, a high-pitched popular-media campaign against "Killer Carbide" immediately went into motion, leaving the impression that the accident was a sinister conspiracy by outsiders. Denial and scapegoating set the tone of the event in the minds of the general populace, for whom, to this day, there is no other side to the story.

When Union Carbide's CEO, Warren Anderson, arrived, he was refused permission to see the plant and instead detained along with his technical team. For more than a year, Union Carbide lawyers and scientists were denied access to critical evidence at their own subsidiary's plant. They could not examine thousands of documents, including company logs that might have reconstructed the chronology of events that night. The plant was sealed by Indian officials, and when documents were released from the Central Bureau of Investigation, some had been so clumsily forged that the attempt was obvious. Union Carbide charges that these logs would never survive scrutiny in a court of law.

Seven years after the tragedy, Union Carbide's payment of $470 million dollars to India still had not been disbursed. The money was tied up in political posturing over the size of the award, although the award had been upheld twice by the Supreme Court of India.

India has consistently refused to allow a full, impartial, and international on-site investigation into Bhopal. Foreign companies point to the incident as evidence for their concern for the right of businesses to manage their own property in India. This increases the likelihood of the subsidiary's management to cover up their mistakes, thus shedding all responsibility onto the parent company. India's "deep-pockets" laws are being interpreted to mean that a foreign corporation can be denied all access to its subsidiary in the event of disaster yet still be held accountable for what went on there.

The issues of accountability and industrial safety raised by Bhopal were never examined in the popular press. Instead, there appeared photos of a statue of a stricken mother and child erected in memory of the victims, and editorial reminders of what happens when India deals with a "killer multinational."

There are many lessons from Bhopal, but two stand out for today's managers on their way to India:

1. This is the age of e-mail and the fax. It is a vital to inaugurate in all of your overseas operations daily electronic transmittals of events that might in any way affect plant operation or reputation. This means employee problems, disgruntled suppliers, local political hostility, the activities of those who manage and move your money, and whatever else might be pertinent in the event of disaster. This evidence may not be admissible in a court of law, but an industrial accident or financial debacle is also on trial in the media, not just in the courts. Your duty to everyone is to record and produce all of the facts that occur.

2. Make very careful pre-emptive media damage control plans in conjunction with local public-relations consultants. These should contain specific guidelines about what you must do and say when faced with a possibly hostile press. Copies should be maintained at your headquarters. It is imperative that local managers not get pushed into situations where they can blurt something under pressure to a press that will negativize it.

The Legal System

The broad basics of India's legal system are described in Chapter 6. Here we will discuss some specific issues that affect daily management. The most common complaint of overseas business firms is that the judicial resolution of commercial disputes is inefficient, lengthy, and expensive. (Bankruptcies filed 50 years ago still have not been resolved, and the cases on the docket as of January 1996 will take until the year 2330 to be resolved at today's processing speed.)

The legal issue most likely to effect overseas investors is variations on the *ultra vires* ("outside the domain") doctrine. Briefly stated, this doctrine renders unenforceable obligations incurred by a company when it acts "outside of its domain." This domain is essentially the company's Statement of Purpose as defined when the company registers. The domain states the primary objectives the business will pursue in its first five years of operation.

If, for example, a company's Statement of Purpose is the manufacture of textiles for export, any activities the company undertakes outside that definition fall into legal no-man's land. An overseas firm whose domain is the processing and cutting of raw diamonds for export could run afoul of the Companies Act if it decided to expand its product line to the creation of finished jewelry. Another example might be a garment-making firm that decides to add leather shoes to its line. Shoes would fall under the export category of Leather Products, not Finished Textiles, and this would be outside the company's original domain.

Most *ultra vires* problems can be avoided by good legal counsel when setting up your company. But be sure to emphasize your awareness of the problem. Such a statement will reinforce to your attorney and accountants that you know the implications of some aspects of Indian business practices.

Exit Problems

Terminating a business tends to be very difficult. When a venture becomes nonprofitable, it is considered to be "sick" and comes under the Sick Industries Act. A board is appointed then to try and revive the company. If losses are experienced for three continuous years, the board *may* allow a certificate to be filed in court allowing the venture to be shut down.

The biggest legal obstacle to bankruptcy is that the rules which apply to it are not provided for in the Companies Act, 1956, but are contained in various regulations and circulars issued by the government. This system itself is legally shaky, but the rules are now ingrained and they can only be removed by an amendment to the Companies Act, which is unlikely in the near future given India's much more pressing financial problems.

Bankruptcies aside, redundancy and factory closures are regulated by the provisions of the Industrial Disputes Act, 1947, and the Industrial Disputes (Amendment) Act of 1982 and 1984. Under these Acts, any worker who has completed a continuous year of service is entitled to a certain minimum compensation for closure or retrenchment (the Indian term for "redundancy"). In businesses employing more than one hundred workers, there can be no retrenchment or closure without the prior permission of the appropriate government body.

Technically, this obstacle is easily surmountable: A company's management can bypass these regulations by separating its operations into multiple subsidiaries each employing fewer than one hundred persons at any one time.

The problem is that these steps will be interpreted by the local press as an example of Western imperialism, arrogance, and rapacity. The fact that Indian businesses also bypass the Companies Act with innumerable (and often delightfully ingenious) stratagems is beside the point. Your management choices must take into account negative interpretation of everything you do. This will include you personally. Your address is likely to be printed, along with photos of your house and children at or near their school. A *paparazzi* mentality exists in India's popular press in which you can be certain that every aspect of your personal life will be held up to scrutiny if your business activities inflame union or worker hostilities.

The wisest strategy—trite as it is to say—is to not get into a situation where you are likely to become a press victim. The burden is on you to be fully aware of what you are getting into personally when carrying out your company's policies. Hence you may find yourself acting as an unwilling devil's advocate in the ranks of your firm, arguing against policies that you know make good economic sense but can inflict greater damage in publicity terms than they do in bottom-line terms.

Entrepreneurship

The entrepreneur-mindedness of the West is only just beginning to make itself felt in India. There are only a handful of venture capital firms. Although the terminology of the modern business revolution is familiar in India, the average executive's orientation is likely to be long-term job security rather than high reward for risk.

You will encounter considerable risk-averse behavior among employees. Local managers will excel at doing what they are asked but will be uncomfortable with suggesting improvements to products or processes. Indeed, suggesting an improvement is considered to be a slight on the original product.

Suppliers and vendors have a mindset that thinks in terms of exclusive relationships. They are likely to take a contractual relationship as an assertion of personal friendship in which suggesting more competitive service is taken as disloyalty rather than efficiency.

Corporate and Business Crime

India is a fairly crime-free country. The robbery-minded tend to prefer doing it with a pen. Drug abuse is minuscule compared with Western and Southeast Asian countries. Mumbai has organized crime of the triad and yakuza type, but much of it is associated with the money exchange, construction, and film worlds. Foreigners are discouraged from going into the political hot spot of Kashmir and will find it very difficult to get into the fractious, often rebellious northeastern states.

Most crime that affects foreigners is of the pickpocket and housebreaking variety. There is virtually no violent crime of the drive-by shooting variety, except in Kashmir. Violence that does reach the news is usually domestic violence exacerbated by alcohol.

Alcohol also tends to figure prominently in embezzlement and loading-dock theft. India has a fairly serious alcoholism problem (also much denied), and very little in the way of the 12–step types of programs that have proven so successful elsewhere. Alcoholics Anonymous World Services at P.O. Box 459, New York, NY 10163, can provide a directory of Indian AA contact addresses.

India's police forces are—in this writer's experience—reliable and honest. House break-ins and similar petty thievery against resident foreigners is given prompt attention and efficient follow-up. India's petty-crime problem is poverty- rather than drug-related, and the police often cannot offer much more than sympathy and directions to the black market where your stolen goods are most likely to show up.

Industrial thievery exists but is not all that common to firms which take the obvious precautions. The security arrangements at EPZs strongly inhibit walkaway leakages of the type that affect the garment industry. It is mandatory to oversee any operations that involve small-sized parcels or pocketable electronic equipment.

Most business people identify the Customs Office as the most corrupt of the government agencies they deal with. Firms complain of unduly long delays clearing imports and, to a lesser degree, exports. Petty corruption is endemic. "Expediting fees" or "personal attention" are common demands. The Indian government has been working with technical support from the IMF to computerize its customs administration, and customs valuation procedures are indeed being reformed. The degree to which these will find their way into actual practice is hard to judge. Investors planning to open export-oriented businesses in India should inquire about the realities of preshipment inspection practices from other exporters.

4

How to Invest in India

GETTING THE MOST CURRENT INFORMATION

The information in this chapter can change quickly. Indian consulates and trade missions in certain countries may not always be up to date on specific matters or able to answer technical questions. The most current investment details are available at the following Internet and telephone/fax addresses (see Appendix A for more complete and many other addresses):

http://www.indiaserver.com/biz/dbi/MEA3.0.html

http://www.indiaserver.com/biz/dbi/MEA25.html

http://www.indiaserver.com/biz/dbi/MEA519.html

http://www.indiaserver.com/biz/dbi/MEA527.html

The Joint Secretary (SIA)
Department of Industrial Development
Tel: 91 11 301 1983 Fax: 91 11 301 1770

The Secretary
Foreign Investment Promotion Board
Tel: 91 11 301 7839; Fax: 91 11 302 6857

The Exchange Control Officer
Reserve Bank of India
Tel: 91 22 266 1602; Fax: 91 22 261 9330

The Executive Director
   Indian Investment Centre
   Tel: 91 11 373 3673; Fax: 91 11 373 2245

Tax and other matters are often freshest from international accounting firms such as Ernst & Young, Price-Waterhouse, Coopers-Lybrand, which maintain liaison offices in India.

Beyond these, an astonishing amount of information is available via the Internet using search-engine keywords such as "India and Investment" and "India Free Trade Zones." This writer's Yahoo and AOL Webcrawler searches turned up over 2,800 citations each on 19 November 1996. A significant number of these were consultants and advisory services within India or managed abroad by nonresident Indians (NRIs) who are familiar with the details of investing in India.

THE BIG PICTURE

The Indian market consists of buying from India, selling to India, technology transfers, franchising, and equity participation. The last of these may be via joint ventures by incorporating a company under the Companies Act in collaboration with an Indian partner as an existing private or public company, or incorporating a new company with a general partner and general participation of the public. Alternatively, a wholly owned company with 100 percent foreign equity may be set up. This chapter covers each of these topics in moderate introductory detail.

Foreign Direct Investment

India welcomes direct foreign investment in every sector of its economy except the strategic sectors of defense, railway transport, and atomic energy. As of November 1996, India's Most Favored Investments were as follows:

- production of goods where India's exports are subject to international quotas, e.g., textiles;
- growing and primary processing of agricultural products;
- mining and primary processing of nonrenewable natural resources;
- timber-based industries using local timber;
- fishing (other than deep-sea fishing);

- construction of residential buildings;
- supply of water;
- mass transportation;
- telecommunications;
- education;
- professional services;
- freight forwarding;
- travel agencies;
- shipping agencies.

India's basic investment policies have changed dramatically since liberalization in 1991, but more moderate improvements were made after the 1996 elections. The basic policies are these:

- Foreign equity up to 100 percent is allowed, subject to certain conditions.
- Automatic approval is granted for foreign equity up to 51 percent in many key areas.
- Foreign investors need not have a local partner (although as a practical matter a local partner is desirable).
- Free repatriation of profits and capital investment is permitted, except for a list of specific consumer-goods industries that are subject to dividend balancing against export earnings.
- Use of foreign brand names and trade marks for sale of goods is permitted.
- Indian capital markets are open to foreign institutional investors.
- Indian companies are permitted to raise funds from international capital markets.
- India has signed bilateral investment protection agreements with investing countries.
- Corporate taxes have been reduced, with further progressive reductions planned.
- Special investment and tax incentives are given for exports and certain sectors such as power, electronics, and food-processing.

All proposals involving foreign direct investment and technology transfer require approvals. Two routes are available for foreign investors for
obtaining these approvals. The first applies to automatic approval cases, in
which up to 51 percent equity holding is allowed in thirty-five specified
industries, and up to 50 percent in the mining sector, provided that:

- Foreign equity covers the foreign exchange requirement for the
  import of capital goods that are new and not previously used.
- For proposals with a technical collaboration agreement, the payment of know-how fees and royalties conform to specified parameters; in such cases approval is given by the Reserve Bank of India
  (RBI) within two weeks.

The second route covers all of the other cases in which the parameters
for automatic approval are not met, for example, where foreign equity does
not cover the foreign exchange requirement for imported capital goods, or
where it is beyond 51 percent, or where it involves activities or categories
other than in the list of specified industries. Such cases are cleared by the
Foreign Investment Promotion Board (FIPB) normally within four to six
weeks. Applications may be made either to the FIPB or the Secretariat for
Industrial Approvals (SIA), or Indian Embassies and consulates abroad.

Equity Investment in Indian Companies

It is not obligatory that foreign investors have a local partner if the
investor wishes to hold less than the full equity of the company—the
remaining portion of the equity may be subscribed by the public.

Foreign Institutional Investors (FIIs) such as pension funds, mutual
funds, investment trusts, asset management companies, nominee companies, and incorporated/institutional portfolio managers or their power of
attorney holders (providing discretionary and nondiscretionary portfolio
management services) are welcome to invest in all of the securities traded
on the primary and secondary markets. Such investments may include the
equity and other securities/instruments of companies that are listed/to be
listed on the Stock Exchanges in India, including the OTC Exchange of
India. These would include shares, debentures, warrants, and schemes
floated by domestic mutual funds.

To undertake these activities, FIIs are required to obtain an initial
registration with the Securities and Exchange Board of India (SEBI), the
regulatory agency for securities markets. In addition, FIIs need to comply

with certain foreign exchange regulations for which they need to file an application with the SEBI addressed to the RBI. The RBI's general permission must be obtained by the SEBI before granting initial registration. The SEBI's initial registration is valid for five years. The RBI's general permission will hold for five years. Both are renewable for similar five-year periods. The RBI's general permission granted under the FERA enables the registered FII to buy, sell, and realize capital gains on investments made through the initial corpus remitted to India, subscribe or renounce rights offerings of shares, invest on all recognized stock exchanges through a designated bank branch, and appoint a custodian for custody of investments held.

Disinvestment is allowed through stock exchanges in India, including the OTC Exchange. In exceptional cases, the SEBI can permit sales other than through stock exchanges, provided that the sale price is not significantly different from the stock market quotations, where available. Over 200 FIIs have been registered with the SEBI, and cumulative net investment by FIIs had reached nearly $2.8 billion by mid-1996. In addition, a number of offshore India funds have been instituted by investment agencies abroad and are listed on international stock exchanges.

Mergers and Acquisitions

Merger activity is monitored by the Company Law Board (CLB), an entity within the Department of Company Affairs. The CLB sets down the criteria to acquire another firm, which in India means obtaining more than 25 percent of its shares. Within four months of an acquisition offer, holders of at least 90 percent of the share value must decide whether to accept the tender offer. Dissenting shareholders have the right to appeal to the courts, which will block the move only if the transaction appears to be manifestly unfair or if majority consent seems to have been induced through fraud or deception. Conversely, the government can order the amalgamation of two or more companies if it believes this to be in the public interest.

In July 1991, the SEBI released guidelines for fresh legislation on mergers and acquisitions to replace the existing laws. The guidelines call for increased public disclosure, open offers to small shareholders at a defined minimum price, and a shift in the power to refuse share transfers from the board of directors to the shareholders. They may be summarized as follows:

- Once 10 percent of a company's equity is bought by a raider, or management control changes, the takeover code gets activated.

- Open public offer is required to buy 20 percent shares, and 10 percent of the amount must put in an escrow account as a guarantee.

- Payments must be made within 30 days of close of offer.

- The minimum offer price is to be based on an average of six-month closing highs and lows, or on a negotiated price for acquiring the target company; the higher one will be the offer price.

- Financial institutions can invite takeover bids if one-half of the company's net worth has been eroded.

- Competitive offers must be made within 21 days of the original public offer.

Until about 1996, most mergers in India were private deals involving promoters, merchant bankers, and financial institutions. The purchase price and percentage of equity obtained remained a matter of speculation. The SEBI has frequently pressured bidders to make open offers to shareholders. In 1992, it was given the power to fine offenders, increasing its leverage. The SEBI guidelines state that, in the event of a takeover attempt, companies cannot refuse to recognize the share transfer on the grounds that it is prejudicial to the interest of the company or public interest. The company will have to call an extraordinary general meeting of shareholders within six weeks of an application for substantial transfer.

Under the Companies Act, however, intercorporate transfers of shares are restricted, although there are some loopholes for investment companies. A company may halt the transfer of its shares if the equity is acquired for speculative purposes or for the takeover of a company's management.

The SEBI has also issued guidelines preventing financial institutions and mutual funds from selling shares amounting to more than 1 percent of paid-up capital to the same entity unless a public announcement is made of the intention to sell. The guidelines were formed in response to the previously common practice by financial institutions of using their large stakes to take positions in merger and acquisition transactions. Several cases have arisen since then in which takeovers were attempted via amassing 1 percent holdings under a variety of dummy companies or via family members.

Trading Companies

Foreign companies may invest in trading companies engaged primarily in export activity. Such trading companies are treated at par with domestic

and trading companies in accordance with the Trade Policy. New companies being set up are required to register themselves with the Director
General of Foreign Trade and acquire certification under the prevailing
Exim policy. This certification is given based on the amount of net foreign
exchange earned in preceding years. The RBI accords automatic approvals
for foreign equity up to 51 percent for setting up trading companies engaged
primarily in export activity; all other proposals that do not meet the criteria
for automatic approval, subject to specified industries, can be addressed to
the FIPB.

Branch Offices

Foreign companies engaged in manufacturing and trading activities
abroad may open branch offices with the necessary permission of the RBI.
These branch offices may be opened for the purposes of:

- representing the parent company/other foreign companies as buy-
ing/selling agents;
- conducting research work in which the parent company is engaged, provided the results of this research work are made available
to Indian companies;
- undertaking export and import trading activities;
- promoting technical and financial collaborations between Indian
and foreign companies.

Project Offices

The project office is the ideal method for companies to establish a
business presence in India for a limited period of time. It is essentially a
branch office set up with the limited purpose of executing a specific project.
Foreign companies engaged in the business of turnkey construction or
installation normally set up a project office for their operations in India.

Liaison Offices

A foreign company can open a liaison office in India to look after its
Indian operations and promote its business interests. Companies engaged
in the sale or manufacture of defense, telecommunication categories, and
shipping (without owning ships) are permitted to open liaison offices with
prior approval of the government. Liaison offices are not allowed to carry
on any business or earn any income in India, and all expenses are to be

borne by remittances from abroad. The approvals for these liaison offices are normally for a period of three years; this period can be further extended.

Foreign companies normally use liaison offices to oversee the company's existing business interests, to spread awareness of the company's products, and to explore further opportunities for business and investment.

Companies wishing to raise foreign equity in existing Indian companies up to 51 percent can obtain automatic approval from the RBI under the following conditions.

When an existing company desires to raise foreign capital up to 51 percent of equity as part of an expansion program, the program must be a high-priority industry and the fresh or additional equity must be part of the financing for its expansion.

- When an existing company wishes to raise foreign equity without an expansion program, the company must be predominantly engaged in high-priority industry activity.
- The increase in equity level must result from expanding the existing company's equity base.
- The foreign equity must be remitted from foreign exchange.
- The foreign equity must be used to import capital goods required for the expansion program.

All other proposals for raising foreign equity in an existing company are subject to prior approval of the Secretariat of Industrial Approvals (SIA). Proposals for raising foreign equity or injecting new foreign equity in existing companies via preferential share allocation to the foreign investor must be approved by the company's shareholders via a special resolution of the Companies Act. Preferential allotment of shares of this type is permitted only at the fair market value of the shares. This price is determined by the average price over the immediate preceding six months at the shares' main listing center. Its price valuation is based on the monthly average of the high and low rates quoted for the shares at this center. When submitting applications for raising foreign equity to the RBI, the company must have this recalculation of its share price certified by a Chartered Accountant.

Investing Customer Agreements

An Investing Customer Agreement is essentially a technique to encourage an otherwise reluctant supplier to build new capacity that primarily serves the buyer. Under this scheme, the buyer makes a sizable lump-sum advance payment to the Indian firm, which is then used by the Indian firm to construct the proposed new capacity. Deliveries are made in the traditional supply relationship. The lump sum represents not only an advance payment on the purchase price for the first few months' shipment, but also a contribution to underwriting the construction of the facility.

Foreign Technology Agreements

The RBI automatically approves foreign technology agreements in all industries within the following limits:

- lump-sum payments up to Rs 10 million ($285,715);
- royalty payments up to 5 percent of domestic sales and 8 percent of exports over a 10-year period commencing from the date of the agreement or over a 7-year period from commencement of production;
- these payments are subject to an overall ceiling of 8 percent of total sales over a period of 10 years from the date of agreement or over a 7-year period from the date of commencement of commercial production.

In case of foreign technology agreements for the hotel and tourism industries, automatic approval of the RBI is available subject to the following:

- technical and consultancy services: a lump-sum fee in dollar amounts up to $200,000;
- franchising and marketing support: up to 3 percent of gross room sales;
- management fees: up to 10 percent of the foreign exchange earnings provided the foreign party contributes 25 percent of the equity (this also covers payments for marketing and publicity support).

Proposals for foreign technology agreements that do not meet these parameters for automatic approval are considered on merit by the SIA, which normally approves such proposals within four to six weeks.

INDIA'S EXPORT PROCESSING ZONES

In India, the terms "Free Trade Zones" and "Export Processing Zones" are synonymous. India offers special incentives to investors to set up units to manufacture goods for export in Export Processing Zones (EPZs). They also may be 100 percent Export-Oriented Units (EOUs) outside EPZs—although 100 percent foreign equity is certainly welcome within EPZs as well. India's EPZs are designed to provide an internationally competitive, duty-free environment at low cost for export production. Each zone provides basic infrastructure and facilities like developed land, standard-design factory buildings, roads, power, water supply and drainage, and customs clearance facilities.

Applications for approval for setting up EPZ units must be submitted to the Development Commissioners of the concerned EPZs (addresses listed below). Applications are usually cleared within 45 days. Further details can be obtained from any Trade Commissioner of an Indian Embassy or High Commission (which can also receive applications for investment proposals for forwarding to the appropriate authorities for approval).

Addresses of Development Commissioners for EPZs & EOIs are:

Santacruz Electronics Export Processing, Mumbai
Zone: Andheri (East)
Mumbai 400 096, India
Tel: (91.22) 836 7143
Fax: (91.22) 832 1169
Jurisdiction: Units situated in Santacruz Electronics Export Processing Zones and approved 100 percent EOUs located in Maharashtra, Goa, Daman, Diu, Dadra, and Nagar Haveli

Kandla Free Trade Zone, Kandla
Zone: Gandhidham
Kutch 370 230, India
Tel: (91.2836) 22994, 23250, 23356, 23281
Fax: (91.2836) 52250
Jurisdiction: Units situated in Kandla Free Trade Zone and approved 100 percent EOUs situated in Gujarat

Madras Export Processing Zone, Chennai (name designated before Madras changed its name to Chennai).
Zone: Administrative Office Building
National Highway
Contact: 45 Tambaram
Chennai 600 045, India
Tel: (91.44) 465 220, 465 230, 465 232
Fax: (91.44) 465 218

Jurisdiction: Units situated in Madras Export Processing Zone and approved 100 percent EOUs situated in Tamil Nadu, Andaman, and Nicobar Islands

Cochin Export Processing Zone, Cochin
Zone: CEPZ Administrative Bldg.
Kakkanad
Cochin 682 030, India
Tel: (91.484) 802 545, 802 571, 802 551
Fax: (91.484) 802 545
Contact: KSHB Office Complex
Panampally Nagar
Cochin 682 030
Jurisdiction: Units situated in Cochin Export Processing Zone and 100 percent EOUs situated in Kerala, Karnataka, and Lakshadweep

Noida Export Processing Zone, Uttar Pradesh & Delhi
Zone: Noida Dadri Road
Phase II
Noida
Distr. Ghaziabad (UP) 201 305
Contact: NOIDA Export Processing Zone
PHD House
Khel Gaon Marg
New Delhi 110 016, India
Tel: (91.11) 685 5061
Fax: (91.11) 685 5061
Jurisdiction: Units situated in Noida Export Processing Zone and approved 100 percent EOUs situated in Delhi, Uttar Pradesh, Punjab, Haryana, Himachal Pradesh, Jammu and Kashmir, Rajasthan, Madhya Pradesh, and Chandigarh

Falta Export Processing Zone, Calcutta
Contact: 2nd MSO Bldg.
Room No. 414
Nizam Palace 234/4
AJC Bose Road
Calcutta 700 020, India
Tel: (91.33) 247 7923
Fax: (91.33) 2263

Jurisdiction: Falta Export Processing Zone and approved 100 percent EOUs situated in West Bengal, Orissa, Bihar, Assam, Arunachal Pradesh, Tripura, Manipur, Meghalaya, Nagaland, Mizoram, and Sikkim

Vishakhapatnam Export Processing Zone
Zone: Udyog Bhavan Complex
Siripuram Junction
Vishakhapatnam 530 003, India
Tel: (91.891) 51259, 545 77
Telex: 0495 334 VEPZ IN
Jurisdiction: Units situated in Vishakhapatnam Export Processing Zone

EPZ Incentives

The incentives for EPZs are also applicable for 100 percent export-oriented units (EOUs), which can be located anywhere in India. India's incentives available for EPZ units include:

- EPZ units can import industrial inputs free of customs duty.
- One-hundred percent foreign equity is encouraged in such units.
- EPZ units are entitled to a tax holiday, that is, they are exempt from payment of corporate income tax for a block of five years in the first eight years of operation. Export earnings continue to be exempt from tax even after the tax holiday is over.
- Industrial plots and standard design factories are available to EPZ units at concessional rates.
- EPZ units are exempt from the payment of central and state sales taxes.

Some of the incentives given to EPZs and EOUs are:

- exemption from customs duty on industrial inputs;
- no import license requirement;
- supplies from the DTA to EOU/EPZ units are regarded as deemed exports and are hence exempt from payment of excise duty (meaning higher quality inputs are available at lower costs);

- subject to fulfillment of certain conditions, EPZs/EOUs are exempt from corporate income tax for any five contiguous years during the first eight years of operation (presently, export earnings also continue to be exempt from tax, even after the tax holiday is over);
- setting up of private bonded warehouses in the seven EPZs is permitted for the purpose of import and sales of goods, including in the DTA, subject to payment of applicable duties at the time of sale;
- trading, including re-export after repackaging/labeling;
- re-export after repair, reconditioning, or re-engineering;
- liberal subcontracting facility allowed: EOUs/EPZs are permitted to subcontract part of their production processes for job work to units in the DTA on a case-by-case basis;
- supplies effected in DTA under global tender conditions, against payment in foreign exchange, to other EOUs/EPZ units and against import licenses, are counted toward fulfillment of the export obligation;
- FOB value of exports of EOU/EPZ units are allowed to be clubbed with that of parent companies located in the DTA for the purpose of getting Trading or Export House status;
- EOU/EPZ units may export goods through Trading and Export Houses or other EOU/EPZ units.

Comparative costs of other Asian EPZs are shown in Table 4.1.

Setting Up an EPZ Facility

Applications for approval of setting up EPZ/EOU units are to be addressed to the Development Commissioners of Export Processing Zones in the case of EPZs and to the SIA in the case of EOUs. Where the proposals fulfill the conditions for automatic approval, they are cleared within 15 days; in other cases, they are normally cleared within 45 days. The government also permits setting up EPZs in the private/joint sectors, including by NRIs and foreign companies. Applications for setting up an EPZ may be made to the Development Commissioner of the EPZ in whose jurisdiction the proposed zone is located.

A number of steps have to be taken for setting up a 100 percent export oriented unit or a unit in the Export Processing Zone. These involve identification of the project; approval of the government agencies, includ-

Table 4.1
Comparative Costs of Asian Free Trade Zones

	Sri Lanka Katunayake EPZ	Vietnam Tan Thuan EPZ	China Shantou Economic Zone	Hong Kong Tai Po & Yuen Long Industrial Estates
Land Costs	$2,500	$110 sq m	$48 sq m	$256–385 sq m
Avg Office & Plant Rents			$1.20 sq m per/mo	
Average Wage	$40–55 mo	$50 mo	$41 mo	$880 mo
Electricity Cap'y & Costs	40 MW	675 MW	$0.10 KWh	$0.11 KWh
Telephone Installation	$265		$547	$69
Water	$0.40 cu m		$0.09 cu m	$0.59–1.29 cu m
Taxes/Fees on Profits	10–15%	10–15%	15%	16.5%
Incentives	No duty on items produced	2–4 year tax holiday	Tax holidays, goods imports duty exempt	
Banks in Zone	3	1	5	11
No. of Ventures	122	40	2,850	117
Approval Time	3 days	2 weeks to 7 mo	3 days	6 weeks
Nearest Airport	5 km	10 km	40 km	10 km

Source: Asiaweek, 13 October 1995

Table 4.1 Continued

Singapore JurongTown Industrial Estates	Malaysia Penang Bayan Lepas FTZ	Indonesia Batam Island Industrial Development Park	Thailand Leam Chaband Development	Philippines Laguna Techno Park
	$16–20 sq m	$4.50–9.90 sq m	$3.70 sq m	$90–94 sq m
	$6.40–8.00 sq m/mo	$7–8.30 sq m		
$1,385 mo	$220–300 mo	$90 mo	$130 mo	$130 mo
$0.05–0.10 KWh	110 MW $0.03–0.10 KWh	77.5 MW $0.05–0.19 KWh	$85 MW $0.04 KWh	$0.09 KWh
	$180	$264		$192
$0.80–1.44 cu m	$0.21–0.60 cu m	$0.28–0.88 cu m	$0.25–0.54 cu m	$0.34–8.55 cu m
30%	30%	10–30% plus 10% in-country VAT	Tax Holiday	35% plus property & business taxes
	5 yr holiday; investment tax credit	No import duties, free forex tfr, easy immigation	Exemp. on import duties, deductions for transport & utilities costs	Tax Holiday, tax credits on supplies & raw goods
150		21	10	4
5,400+	475	4,496	1,000+	51
1 month	2–3 months	2–3 months	4–5 weeks	14–21 days
10 km	8 km	10 km	150 km	47 km

ing the Department of Industrial Development; obtaining a Green Card; and execution of bonds with customs authorities followed by actual implementation work.

Preparing a Techno-Economic Feasibility Report for a 100 Percent EO Unit

Preparation of a techno-economic feasibility report (often termed a "project report") of a 100 percent EO Unit is essential for its successful launching. It is all the more important for new units, as they have to submit a copy of the project report with their application for a 100 percent EO Unit.

There is no definitive format for a project report of a 100 percent EO Unit, but it should cover at least the following topics (as appropriate):

Out:

A. Introduction and importance of categories for which the unit is to be established
B. Promoters' profile, including that of the directors and various divisions of the promoting company
C. Project identification
   (a) Product
       (i)   Reasons for identification of product
       (ii) Business promotion efforts of the promoters
       (iii) Potential of the item
       (iv) Advantages of new unit over existing units
   (b) Land location
   (c) Building
   (d) Plant and machinery
   (e) Power
   (f) Water supply
   (g) Process of manufacture
   (h) Raw material, requirement, and sources
   (i) Indian relevance
   (j) World relevance
   (k) Projections for the year 2000
   (l) Human resource requirements
   (m) Marketing potential and selling arrangements
   (n) Cost of project and means of finance
   (o) Financial forecasts
   (p) Summary and conclusions

A. Project estimates
   (a) Cost of land
   (b) Cost of buildings
   (c) Cost of plant and machinery
   (d) Cost of miscellaneous fixed assets
   (e) Preliminary and pre-operative expenses
   (f) Provision for contingencies
   (g) Margin for working capital
   (h) Cost of raw material
   (i) Cost of power connection
   (j) Factory wages
   (k) Factory supervisory and staff salaries
   (l) Administrative staff and salaries
   (m) Average selling price
   (n) Value of scrap sales
   (o) Calculation of interest and repayment of long-term loans
   (p) Depreciation provision
   (q) Profitability statement
   (r) Projected balance sheet
   (s) Projected funds flow statement
   (t) Break-even point calculation
   (u) Project pay-back period
   (v) Debt service coverage ratio
   (w) Analytical and comparative ratios
   (x) Assumptions made
   (y) Process flow chart
B. Export statistics
C. Directors of promoter company

FORMS OF INDIAN BUSINESSES

India's principal forms of business organization follow the general forms used worldwide:

- public and private companies,
- partnerships,
- sole proprietorships.

The most common type of large business in India is a limited liability company. Unlimited companies and companies limited by guarantee are relatively uncommon. Companies incorporated in India and branches of foreign corporations are regulated by the Companies Act of 1956. The Registrar of Companies (ROC) and the Company Law Board (CLB)—both of which are part of the Department of Company Affairs—are responsible for ensuring compliance with the Act.

Indian law makes an important distinction between a "corporate body" and a "company." A *corporate body* may include foreign companies incorporated outside India. A *company* can be a public or private company with limited or unlimited liability. A company can be limited by shares or by guarantee. In the former, the personal liability of members is limited to the amount unpaid on their shares, while in the latter, the personal liability is limited by a pre-determined amount. Several basic forms of companies come under the Act:

- private companies;
- public companies;
- foreign companies;
- holding and subsidiary companies (private or a public).

Private Companies

A private company incorporated under the Act has the following characteristics:

- The right to transfer of shares is restricted.
- The maximum number of shareholders is restricted to fifty (excluding employees).
- No public offering can be made to subscribe to its shares or debentures.

Private companies are less regulated than public companies because they deal with relatively smaller amounts of public money. A private company is deemed to be a public company if:

- Twenty-five percent or more of its paid share capital is held by one or more public companies.
- The private company holds 25 percent or more of the paid-up share capital of a public company.

- It accepts or renews deposits from the public.
- Its average annual turnover exceeds Rs 100 million ($2.85 million).

Foreign Companies

Foreign companies are any that have been incorporated outside of India. They are required to comply with certain rules under the Act. Hence liaison and project offices and branches of foreign companies in India are regulated by the Act. Foreign companies have to register with the Registrar of Corporations (ROC) in New Delhi within 30 days of setting up a place of business in India.

Holding and Subsidiary Companies

A holding company must publish information on its subsidiaries but is not required to prepare group financial statements. A subsidiary of a public company loses most of its privileges and exemptions. A company is said to be a subsidiary of a holding company if:

- The composition of its board of directors is controlled by the holding company.
- More than one-half of its voting power is controlled by the holding company.
- It is itself a subsidiary of yet another subsidiary of the holding company.

Corporations

Incorporation, which normally takes approximately four to six weeks, requires the following:

- obtaining approval for the proposed name of the company;
- drawing up the Memorandum and Articles of Association;
- getting the appropriate persons to subscribe to the Memorandum (seven persons for a public company, and two for a private company);
- paying a registration fee to the ROC;
- receipt of Certificate of Incorporation from the ROC;

- for public companies, applying for and receiving a certificate from the ROC authorizing it to commence business, issued after fulfilling certain conditions set forth by the Act.

Memorandum of Association

The Memorandum of Association (MOA) is the constituting document of a company. It defines the basic features of the company, including:

- the company name plus the term "Limited" if the company is public and "Private Limited" if the company is private;
- the objects or purposes of the company;
- the amount of registered and authorized share capital of the company.

Amending a Memorandum of Association, once published and therefore a public document, is a complex and time-consuming process. Get it right the first time.

Articles of Association

The Articles of Association regulate the internal management of a company. They define the powers of its officers and establish the contract between the company and its members. All companies (other than public companies limited by shares) must register their Articles of Association. If a public company limited by shares does not provide its own articles, model articles included in the Act will be applied to that company.

Issuing Capital Shares

Shares or debentures offered to the public must be listed on a minimum of one recognized stock exchange. Public companies seeking to be listed on a stock exchange must incorporate the stock exchange listing rules in their Memorandum and Articles of Association. These provisions govern matters such as forms of the transfer of the company's securities. One listing requirement is a minimum issued share capital of Rs 30 million ($857,142), out of which a minimum of 60 percent must be offered to the public. This rule is relaxed by the government in case of a foreign company's participation.

Types of Share Capital

There are two kinds of share capital:

- preference share capital (preferred stock);
- equity share capital (common stock).

This restriction does not apply to private companies that are not subsidiaries of a public company. Private companies are also free to issue other kinds of share capital. Redeemable preferred shares, for example, must be redeemed within 10 years out of retained earnings available for dividends.

Pricing new issues of share capital is substantially free from the government's administrative control. The nominal value of shares is not prescribed by the Act, but there is a generally held convention that this value is normally Rs 10 per share for equity shares and Rs 100 per share for preferred stock. Shares can be issued at par, at a premium, or at a discount (a company must have permission from the regulatory authorities to issue shares at a discount). A public company cannot purchase its own shares or provide financial assistance to purchase or subscribe to its shares or the shares of its holding company.

The amount of capital a company can issue is limited by the authorized capital specified in its Memorandum of Association. No ceiling or floor on this amount is required when preparing the Memorandum. A company can thereafter increase its authorized capital only if a clause to this effect is part of its Articles of Association. The normal means to increase subscribed capital is by offering a rights issue, which is subject to the condition that the new shares first must be offered to existing shareholders in proportion to their share holding.

Companies can also increase their subscribed capital by issuing bonus shares out of earnings retained to pay dividends.

Debentures and Public Deposits

Companies can raise funds by issuing debentures, bonds, and similar debt securities. Convertible debentures are one of the most common instruments issued. Debentures can be redeemable or perpetual, bearer or registered, convertible or nonconvertible. Debentures do not carry voting rights.

Companies can also raise funds by accepting deposits from the public; the Companies Act defines the manner and the source from which deposits can be invited and accepted.

Issuing Stock

Shares can be issued freely as long as companies comply with the Stock Exchange Board of Inspection (SEBI) disclosure requirements in their prospectus. A draft of the prospectus must be approved by the stock exchange and the SEBI before it is filed with the ROC. The SEBI is responsible for regulating the securities market and protecting investors' interests.

Transfers of Shares

A company's shares must be freely transferable before it may be listed on the stock exchange. To transfer shares, the share certificates themselves plus specified transfer documents must be submitted for transferring shares. Approval is required before a company can issue or register share transfers to nonresident Indians and foreigners. All companies must maintain a register of their shareholders. If permitted by their Articles of Association, they can also maintain such a register in foreign countries.

Periodic Meetings

The following regular meetings must be held:

- statutory meetings for all public companies (and private companies in certain circumstances) after commencing business;
- an annual general meeting for all companies at least once every 15 months;
- extraordinary general meetings held at the request of members holding at least 10 percent of the voting power.

The timing, place, and notice of such meetings, and the manner in which they are to conducted, are prescribed by the Companies Act. Approval of shareholders is obtained through two types of resolutions:

- ordinary resolutions, in which a simple majority is sufficient;
- special resolutions in which the votes cast for a resolution must be at least three times those against.

Special resolutions must approve the issue of fresh capital, conversion of a company from private to public, converting debt to equity, or amending the Memorandum of Association or Articles of Association. The board of directors should meet once every quarter, with additional meetings as necessary.

Boards of Directors

The board of directors is responsible for the management of a company. The board must be composed of individuals who meet certain specified criteria. A public corporation must have at least three directors; private companies should have at least two. A director need not own any shares unless specified by the Articles of Association. The Companies Act specifies the retirement of at least one-third of the directors every year; this provision does not apply to private companies unless they are subsidiaries of a public company. Directors can be reappointed or replaced by the shareholders at an Annual General Meeting.

Foreign nationals can be appointed as non-executive directors without prior government approval if they are not required to have any share holding. Appointing foreign nationals as full-time (executive) directors requires prior government approval. A person who meets the criteria specified in the Companies Act can be appointed as managing director or full-time director without any prior government approval.

Every public company and private subsidiary of a public company with a paid-up capital of Rs 50 million ($1.43 million) or more is required to appoint a full-time or managing director. Every company with a paid-up share capital of Rs 5 million ($142,857) or more must appoint a full-time qualified company secretary. The board of directors is not personally liable for the acts of a company except for acts of gross negligence or fraud.

Management Compensation

Limits on management compensation by public companies or their subsidiaries is laid down by the Act. Companies with adequate net profits can freely structure the remuneration of their managerial personnel, provided the total remuneration thus paid does not exceed 10 percent of the net profits (5 percent of the net profits if there is only one beneficiary). The company's net profits are computed as prescribed in the Companies Act. A company does not require approval if the remuneration to an Indian citizen is below certain limits. However, for companies with losses or inadequate net profits, management compensation is subject to limits based on its capital.

Intercompany Loans

Loans made by a public company to companies under the same management should not exceed 20 percent of its capital and free reserves; this limit is 30 percent if loans are given to companies that are not under the same management. Any extension of this limit requires government approval. This limit includes guarantees or securities provided on behalf of another company. Companies are considered to be under the same management if any of the following situations exist:

- Both companies have the same managing director or manager.
- The majority of the directors of both companies are the same persons.
- More than one-third of the voting power of each company is vested in the same person or corporate entity.
- The holding company of which the subject company is a subsidiary and the second company are under the same management.
- The directors and their relatives hold a majority of the shares in both companies.

Purchases of Other Company Stock and Bonds

Public companies and their subsidiaries may purchase a maximum of 30 percent of the capital of a company; more than this amount requires the prior approval of the government. The aggregate investments by a company in all other companies must not exceed 30 percent of its subscribed capital and free reserves. Companies under the same management are included in this definition. Any investment beyond this limit requires prior approval of the government.

OBTAINING INVESTMENT APPROVALS

The Indian Investment Centre (IIC)

Foreign investment is a major objective of India's economic reform program. The Indian Investment Centre (IIC) promotes foreign investment in India and advises overseas investors on setting up industrial projects by providing information regarding investment opportunities, the latest investment policy, taxation laws, and incentives. The IIC also helps foreign companies in finding Indian partners.

Over the past five years the government has liberalized import provisions and simplified approvals. The key features of the foreign investment laws as of mid-1996 are:

- Foreign equity participation in high priority industries and export trading companies: raising from previous restriction of 40 to 51 percent for high-priority industries.

- Up to 25 percent foreign equity participation allowed in small-scale industry.

- Foreign investment allowed in critical infrastructure sectors such as energy, hydrocarbons, and petroleum.

- Joint ventures are permitted to explore and produce oil and gas products.

- There is automatic approval for technology agreements.

- No permission is required to hire foreign technicians.

- The income tax for foreign companies is 25 percent for dividend and interest income and 30 percent for royalties and fees for technical services (compared with 45 percent for domestic companies).

- Foreign remittances are allowed through authorized dealers.

Depending on its product or service, a foreign company investing in India must submit its application to the following governmental bodies. Normally these approvals are automatic.

Reserve Bank of India (RBI)

RBI approval is required for the following investments:

- up to 51 percent in the equity of new companies in high-priority industries;

- an increase of up to 51 percent in existing companies in high-priority industries;

- up to 51 percent foreign equity in new and existing trading companies primarily engaged in export activities;

- full 100 percent equity participation by NRIs in new investments or expansion or diversification of high-priority industries whose profits will be repatriated overseas.

The Secretariat for Industrial Approvals (SIA)

The SIA must approve the following investment types:

- full 100 percent foreign equity in 100 percent Export-Oriented Units (EOUs);

- foreign investment proposals outside the jurisdiction of the RBI.

Foreign Investment Promotion Board (FIPB)

The government has set up a special board known as the Foreign Investment Promotion Board (FIPB). This is a specially empowered Board in the office of the Prime Minister created specifically to speed up the approval process for proposals relating to foreign investments in India. The FIPB is headed by the Principal Secretary to the Prime Minister and has as its members the Finance Secretary, the Commerce Secretary, and the Secretary for Industrial Development. Secretaries of ministries under whose jurisdictions specific investment proposals fall are also invited. No special application form is needed for applying to the FIPB. Proposals can be sent directly to the Prime Minister's Office or through any of India's diplomatic missions abroad. The FIPB negotiates with large multinational companies as follows:

- investments considered in totality;

- investments that are free from predetermined parameters or procedures.

The FIPB has the flexibility to examine proposals in totality or those that are free from predetermined parameters or procedures. Its approach is liberal for all sectors and all types of proposals. Proposals that are rejected by the FIPB are very few. A large number of the proposals cleared involved 100 percent equity participation by foreign investors. The FIPB's clearance of foreign investment proposals is based on the investment proposed, the technology, the export potential or import substitution factors, the foreign exchange balance sheet, and the employment potential. The totality of the package proposed is examined and approved on its merits. The FIPB's approach is liberal, flexible, and open to negotiations. The FIPB normally processes applications in four to six weeks.

TRADE POLICY AND REGULATIONS

India and the World Trade Organization

India, along with 110 other countries, authenticated the results of the Uruguay Round by signing the Final Act at Marrakech in 1994. India intends to abide by the obligations arising out of the agreement on Trade Related Aspects of Intellectual Property Rights (TRIPS), which form part of the Uruguay Round Agreements.

Overall Trade Policy

The Industrial Policy Resolution of 1956 and the Statement on Industrial Policy of 1991 are the basic framework for the overall industrial policy of the government. In the initial stages of India's development, industrial growth was regulated by granting industrial licenses. The system of obtaining government approvals in a large segment of industrial activity was progressively liberalized over the 1980s. This process culminated in the 1991 policy changes that substantially abolished industrial licensing and other measures facilitating foreign investments and technology transfers.

Industries Reserved for the Public Sector

The private sector can operate in all areas except those of strategic importance. The list of industries reserved for the public sector has been reduced to the following:

1. arms, ammunition, and allied categories of defense equipment, defense aircraft, and warships;
2. atomic energy;
3. coal and lignite;
4. mineral oils;
5. minerals specified in the Schedule to the Atomic Energy (Control of Production and Use) Order, 1953;
6. railway transport.

Private participation is permitted in some specific areas in this list as well, such as mining, oil exploration, refining and marketing, and certain rail transport sectors.

Industries for Which an Industrial License Is Required

The requirement to obtain a manufacturing industrial license is limited to:

- industries reserved for the public sector;
- fifteen industries of strategic, social, and environmental importance;
- industries reserved for the small-scale sector.

All other industries are exempt from licensing except for certain restrictions on locating in metropolitan areas, such as:

1. coal and lignite;
2. petroleum (other than crude) and distillates;
3. distillation and brewing of alcoholic beverages;
4. sugar;
5. animal fats and oils;
6. cigars and cigarettes of tobacco and manufactured tobacco substitutes;
7. asbestos and asbestos-based products;
8. plywood, decorative veneers, and other wood-based produce such as particle board, medium-density fiber board, and block board;
9. tanned or dressed fur skins, chamois, and leather;
10. paper and newsprint except bagasse-based units;
11. electronic aerospace and defense equipment of any type;
12. industrial explosives including detonating fuses, safety fuses, gunpowder, nitrocellulose, and matches;
13. hazardous chemicals;
14. drugs and pharmaceuticals (according to Drug Policy);
15. entertainment electronics (VCRs, color televisions, CD players, tape recorders).

Foreign Technology or 51 percent Foreign Equity Agreements

1. Metallurgical industries (a) ferro alloys, (b) casting and forging, (c) non-ferrous metals and their alloys, (d) sponge iron and

pellets, (e) large diameter steel welded pipes of over 300 mm diameter and stainless steel pipes, (f) pig iron.

2. Boilers and steam generating plants.

3. Prime movers (other than electrical generators): (a) industrial turbines, (b) internal combustion engines, (c) alternate energy systems such as solar, wind, etc., (d) gas/hydro/steam turbines up to 60 MW.

4. Electrical equipment: (a) equipment for transmission and distribution of electricity, including power and distribution transformers, power relays, ht-switch gear synchronous condensers, (b) electrical motors, (c) electrical furnaces, industrial furnaces and induction heating equipment, (d) x ray equipment, (e) electronic equipment, components including subscribers' and telecommunication equipment, (f) component wires for manufacture of lead-in wires, (g), hydro/steam/gas generators/generating sets up to 60 MW, (h) generating sets and pumping sets based on internal combustion engines, (i) jelly-filled telecommunication cables, (j) optic fibre, (k) energy efficient lamps, (l) midget carbon electrodes.

5. Transportation: (a) mechanized sailing vessels up to 10,000 DWT including fishing trawlers, (b) ship ancillaries, (c) commercial vehicles, public transport vehicles, automotive commercial three wheeler vehicles, industrial locomotives, automotive two wheelers and three wheelers, automotive components/spares and ancillaries (d) shock absorbers for railway equipment, (e) brake systems for railway rolling stock and locomotives.

6. Industrial machinery and equipment: (a) Machine tools and industrial robots and their controls and accessories, (b) jigs, fixtures, tools, and dies, (c) engineering production aids such as cutting and forming tools, patterns, dies, and tools.

7. Agricultural machinery: (a) tractors, (b) self-propelled harvester combines, (c) rice transplanters.

8. Earth moving machinery: (a) earth moving machines, (b) construction machinery and components.

9. Industrial instruments: (a) indicating, recording and regulating devices for pressure, temperature, rate of flow, weights, levels, and the like.

10. Scientific and electromedical instruments and laboratory equipment.

11. Nitrogen and phosphate fertilizers:

12. Chemicals (other than fertilizers): (a) heavy organic chemicals including petrochemicals, (b) heavy inorganic chemicals, (c) organic fine chemicals, (d) synthetic resins and plastics, (e) man made fibers, (f) synthetic rubber, (g) industrial explosives, (h) technical grade insecticides, fungicides, weedicides, and the like, (i) synthetic detergents, (j) miscellaneous chemicals for industrial use only such as: (a) catalysts and catalyst supports, (b) photographic chemicals, (c) rubber chemicals, (d) polyols, (e) isocyanates, urethanes, etc., (f) specialty chemicals for enhanced oil recovery, (g) heating fluids, (h) coal tar distillation and products, (i) plants for manufacturing industrial gases, (j) high altitude breathing oxygen and medical oxygen, (k) nitrous oxide, (l) refrigerants gases such as liquid nitrogen, carbon dioxide, etc., In large volumes, (m) argon and other rare gases, (n) alkali/acid resisting cement compounds, (o) leather chemicals and auxiliaries.

13. Drugs and pharmaceuticals according to drug policy.

14. Paper and pulp including paper products and industrial laminates.

15. (a) automobile tires and tubes, (b) rubberized heavy duty industrial belting of all types, (c) rubberized conveyor belting, (d) rubber reinforced and lined fire fighting hose pipes, (e) high pressure braided hoses, (f) engineering and industrial plastic products.

16. Plate glass and glass products: (a) glass shells for television tube, (b) float glass and plate glass, (c) high tension insulators, (d) glass fibers of all types.

17. Ceramics for industrial uses.

18. Cement products: (a) Portland cement, (b) gypsum boards, (c) wall boards.

19. High technology reproduction and multiplication equipment.

20. Carbon and carbon products: (a) graphite electrodes and anodes (b) impervious graphite blocks and sheets.

21. Pre-tensioned high pressure pipes.

22. Rubber machinery.

23. Printing equipment.

24. Welding electrodes other than those for welding mild steel.

25. Industrial synthetic diamonds.

26. (a) photosynthesis improves, (b) genetically modified free living symbiotic nitrogen fixers, (c) pheromones, (d) bio-insecticides.

27. Extraction and upgrading of mineral oils.

28. Pre-fabricated building material.

29. Soya products: (a) soya texture proteins, (b) soya protein isolates, (c) soya protein concentrates, (d) other specialized products of soybeans, (e) winterized and deodorized refined soybean oil.

30. (a) certified high yielding hybrid seeds and synthetic seeds, (b) certified high yielding plantlets developed through plant tissue culture.

31. All food processing industries other than milk food, malted foods, and flour, but excluding the categories reserved for the small-scale industries sector.

32. All categories of packaging for food processing industries excluding the categories reserved for the small-scale industrial sector.

33. Hotels and tourism-related industry.

34. Electronics software.

Technology Transfer Agreements

The RBI grants automatic clearance to foreign-technology agreements in which lump-sum payments and royalties fall within approved limits. Proposals outside these parameters must seek approval via application to the FIPB or the SIA. On approval, a licensee may obtain the necessary foreign exchange at market rates for remittances from any authorized exchange dealer.

India is more receptive to royalty arrangements that offer continued access to technical know-how and new research and development, rather than the right only to exploit a patent. The government also requires sub-licensing clauses in order to avoid the licensing of similar technology by two different manufacturers, particularly in industries using less-sophisticated technology. To encourage the sub-licensing of know-how, the

Ministry of Industry has decided in principle to drop the secrecy clause from all new foreign-licensing agreements, and has stipulated that a non-restriction clause be incorporated into new contracts. Sub-licensing agreements usually offer lower royalty rates than the original arrangement.

Foreign multinationals should note that an Indian firm that enters into a foreign collaboration requiring more than Rs 20 million ($572,140) worth of technology is required to:

- Involve in the negotiating process of technology acquisition either competent R&D personnel from within their enterprise or researchers from any other R&D institution.

- Submit a time-bound program for technology absorption, adaptation, or improvement within six months of the approval of the collaboration.

- Establish in-house R&D facilities or enter into long-term consultancy agreements with any relevant R&D institution within two years of approving the collaboration.

- Ensure that the agreement gives indigenous R&D institutions free access to the production unit of the enterprise (the proceeds of a 5 percent levy on all payments made towards technology imports is used to promote R&D).

A licenser can renew a licensing contract easily enough if it agrees to make new technology or processes available or permits the licensee to export to areas not covered by the original agreement. Under Indian regulations, former licensees may continue production after the licensing contract expires without further payments to the licenser—even if the product is still protected by Indian patents.

Restrictions on Payments for Foreign Technology

Automatic approval for foreign technology agreements is possible if lump-sum payments are not greater than Rs 10 million ($285,715) and royalties are no more than 5 percent on domestic sales and 8 percent on exports. Restrictions on payments include an overall limit equal to 8 percent of sales over a 10-year period starting from the agreement date, or a seven-year period starting from the date of production. For agreements involving the transfer of high technology, the lump-sum payment is limited to a maximum of 50 percent of the total royalty fee. The FIPB or the SIA may authorize higher rates for ventures that will export most of their output.

Since lump-sum payments may be approved for drawings, documentation and other forms of know-how, foreign collaborators can itemize and ask for separate fees or cash payments to cover each major aspect of technical assistance. In evaluating the reasonableness of such payments, the SIA calculates whether the lump sum and the recurring royalty, if any, constitute an acceptable proportion of the value of production. Fees are generally paid in stages: one-third when the agreement is signed; one-third when the documents are transferred; and the remainder either when production commences or 48 months after the signing, whichever is earlier.

Capital Goods Imports

Capital goods, barring a few categories on the negative list, can be freely imported into India without license, subject to payment of relevant duty, except for a small list consisting of:

- Prohibited categories (three categories) whose import of which is not allowed.
- Restricted categories (72 categories), the import of which is allowed against an import license or under general schemes notified separately.
- Canalized categories (seven categories), import of which is permitted only through designated agencies.

Quantitative restrictions on imports of capital goods and intermediates have been almost completely removed. The import of second hand capital goods is allowed, provided they have a residual life of five years. Import of all categories except those on the prohibited list is permitted free of duty for export production under a duty exemption scheme. In order to facilitate approval of import proposals, input-output norms for more than 3,000 categories have been announced. Import of capital goods (either new or second hand) is also permitted at a concessional customs duty of 15 percent under the Export Promotion Capital Goods (EPCG) scheme.

Phased Tariff Reductions Through 2005

The government is committed to the phased reduction of tariff to international levels. There has been a consistent decline in these rates from peak rates of 300 percent in 1991 to 65 percent at present. Capital goods imports which once were subject to tariff rates of around 100 percent now face duties in the range of 20–40 percent, with the basic import duty on general capital goods at 25 percent. Import duties on equipment are even lower for projects in specific sectors and nil for export oriented projects.

Exports

Export of goods is allowed freely, except for a few categories in a Negative List of Exports:

- Prohibited (10 categories) which are not permitted for religious or environmental considerations.
- Restricted (29 categories and 38 sub-categories) which may be exported with the proper license.
- Canalized (six categories and 18 sub-categories), export of which is permitted through designated agencies.

Special Export Incentives

Exports are the centerpiece of India's trade policy. India's export promotion package compares favorably with incentives offered elsewhere in the world:

- Export profits are exempt from income tax computed in proportion of export turnover to total turnover.
- Higher royalty payments of 8 percent (net of taxes) are permitted on export sales as compared to 5 percent on domestic sales.
- Export commissions up to 10 percent are permitted.
- Capital goods may be imported at concessionary duties if they are later re-exported.

The scheme also applies to hotels, restaurants, travel agents and diagnostic centers. Inputs required to be imported for export production are exempted from customs duty under the Advance License Scheme, which allows free transfer of Advance Licenses and can be availed of by any exporter. Export-Oriented Units (EOUs) and Export Processing Zones (EPZs) enjoy special incentives such as duty free imports of capital goods and raw materials for the purpose of export production.

THE INDIAN TAX SYSTEM

The authority to levy taxes is divided between the Union government and the State governments. The former levies direct taxes such as personal income tax, corporate tax, and indirect taxes such as customs duties, excise duties, and central sales tax. The states are empowered to levy state sales tax apart from various local taxes such as entry tax and octroi taxes on intrastate trade.

India has signed Organisation of Economic Cooperation and Development (OECD) tax treaties with over 45 countries. These treaties generally provide for the complete exemption of profits from the operation of ships and aircraft. The result is a relatively lower tax cost for foreign companies doing business in India than for domestic companies.

In recent years India's tax system has become more broad-based. Tax revenue as a percentage of GNP has been consistently increasing with more and more revenues coming from indirect taxes, notably customs and excise.

A summary of India's most important tax laws is given in Table 4.2:

Table 4.2
India's Most Important Tax Laws

Type of Tax	Regulatory Act	Administrator
Income Tax	Income Tax Act of 1961	Central Board of Direct Taxes (CBDT)
Wealth Tax	Wealth Tax Act of 1957	CBDT
Gift Tax	Gift Tax Act of 1958	CBDT
Excise Taxes	Central Excise and Salt Tax of 1944	Central Board of Excise and Customs (CBEC)
Customs	Customs Tax Act of 1962	CBEC
Sales Taxes	Central Sales Tax of 1956	Union government
State Sales Taxes	Various state tax acts	State governments

Direct Taxes

Corporate or personal income earned during any portion of a tax year is subject to income tax. The tax a company's income depends on its domicile. Indian companies are taxable in India on their worldwide income. Foreign companies are taxed on income from their Indian operations and income that is deemed to arise in India (see Table 4.3). Royalty, interest, gains from sale of capital assets located in India (including gains from sale of shares in an Indian company), dividends from Indian companies and fees for technical services are all treated as income arising in India.

Table 4.3
India's Tax Rates on Corporate Income

Type of Company	Tax Rate
Closely held domestic	40 percent
Widely held domestic	40 percent
Foreign owned	55 percent

Domestic companies with taxable income exceeding Rs 75,000 are assessed a surcharge of 15 percent.

Taxable Income

The main source of income of a company is normally from its business operations. Taxable income is calculated according to the rules for each class of income and then aggregated to determine total taxable income. These classes of income could include, for example:

- income from commercial or residential property;
- capital gains;
- royalties, license fees, and similar other sources.

Withholding Tax

Taxes due are required to be deducted at their source from payments made to non residents and foreign companies, at rates specified under the domestic law or tax treaties (see Table 4.4).

Table 4.4
Selected Withholding Rates from Payments to Non Residents

Payment Category	Percent of Tax Withheld
Technical services fees	30
Royalties	30
Dividends	20
Interest	20
Other	55

Depreciation and Deductibles

Expenses incurred wholly and exclusively for business purposes are generally deductible. Some of these are depreciation on fixed assets, interest on borrowed funds during that financial year, and so on (see Table 4.5).

Table 4.5
Selected Depreciation Rates

Depreciable Asset	Percentage Rate
Buildings	5 to 100
Machinery	25 to 100
Furniture and fittings	10 to 15
Vehicles	20
Pollution control equipment	40
Energy saving devices	100
Ships	10 to 20

Certain expenses are specifically disallowed or the amount of deduction is restricted:

- entertainment;
- interest or other payments to non residents without deducting withholding tax;
- corporate taxes paid;
- indirect general and administrative costs of a foreign head office.

Set-Offs and Loss Carry-Forwards

Business losses incurred in a tax year can be set off against any other income earned during that year, except capital gains. Unabsorbed business losses can be carried forward and set off against business profits for eight years. Unabsorbed depreciation losses can be carried forward indefinitely. Carry forward is not available to closely-held (private) companies in which there has been no continuity of business.

Tax Holidays and Other Incentives

India's tax holidays and other incentives reflect the government's shifting emphasis on arenas of business development. These can significantly reduce the effective tax rates for the beneficiary companies. Some examples are:

- five year tax holidays for power projects, firms engaged in exports, new industries in certain (usually underdeveloped) states, and new industrial units established in Export Oriented Units (EOU) and units in Free Trade Zones (FTZ);

- tax deductions of 100 percent of export profits;

- deduction of 30 percent of net income for 10 years for new industrial undertakings;

- deduction of 50 percent on foreign exchange earnings from construction companies, hotels, and royalties and commissions from foreign exchange;

- deduction of certain inter corporate dividends up to the full amount of a declared dividend.

INDIRECT TAXES

Excise Duties

Despite liberalization, companies continue to pay a variety of taxes on manufactured goods.

- **Central excise tax.** This is paid on the "declared price," i.e. the cost of goods plus the company margin.

- **Central sales tax.** This is levied when goods owned by one person/entity are bought by another person/entity and transported to another state.

- **Local/state sales tax and, in most cases, an octroi tax.** The latter is a municipal tax levied on goods entering a city/town. As there are varying rates of state sales and octroi taxes, many fast-moving consumer products until a few years ago carried the label '*Recommended Retail Price: Rs X; Local Taxes Extra*' on them.

All manufacturers are required to register under the Central Excise Rules of 1944. This registration is valid as long as production activity continues; no renewals are necessary.

The Modified Value Added Tax of 1985 (MODVAT)

India's excise duties are based on the Central Excise and Salt Act of 1944, the Excise Tariff Act of 1985, and the Modified Value Added Tax

(MODVAT) of 1986. The rates duties vary according to the item, the nature of the manufacturer, and the place of sale. The rates are either *ad valorem* (a fixed percentage of the cost of production), specific (a fixed rate based on the item), or a combination of both.

MODVAT applies only to a limited number of categories. Its objective is to inhibit multiple duties on goods subject to excise taxes which are then used to produce other excisable goods. The exemptions now include capital goods and petroleum products. MODVAT is based on credit for taxes paid on raw materials on which excise has been paid. This credit sets off the excise due on subsequent products. Duties paid on imports are eligible for MODVAT credit.

Customs Duties

The Indian tariff system is based on the Customs Cooperation Council nomenclature in which most taxes are *ad valorem*. Customs duties are levied on imports at rates specified in the Annual Budget. The maximum rate of customs duty for 1995–96 is 65 percent, except on baggage (see Table 4.6).

Table 4.6
Some Example Customs Duties

Product	Tax Rate (%)
Machinery	30 to 40
Ferrous and other metals	10 to 50
Miscellaneous chemicals	15 to 50
Drugs	30 to 60
Pesticides	30 to 60
Electronic equipment	30 to 40
Telecommunications equipment	20 to 50
Petroleum and coal products	15 to 35

Under the Export Promotion Capital Goods scheme (EPCG), capital goods can be imported at concessionary duties.

Sales Tax

Sales tax is levied on the sale of a commodity which is produced or imported and sold for the first time. Products subsequently sold without being processed further are exempt from sales tax. Sales tax is levied by either the Central or the State government. Central Sales tax of 4 percent is generally levied on all inter State sales. State taxes on sales made within the State range from 4 percent to 15 percent. Sales tax is charged on works contracts in most States; the value of contracts subject to tax and the tax rate vary. Exports and services are exempt from sales tax.

Service Taxes

A service tax at the rate of 5 percent has been levied on services of telephones, insurance (other than life insurance), and stock brokers. The tax will be charged on the amount of telephone bills, the net premium charged by insurance companies and the brokerage or commission charged by stock brokers for their services.

Other Taxes

Transfer of assets attracts stamp duty. Some states also impose real estate taxes based on assessed value. Real estate taxes are also imposed by municipalities and octroi is charged on goods entering their jurisdiction. Interest tax is levied on banking and financial services companies.

Special Incentives Granted by India's States. In keeping with India's federal system, a number of investment incentives are provided by the state governments in addition to the benefits offered by the Centre. While the details of the incentives package often varies from one state to another depending upon a particular state's perception of its investment priorities, the package includes an element of subsidy to promote industrial development, as well as tax breaks accompanied by exemption/deferment of specific duties.

Capital Investment Subsidy. Capital investment subsidy is provided by nearly all the state governments. The subsidy ranges from Rs 15 lakh ($42,857) to Rs 7.5 lakh ($214,285) and is available on the basis of location and size of the eligible units which have set up approved projects specified by the various state governments. Specific benefits are also available for electronics, food processing, agro-based industries, industries in identified backward areas, pioneer and prestigious units as specified under various state rules.

Sales Tax Exemption/Deferment Scheme. Further incentives are provided in the form of sales tax exemption and deferment schemes. Units may be exempted from paying sales tax on purchases of capital goods and raw materials. Further, units may also be exempted from having to charge sales tax on sales of final products by the units for a specified time period. Alternatively, the unit may collect tax on sales in the ordinary course of business, but not remit the same to prescribed authorities for a specified period. In this way the unit enjoys financial assistance in the form of a loan from the prescribed authority. Sales tax exemption/deferment is available for a period ranging from five years to 15 years from the date of commercial production.

Electricity Duty Exemption and Power Concessions. This incentive is available for one to 12 years, either in the form of exemption from duty payable or refund of electricity duty paid for a specified time period.

Other Tax Benefits

In addition to the various benefits and incentives listed in the preceding paragraphs, there are several other tax benefits which are available to foreign investors:

New Industrial Undertakings. For any new industrial undertaking set up as a company anywhere in India, a deduction of 30 percent of the profits of the new undertaking will be allowed in computing the company's total income for the first 10 years of operation. This concession is provided for undertakings manufacturing any items listed in the Eleventh Schedule to the Income Tax Act.

New Power Projects. Complete tax holiday for profits from new power projects for first five years of operation.

Special Income Categories. Income earned as dividends, royalties, technical service fees and interest on loans received by foreign companies is taxed at concessional rates. Dividend income received by a company incorporated in India from another domestic company is exempted from tax to the extent of the amount distributed as dividend by the former. Dividends received by foreign companies are taxed at the flat rate of 25 percent. Where foreign companies receive interest on money borrowed or royalty fees for technical services from an Indian concern, they are charged the concessional rates of 25 percent on interest income and 30 percent on royalty and fees for technical services.

BANKING AND FINANCE

Overview of India's Banking System

The Reserve Bank of India supervises all banking operations in the country. There are 78 scheduled commercial banks (including foreign banks) which, together with 196 Regional Rural Banks, have over 61,000 branches in the country. All major international banks operate in India. There are 24 foreign banks with 147 branches.

Commercial banks are the major source of short term finance for working capital. They also provide a range of other services including capital market advisory services, foreign exchange services, investment consultancy, personal banking services, portfolio management, factoring, leasing, and venture capital. This network is being rapidly expanded and modernized with a view to improving the efficiency and quality of services.

In mid 1991, the government appointed a Committee to examine all aspects of the structure, organization, functions, and procedures of the financial sector and suggest reforms. The Committee made far-reaching recommendations which have been implemented or accepted in principle by the government. Some of these are:

- Nationalized banks have been permitted to raise fresh capital through public issue of shares.

- Permission has been granted for the formation of private banks in collaboration with foreign banks or as subsidiaries of foreign banks.

- Banks are required to comply with international accounting standards and adequate disclosure norms.

Other Financial Institutions

An integrated network of other financial institutions caters to the long and medium term financing needs of industrial projects via project loans, underwriting, deferred payment guarantees, leasing, venture capital and other financial products. There are five major financial institutions:

- Industrial Development Bank of India (IDBI)
- Industrial Finance Corporation of India (IFCI)
- Industrial Credit and Investment Corporation of India (ICICI)
- State Financial Corporations (SFCs)
- State Industrial Development Corporations (SIDCs)

State-level institutions service mainly the medium and long term financing needs of small and medium sized units through project loans, underwriting, and direct subscription to shares and bonds of industrial units, deferred payment guarantees, discounting and rediscounting of machinery bills, leasing and venture capital, etc.

In addition, a number of specialized financing agencies have been set up to meet the requirements of specific industries:

- Risk Capital and Technology Finance Corporation (RCTFC)
- Technology Development and Information Company of India (TDICI)
- Export and Import Bank of India (Exim Bank)
- Small Industries Development Bank of India (SIDBI)
- Shipping Credit and Investment Corporation of India (SCICI)
- Tourism Finance Corporation of India (TFCI)

Insurance Companies

There are six insurance companies in India, all government owned. The Life Insurance Corporation of India (LIC) and the General Insurance Company (GIC) are responsible the country's life insurance. GIC is a holding company for four subsidiary companies and is responsible for general insurance. Recent reform measures or suggestions the entry of the private sector and the conversion of LIC, GIC and its four subsidiaries into companies, with the government retaining a 50 percent stake in each of them, with the balance to be owned by the public. A government committee has suggested that foreign-owned insurance companies be allowed into India via joint ventures with Indian partners. All insurance companies would be subject to the provisions of the Insurance Act.

Capital Markets

With over 20 million shareholders, India has the third largest investor base in the world after the United States and Japan. Over 6,500 companies are listed on the stock exchanges, which are serviced by approximately 5,600 stock brokers. India's equity markets are regulated by the Securities and Exchange Board of India (SEBI) under the provisions of the Securities Contracts (Regulation) Act of 1956 and the Securities and Exchange Board of India Act of 1992. SEBI regulates and promotes the securities market and protects the interests of investors via guidelines for capital issues, disclosure by public companies, and investor protection. SEBI is a powerful independent body that has revolutionized the functioning and regulation of the Indian capital markets. Tax and other incentives channel investment into the capital markets, from which Indian companies have raised large amounts of capital in recent years.

There are 23 recognized stock exchanges in India, including the Over the Counter Exchange of India (OTCEI) and the National Stock Exchange of India (NSE). OTCEI is a fully automated nation-wide trading exchange that enables small and new companies to raise funds through public issues. NSE is intended to function as a model exchange and to provide nationwide services to investors. It has two trading segments: the Wholesale Debt Market (WDM) and the Capital Market (CM). WDM is a facility for institutions and corporate bodies to enter into high value transactions in instruments such as government securities, treasury bills, public sector undertaking bonds, commercial paper, certificates of deposit, and similar instruments. It commenced operations in June 1994 and is a fully automated screen-based trading system intended to bring the Indian Stock Market in line with international markets. The Securities Trading Corporation of India (STCI) was set up to develop an active secondary market in government securities and public sector bonds.

Credit rating requirements for debenture issues, fixed deposits and commercial paper are served by the Credit Rating and Information Services of India Limited (CRISIL), Investment Information and Credit Rating Agency (IICRA), and Credit Analysis and Research Agency (CARE). These provide an independent rating. Their primary concern is rating debt obligations so investors can assess timely payments of interest and principal on debt instruments. These ratings are instrument specific and not for the company as a whole. They are compulsory for debenture issues, fixed deposits and commercial paper. Custodial services are provided by the Stock Holding Corporation of India Ltd., and certain foreign banks.

Mutual funds are a significant source of investment in both the government and corporate securities and are within the regulatory framework of SEBI. The primary institution in this field has been the government-owned Unit Trust of India (UTI). SEBI has approved more than 20 private sector sponsors to set up unit trusts.

A variety of money market instruments are available, including Commercial Paper (CP), Certificate of Deposits, gilt edged securities, and Treasury Bills. RBI has suggested flotation of money market mutual funds, offering opportunities for safe investments to investors irrespective of the condition of the money market. In addition to traditional sources such as cash credit, short term financing is available through inter corporate deposits, bill discounting, factoring, export financing, and commercial paper. The minimum net worth necessary Rs 40 million ($1.14 million). A company can collect money through CPs up to 75 percent of its permissible working capital credit limits.

Venture Capital

India's private equity market has entered an era of growth and change. Uncertainties linger in areas such as repatriation of profits, double taxation, and bureaucratic meddling. What seems equally clear is that despite the fact that the country's 40-year love affair with socialism has soured, its latent economic nationalism has become increasingly tempered by the realities of global competition. Fueling these changes is a surge in overseas private equity coupled with capital market forces—falling share prices and rising interest rates—and government restrictions which have dried up domestic equity funds.

According to the *Asian Venture Capital Journal*, the amount of private equity in India leaped fivefold from a base of $150 million in 1993 to over $800 million by the end of 1995. Aiding these market forces, or because of them, the Indian Venture Capital Association now counts 24 funds—10 offshore, eight state controlled, and six private sector funds.

Traditional venture capital activities funding seed and development capital situations, IPOs, and buyouts. The sectors attracting the most VC attention are:

- food processing—agro-based industries, frozen foods;
- auto components—outsourcing auto components;
- metal-based engineering foundries and forging;
- IT industry—software, service companies;
- pharmaceuticals.

India can be a difficult place to do VC business in. Applicants must acquire as many as 32 separate approvals, each of which must be resubmitted to the original official for verification. Antiquated infrastructure, power failures, and endemic corruption all loom as obstacles for venture capitalists.

Some Examples of Venture Capital Funds

Indian venture capital funds are often limited-purpose, limited duration pools. Over any given year a number of funds may come into existence or terminate. The following list is a brief sampler drawn from listings published in the third quarter of FY 1995. These funds are listed only as examples of the type and size of funding that might be floated at any given time. They may have ceased to exist at the time of reading. There also may be many other VC firms operating by the time the reader sees this.

Fund Name: AIG Indian Sectoral Equity Fund
Target Amount: $150 million
Launch Date: June 1995
Fund Manager/Advisor: IL & FS/AIG

Fund Name: Canbank Venture Capital Fund (1996)
Target Amount: Rs 350 million ($11 million)
Launch Date: Early 1996
Fund Manager/Adviser: Canbank Venture Capital Fund

Fund Name: HSBC India Fund
Target Amount: $50 million
Fund Manager/Adviser: HSBC Asset Management

Fund Name: India Private Equity Fund
Target Amount: $105 million
Launch Date: 1996
Fund Manager/Adviser: Pathfinder Investment, Chase Capital, Oppenheimer & Co.

Fund Name: Indus Venture Capital Fund II
Target Amount: $50 million
Launch Date: 3rd quarter 1995
Fund Manager/Adviser: Indus Venture Management

Fund Name: South Asian Regional Apex Fund (SARA Fund)
Target Amount: Rs 1,000 million ($32 million)
Launch Date: August 1995
Fund Manager/Adviser: Creditcapital Venture Fund (India)

The Mauritius Tax Incentive

In 1994 India's finance ministry was surprised to find that the tiny (population 1 million) island of Mauritius turned up in its charts as the fourth-largest source of FDI to the country, with a total of 5.3 billion rupees ($165 million in 1993 dollars) in approvals.

Mauritius seemed not the most plausible spot for such sizable investments, even given the size of its populace which emigrated there from India in the last century.

It turned out that Mauritius had quietly been turning itself into a key tax haven targeting the emerging market of India just as Cyprus is a major offshore center for emerging markets in Central and Eastern Europe, and Malta has become a chief conduit for money aimed at North Africa.

Investments in India were routed through companies registered in Mauritius by a host of international firms and banks—examples being Enron, General Electric, and Merrill Lynch. Since 1994, the number of ashore companies registered in Mauritius has risen from 10 to over 2,500, including 45 ashore investment funds with $4 billion in assets destined for India.

Mauritian inducements include exemptions from profit tax, stamp duties, and capital-gains tax—in stark contrast with India's 65 percent capital-gains tax on assets held for less than a year. Indeed, much FDI into India since 1992 has been routed through the island. India and Mauritius; signed a double taxation avoidance treaty in 1983 which offered a number of benefits to investing companies based in Mauritius. Ironically, the original agreement was designed to encourage investment into Mauritius from India. The canny Mauritians turned their plans to make the island over into an offshore tax-friendly, jurisdiction into a primary facilitator of investment into India. Arthur Anderson & Co. was not long in seeing the advantages to this and has since become the major assembler of investments into India via Mauritius.

If a Mauritian offshore company owns 10 percent or more of the equity of an Indian company, a withholding tax rate of 5 percent is levied on the dividend paid out of India to the Mauritian company. If the share holding is less than 10 percent, the tax rate is 15 percent. India's tax on dividends is 20 percent. In India, foreign institutional investors are taxed at 10 percent on long-term capital gains and between 30 and 55 percent on short term gains. (Domestic companies pay 20 percent on long term gains and 45 percent on short-term gains.) However, under the treaty with Mauritius, capital gains on the sale of shares in India are not taxed in India but rather according to Mauritian law. Under that law, a Mauritian offshore company pays 0 percent tax on capital gains. Hence a Mauritian company that sells shares in an Indian company does not pay capital gains tax.

Soon Indians began investing in their own country via Mauritius in order to exploit this tax advantage. The Indian government was hardly thrilled. The Mauritian government was sensitive to complaints by Indian parliamentarians that Mauritius is costing India lost tax. In actual fact the country's finance ministry is still quietly encouraging the process.

The Authority for Advance Rulings in Delhi, which gives opinions on tax matters to nonresidents which are binding on both the applicant and the income-tax department, cannot give opinions if it thinks a scheme is meant for tax avoidance. After several complex cases forced the issue of clarification, the Authority has now stated that genuine commercial-based transactions can avail of tax concessions from the treaty provided there is a genuine need for the Mauritian company, for example, if subscribers to an offshore fund are in various countries and Mauritius is the most appropriate low-cost offshore financial center and such subscribers could not directly invest in India because of various approvals and exchange control restrictions. In examples like this the Mauritian company is clearly not a tax dodge and could legitimately benefit from the tax breaks under the India treaty.

Mauritius has signed double taxation treaties with 16 countries and is negotiating with another 11. Mauritius did its homework well by studying offshore structures around the world and incorporating their best advantages. Under section 15 of the Mauritius Offshore Business Activities Act 1992 and section 130 of its International companies Act 1994, confidentiality of the companies is guaranteed. There are no registers of offshore companies available for public inspection. The island has now done away with the class of companies called "exempted companies" which were being used as shell companies and had the potential to become a money laundering conduit. Mauritius requires companies to have two local directors on their board. Mauritius is part of the COMDESA trade bloc which has a clearing and payments mechanism that enables exporters from member states to invoice in a currency of their choice, hence there is an assured repayment of exports even to high risk countries. Mauritius is a springboard for entry into Africa, where many expatriate Indians live and do business. Companies operating out of Mauritius can access EEC countries without quotas and duties since Mauritius is a member of the Lomé Convention.

5

Doing Daily Business

MAKING CONTACTS

Initiating a business connection in India follows the pattern that is generally prevalent throughout Southeast Asia. You can write a letter or send a fax to a prospective contact in India without first being introduced, but mentioning a referral may result in a faster response. A "cold" letter or fax should briefly introduce your company and state your reasons for writing. Direct your first communication to the most senior person possible—usually the department head if it is a large corporation and you wish to provide a product or service. For smaller companies, or if your interest is in developing an export relationship, address your letter to the Managing Director.

If you fax, be sure never to give the impression that your communication is a "spam" addressed blindly to numerous recipients. Some companies have gone to India and faxed everyone in the local phone directory with news of their arrival and business hopes. As one wary business owner put it, "I do my shopping where I can see the face of the man doing the selling."

First contacts by E-mail are usually made by project managers or similar people directly involved with an individual in India who manages the local end of a mutual project. E-mails of this kind can be specific to the matter at hand, especially between professionals such as engineers, accountants, and so on. (E-mail correspondence in India is often called a "zip," as in, "I received your zip yesterday. . . .")

If your first letter mentions a referral, be sure not to hint that you presume the addressee will thereupon work with you. Few Indians respond well to hints of implied obligation.

Follow up your letter with a telephone call as soon as practicable. Indians may seem noncommittal during a follow-up call. They do not know you yet. However, a certain "distance" does not imply lack of interest in your proposals. They simply do not commit themselves to anything or begin an extended discussion over the phone. One reason is the ever-present possibility of the connection going dead. In many cases, the phone seems to exist mainly to make appointments. Only after your affairs are running rather smoothly does telephoning come into play as a daily communication tool.

FIRST IMPRESSIONS

First meetings usually occur at their office or your hotel lobby if the latter is more convenient for both parties. Do not be put off if your counterpart orders tea or coffee in a rather brusque manner from the hotel staff. In this context the waiter is a surrogate peon for the office *chai-wallah* ("tea boy") and is dismissed just as peremptorily. (The term "peon" is a functioning term in India; it roughly translates to the American term "gofer.")

Indian business people tend to be rather proud of their accomplishments and acquaintances. To some this comes off as boastful. It is not. It is the local equivalent of showing someone the pictures of your wife and children in a wallet—which in many countries would be taken as a none-too-subtle attempt to display how fat your wallet is. Hence, be aware of implied perceptions at both ends—some things that you may take as perfectly normal are seen quite otherwise by locals.

Hence when a profusion of name-dropping occurs soon after sitting down to a meeting, what is really being communicated is that your Indian counterpart really knows how business is done locally, and with whom. Indians also use name-dropping to establish pecking order and simply to catch up on the doings of acquaintances they have not seen in awhile.

On the other hand, there is an indefinable point when name-dropping becomes fishing. A first acquaintance who goes on and on about his extensive connections may really be trawling to see how much you really know about doing business in India.

A PROTECTIVE PAPER TRAIL

If you are in India as an independent business person or free agent soliciting on behalf of other businesses "on spec," you are vulnerable to people waiting for you to establish a clientele they can then muscle in on. You need to budget ahead of time for the services of an attorney who can act as advisor and also repository of not merely critical transactions but any item that establishes a credible paper trail. If, as most visitors do, you have business cards printed locally, add this attorney's name and telephone as "Acting Counsel" or other terminology the attorney suggests.

Then mail or fax a copy of *every* meeting's schedule and notes, a spare copy of the business cards of people with whom you discuss your plans, and every item of correspondence or contract. As negotiations advance with a prospective client, you should be sure to casually drop the fact that you have such an attorney. The appropriate context is when presented with a contract or other document that implies a money transfer. The appropriate words are on the order of, "I'll have to see this to my attorney for clearance, but you can be sure to hear from me within a few days."[1]

MEETING PEOPLE

In general, avoid doing important business near one of India's major holiday periods, such as Diwali at the beginning of November. (See the list at the end of this section.)

It is fairly common for Indian executives to arrive at the office late in the morning and stay late at the end of the day. This often has to do with family obligations like getting the kids to school—Indians tend to put the happiness of their children above daily business details. Hence it is best to not schedule appointments earlier than 10:00 a.m. Also avoid the lunch period between noon and 2:00 p.m.

Indians are often late to appointments. *Some* executives do not mind if foreigners show up a few minutes late. Better to bring a copy of a local Indian business magazine while you cool your heels so you will have an ice-breaker when the meeting does begin.

Do not make assumptions about a person's position based on sex. The majority of Indian businesses are family-owned and many a widow takes over her deceased husband's job. There are many senior female managers, and men are secretaries more often than women (especially in government bureaucracies). India suffers from the same global syndrome of the cutie-pie at the receptionist desk being the least knowledgeable person in the company answering the most sensitive questions.

American business women are held in a kind of awe by many Indian business males. At one time they were held in about equal regard as men. But ever since the Indians' experience with Rebecca Mark, the Chairman of Enron, American women executives are now esteemed for their ability to work subtly behind the scenes. Ms. Mark and Enron were crudely rebuffed by Maharashtra state pols over what they considered to be a neocolonialist approach to India's water resources. The details of the Dabhol story are now history, but what the average Indian business person remembers is that Ms. Marks did not raise her ire, thought coolly, and ended up with both Enron and Maharashtra state getting a better deal in the long run. As an Indian colleague put it, "I see why Americans invented separate checking accounts." One of the things Indians liked most about her style was that she did not restructure the deal maliciously: Her opponents profited as handsomely as Enron.

THE LORE OF LAST NAMES

Indian surnames can indicate many things. Sometimes they hint at the part of the country where the person originated.

All orthodox Sikhs have Singh as part of their name. However, there are other Singhs as well. "Singh" means "lion" and is often associated with higher castes. In Bihar, Singh is associated with the land-owning castes. In Rajasthan, Singhs without turbans are from the former royal family and often live next door to Singhs with turbans but no royal blood who are wealthier.

So-called "-jee" suffixes like Banerjee are high-caste Bengali names; "-se" names like Ghose are from Bengal but not high-caste. "Kar" names like Chandraskar are typically Maharashtran high-caste. Jewish-sounding names like Solomon and David are from the Syrian Christian community of Kerala; Menon is a Keralan Hindu name.

A name with many strung-together syllables like Kurunadhihi or Suri-arachchi or Ponnambalam is likely to be from Tamil Nadu, where the ancient Dravidian language Tamil is spoken. Some Tamils aver that Dravidian was the original mother tongue of India before the Aryan language and mythology influenced Northern India, and to this day *Dravida Desam* ("Dravidian Homeland") is a rallying cry for separatists there. The literature and philosophical outpouring of Dravidian India has unfairly been overshadowed by the attention showered on the Sanskrit literature of the north.

TITLES

Use formal titles and surnames with senior government officials regard-less of how long you have known them. In private business, unless you have been invited to say otherwise, always use a proper title such as "Dr.," "Mr.,"

"Mrs.," or "Miss," with the person's surname. If you do not know or cannot recall the surname, using "Sir" or "Madam" discreetly asks for it. "Doc" for "Dr." is not done. "Ms." has never caught on. A "Mrs." is a high distinction in India, and a "Miss" will not object to being called one.

GREETINGS

Indian business people greet with a handshake in office settings. Outside the office, the *namaste* (pronounced "namastay") is preferred. This is an ancient greeting carried out by placing both palms together as in a prayer at chest level and accompanied by a slight nod of the head. When greeting senior government officials, the namaste is more appropriate. In casual situations such as a chance encounter with an acquaintance on the street, the namaste hints at your familiarity with Indian etiquette. In smaller towns and rural areas, the namaste will mostly be used in lieu of a handshake.

Business cards are exchanged at the first meeting, although not necessarily at the beginning of the meeting. The usual style is to hand the card with the right hand, although the Asian style of presenting it formally with both hands with the lettering facing the recipient also occurs. Using that method is a subtle way of communicating your familiarity with other Asian countries. Leaving the card on the desk in front of you during the meeting is a sign of respect—and also is a quick aid in case you forget the name.

Gifts are not advised at initial meetings, as they may be interpreted that you assume that your counterpart is no better than a bribe-greedy bureaucrat. Indian business people regard themselves psychologically as Ksatriyas (descendants of the warrior castes) while government workers are considered Shudras (the difference between these and common laborers is that they sweat over a pen instead of a shovel).

On the other hand, sample products are perfectly appropriate because they give the meeting reality.

OPENERS

Most meetings begin with light chat on topics like travel, international business conditions, and the shares markets. It is useful to ask how the BSE (Bombay Stock Exchange) is doing, as it is the bellwether exchange (like the NYSE in the United States), as well as also a perennial source of scandals that can liven a conversation no end. Indians love relating their worldly experiences and will quickly share overseas reminiscences with you. Unless your business is church vestments, it is wise to avoid religions.

Cricket, on the other hand, is a sure winner (even if the Indian teams are not), and it is useful to acquire some knowledge about the terminology of the game, even though the details may be over your head.

Indians are usually better informed about the West than the other way around. Western ignorance of matters Indian is often an insult to them—as you might well be if an Indian host began to extol the virtues of the Los Angeles Forty-Niners or the dramatic quality improvements in the autos being designed these days by Grand Rapids. Indians perceive their country as a global power—as indeed India is—and are slighted when others frame India's political presence in the same type of terms that they use for India's poverty problems. The best display of interest is how India's enormous heritage of the past is being transmuted into business culture today.

You can begin to discuss business details in a few minutes, although a busy host will often proceed to business immediately. Most executives are busy and value their time (although not everyone else's!). If you are only interested in general fact-finding and relationship-building, make sure that your Indian counterpart knows this in advance—this is usually considered a subject better suited to lunch or an after-hours drink than to the middle of a busy business day. Even then, maintain a formal tone. Indians want to be regarded as serious business contenders.

THE CORPORATE PECKING ORDER

Most businesses in India are privately owned, tightly managed, and strongly hierarchical. Indeed, your Indian hosts will delight in any questions you ask about Indian management thinking, since the merits of Indian management styles versus the latest theory from Harvard is a subject of hot interest in the business press. Indians quite rightly feel that their extraordinarily diverse institutional memory running back some 3,000 years has produced some management ideas that the rest of the world has unfairly ignored.

Government-controlled corporations—the source of many bribery scandals—are increasingly out of the picture for the average business person arriving in India today. They operate only in specific industries and face much press scrutiny as their Congress power base erodes beneath them.

In private family-owned companies, the key decision-maker is almost always the senior male family member of the family or his widow. "Micro-management" takes on real meaning when dealing with an Indian chairman or managing director. It is best to prepare your presentation with more detail-awareness than you would at American or European meetings.

The typical business hierarchy consists of the chairman, a managing director/president, a general manager/vice president, deputy general managers, managers, and officers. In the lower ranks, titles often imply more authority than actually exists, as is the case with "vice president" in American banking circles.

The senior person in the firm is usually the chairman, although these often exert little daily operational responsibility; that function usually befalls to the "MD" or managing director. The American equivalent is the difference between the president and the CEO. Usually the MD has day-to-day authority; those down at the vice-president level and below have negligible real power and are often relatives for whom no one can find a better use.

As with India's low-caste laborers, no one who has ever eyewitnessed a senior executive's day would ever accuse him or her of living the easy life. They work hours of the kind usually associated with yuppies in U.S. real estate. A good deal of their time is given over to micromanagement. If you are ever in a mood to contemplate the results of the unitary authority model compared with the U.S. diversified authority model, the Indian private company is worth a few hours of your time. As one manager wryly put it, "We call it MSA—Management by Stomping Around."

This, like many aspects of Indian business that mystify foreigners, has strong historical roots, and only by studying India's history can you understand India today. Power display is a fundamental component of the caste mechanism. Its use is to visibly define the limits of knowledge—remember that the caste system is in part a system for preserving knowledge niches. Indian business people display their authority with the same visibility that their ancestral Ksatriyas did. This filters down into the distinct class structure at the office, which can be likened to India's historical court life and its myriad viziers, muftis, pandits, and others who shielded potentates from the truth.

Classes exist apart from caste considerations in India's business environment just as they did in the ancient courts. This is because many of today's self-made men opted for their careers because their birth caste was onerously restrictive or no longer truly functioning. For example, when the European demand for cinnamon resulted in huge plantations in Indonesia and the trade with India fell off, the cinnamon-peeler caste found itself without a profession. Many turned to land development and today many real estate developers have ancient peeler-caste names.

One old caste habit that entered directly into business was that the more elite you are, the less physical and more mental work you do. Superiors will not engage in physical work—it is perceived to be beneath them. Subor-dinates who do physical work are treated in a condescending manner and respond with the proper subservience. This explains why a boss buzzes for the peon to bring him the file folder that is just out of reach across his desk and why the peon is so happy to hand it across that desk as if the desk were a continent; psychologically, it is.

Such sharply defined roles often have a certain utility. The boss who tells the peon to ring up someone on the phone is actually saving himself wasteful moments of tedium while the phone exchange decides if it wants to let him through. What may seem inefficient to Western eyes is often a very pragmatic response to Indian circumstances. Indians think that Americans are crazy to get in the car to drive to the store to do a week's shopping when Indians shop for just what they need for the next meal; it is fresher that way.

SOCIAL BUSINESS

Dinners are the preferred meal for business socializing, although business lunches are acceptable. Indians think that the concept of power breakfasts, as an engineer friend of mine from Tamil Nadu so aptly put it, "is an idea only a monkey could dream up since only monkeys are so uncertain of themselves they have to start off the day pounding their chests."

The best places to dine are restaurants suggested by your counterparts. Express an interest in "authentic Indian cuisine" (or, even better, a regional cuisine) and you can be sure your acumen will be rewarded. Foreign women can invite Indian men to a business dinner, but they should invite others from the same company rather than just the one man. Most Indian men do not invite their wives to business dinners, although couples are the norm at social dinners.

The one who does the asking does the paying. Indian business people will offer to "pick up the tab" (sounding like the 1950s movies where they learned the term), but you should insist that it is your "honor" to pay. The use of the term "honor" throws the event into an entirely different light.

Alcohol is not served during most Indian meals. For one, it kills the palate for the nuances of the flavors, and is in turn killed when those flavors include India's wide array of chilis. Most business people will take a scotch before dinner and a cognac after. Beer is becoming more popular as the exotic locales in beer ads turn up in more business magazines. Indian women are unlikely to drink, but this is changing.

BRIBES

The Indian attitude is that bribes go to petty officials earning petty money by doing petty things for petty cash. The bribe's social virtue is that it keeps people thinking so small that they never think to expect much greater.

This writer's interviews with Koreans, Malaysians, and Singaporeans doing business in India indicate that Indian business people are very upright by the standards of Asia in general. The heavy skims that come from the Indian business community are usually in connection with the fees for exclusive market areas, distributor access to the retail market, and commission/kickback schemes. In this light they can be considered an overpriced service akin to the fees asked by lawyers. Surprisingly, India has no deeply entrenched syndicate crime of the mafia, triad, and yakuza types, although Mumbai is making a determined effort to resemble Chicago in the 1930s.

Subtlety in corruption certainly cannot be said for India's political peons and desk *wallahs*. Petty graft is widespread. That petty bureaucrats do not get paid much is true enough, but what is more pertinent is that wheedling money from you is a minion's way of getting you down to their level so that you can see what life is like there. They think it abhorrent to subsidize your hotel-room lifestyle from their peon incomes. Thinking in India does not always make sense, but it is usually understandable.

The conventional advice is to develop a company policy for graft and adhere to it. That is about as useful as conventional advice anywhere. The realistic advice is to find a local manager to handle the "expediting" factor of doing business. Nobody minds paying a handsome fee to Federal Express to get it there on time.

However, never directly offer money to a business person or government official yourself. Never fax or write your parent organization about graft and related issues. Instruct them to similarly refrain. If you have to discuss it, do it over the telephone or wait for a face-to-face meeting. Your fax machine is the one place you do not want to leave a paper trail.

GIFTS

Appropriate gifts are not bribes and are not seen as such. After a deal is closed, or if leaving the area, it is acceptable to exchange something like a good-brand fountain pen or one of the upscale ball-point pens, expensive liquor (VSOP is a useful acronym), and especially fine crafts from your home country A very thoughtful gift is 1-1/2, 2-1/2, or 5 yards of really high-quality 54-inch-wide fabric from your home country (and not wool!). Whether suiting material for a man or fine dress-making fabric for a woman, this is the type of unusual gift that will stick out in your counterpart's mind. The above lengths will make, respectively, a man's trousers or a woman's blouse, a man's jacket or a woman's skirt, or a full suit for either. It packs easily, and their tailor will bless you forever for presenting him with something unique to work with.

Money gifts are given for relatively few social events such as weddings. It is bad luck to give even amounts such as Rs 100 or Rs 1000; always add 1 to make the amount Rs 101 or Rs 1001. The numbers 108 and 1008 are especially auspicious to Hindus and Buddhists, even though they are "even" amounts. Ask a local counterpart about the appropriate amount for any particular event; too little can be perceived as an insult, too much as—well, too much.

DRESS CODE

For men, a suit and tie is appropriate for the first meeting. Thereafter, follow the lead of your local counterparts. In many instances, particularly in the warmer months, a shirt and tie but no jacket is fine. For women, suits, dresses, or skirts and blouses are appropriate. Despite their overall conservative bent in the matter of dress, Indians prefer bright colors.

Most Indian women wear traditional Indian sarees. There is quite a lore and legend about sarees, and one good small-talk opener at dinners is to ask a woman to explain all about her own.

For many purely social events, Indians are delighted when foreigners wear traditional Indian garments such as a silk Nehru jacket for men or a saree or *salwar khameez* (long jacket and pants) for a woman.

Your hotel can help you find a tailor if you want something custom-made. Indeed, once you find a good tailor you will never buy another off-the-rack garment as long as you are there. First, you get to choose the exact material you prefer. Second, the tailor can adjust for every minor difference in your body. Third, the fit and finish will be incredible by any previous standard you ever had, unless you shop at Harrod's. Each pocket, for example, will be made of strong muslin and double-stitched all the way around, and the pleats will be perfect even if your hips are not. Fourth, the price will be well beneath what you will find in the ready-to-wear shops. And finally, your Indian business associates will see that you know enough about India to know where to get a decent "pak" or suit made. In short, you have "arrived."

WORKING HOURS

India has a five-day work week, although this differs by industry and region. Most businesses, banks, and government offices are open from 10:00 a.m. to 5:30 p.m., Monday to Friday. City offices may be open from 8:00 a.m. to 6:00 p.m. On Saturdays, some businesses are open for a half-day, others for a full day. There is a one-hour lunch break on all days. Office workers usually work 40 hours per week, while factory and industrial workers work a 48–hour week. Due to inadequate power supply, factories often have staggered schedules with different factories in a district closing on a different day of the week.

Shops are usually open daily from 10:00 a.m. to 7.00 p.m. and are also closed one day per week; the day differs between regions and within cities.

MAJOR HOLIDAYS

Try to avoid business visits during major holiday periods. Each state or region has local holidays. Also, check before you travel as a holiday approaches; many businesses and schools close for big holidays, and obtaining train and air reservations can be difficult.

January 1	New Year's Day
January 26	Republic Day
February/March*	Ramadan
February/March*	Eid-ul-Fitr (end of Ramadan)
March*	Holi
April 1	Annual Closing of Bank Books
April†	Good Friday and Easter
May/June*	Eid-ul-Azha (Feast of Sacrifice)
July/August*	Muharram
August/September*	Prophet Muhammad's Birthday
August 15	Independence Day
September 30	Half-year closing of bank accounts
September/October*	Durga Puja Dussera
October 2	Mahatma Gandhi's Birthday
October/November	Diwali (Festival of Lights)
November/December†	Guru Nanak's Birthday
December 25	Christmas Day

*Based on the lunar calendar and differ from year to year.
†Observed on the first Friday and first Sunday after the Easter full moon.

NOTE

1. Many Americans would be inclined to use the term, "I'll have to run this past my attorney. . . ." Be careful with slang that might be ambiguous or mystifying. It is best to use precise formal English in business and save the slang for dinner afterward.

6

Basic Indian Business Law

HISTORY

Today's legal system in India is largely of British parentage. It originated in two charters granted in 1600 by Queen Elizabeth I and in 1609 by King James I of England to the East India Company (EOC). The Company was authorized to "make, ordain and constitute such and so many reasonable laws, constitutions, order and ordinances as to them . . . shall seem necessary . . . so always that the said laws, orders, ordinances, imprisonments, fines and amercements be reasonable and not contrary or repugnant to the laws, statutes, customs of this Our realm."

The EOC established trading outposts or factories in various places in India with the approval of the Moghul rulers of the time. According to a 1618 treaty between England and the Moghuls, the EOC was also given the authority to adjudicate disputes between its British employees and other Englishmen living in the company's first factory at Surat. Over time, the EOC expanded its commercial and political interests until they were tantamount to sovereign powers over the territories under its control. The EOC lost this status with the British Parliament's Government of India Act of 1858, which transferred to the Crown the Company's sovereignty over large tracts of Indian territory. In 1947, the British Parliament enacted the Indian Independence Act under which India and Pakistan were declared to be separate and independent dominions.

214 Doing Business in Today's India

INDIA'S CONSTITUTION

The Constitution of India came into force on January 26, 1950. It provided for a federal structure with the Westminster form of Parliamentary democracy at the central and provincial levels of government. The Constitution deals with the structure, functions, and powers or the organs of the Union and the States, and their interrelationship with each other. The Indian Federation consists of the Union of India—the Central Government—with the capital at New Delhi and twenty-five states, each with its own capital. In addition, there are seven self-governing union territories.

Legislative powers are divided between the Centre and the states. List I (the Union List) of the Seventh Schedule describes matters over which the Parliament of India has exclusive jurisdiction to enact laws. List II (the State List) consists of matters over which State legislatures can only enact laws. List III (the Concurrent List) is composed of the matters over which the Centre as well as the States may legislate. Certain Residual Powers are reserved for the Parliament. In the event of a conflict between the federal and provincial laws, the former prevail.

The regulation of foreign and interstate commerce falls within the exclusive domain of the Parliament. This is the root cause why commercial and political affairs are so inextricably mixed in India. The executive power of the Union Government extends over matters that are within the competence of the Parliament of India and the executive power of the states.

Indian states are delineated mostly along linguistic lines—hence the phenomenon of Malayalam speakers being mostly in Kerala, Tamil speakers in Tamil Nadu, Kanada speakers in Karnataka, and so on. States are entitled to have their own government-owned and -operated industrial development corporations, which some states like Gujarat do extensively, while others such as Bihar have lower profiles. Generally, an industrial enterprise may be opened only within the territorial limits of a state.

After the 1991 liberalization of the industrial policy these industrial development corporations began offering incentives for investment within their states.

Constitutional Safeguards

Part III of the Constitution enshrines fundamental rights such as the right to equality, the right to freedom, rights against exploitation, the right to freedom of religion, and the numerous cultural and educational rights of minorities. Any part of a law inconsistent with the fundamental rights is void.

The Supreme Court has power to issue directions, orders, or writs, including writs in the nature of habeas corpus, mandamus, certiorari, prohibition, and quo warranto, for the enforcement of these fundamental rights. The High Courts have the same power to issue these writs not only for the enforcement of the fundamental rights, but for any other purpose. All legislation and executive actions, federal or state, are subject to judicial review if they infringe on any of the fundamental rights. The right to petition the Supreme Court for the enforcement of fundamental rights is itself a fundamental right.

However, it is important to realize that among the above fundamental rights, the right to hold property is not a fundamental one. Article 300A, "no person shall be deprived of his property save by authority of law," was introduced by the 44th Amendment to the Constitution. This replaced the right to property as guaranteed by Article 31. There are numerous questions related to whether there is an obligation of the states to pay compensation for compulsory acquisition of property. Some legal authorities argue that there is an obligation to pay full compensation; others aver that under international law an alien's property cannot be expropriated except on the payment of just, adequate, and prompt compensation. In 1992, India became a signatory to the Convention on Establishing Multilateral Investment Guarantee Agency sponsored by the World Bank, which guarantees bilateral investment agreements with major investing countries.

The Constitution's Article 19(1)(g) guarantees to citizens the right "to practice any profession, or to carry on any occupation, trade or business." Article 301 provides that "trade, commerce and intercourse through out the territory of India shall be free." Hence, while Article 19(1)(f) guarantees the right to carry out trade, Article 301 makes India one single economic unit for trade purposes. Therefore, only the Parliament is competent to impose restrictions on interstate commerce in the public interest; the states have no such jurisdiction.

Similarly, Article 286 provides that "no law of a State shall impose or authorize the imposition of a tax on the sale or purchase of goods where such sale or purchase takes place—(a) outside the State; or (b) in the course of the import of goods into, or export of goods out of, the territory of India."

Role of the Supreme Court

A substantial body of jurisprudence has emerged on the interpretation and enforcement of fundamental rights and the development of a viable constitutional law and administrative law. The Supreme Court plays a seminal role in interpreting the Constitution and in maintaining a balance between the rights of citizens and the requirements of the state. It has developed or improved on many traditional doctrines of the constitutional law and administrative law, such as the principles of "natural justice" consisting of *audi alteri partem* ("hear the other party"), promissory estoppel, natural justice, and so on. The law declared by the Supreme Court is binding on all Courts in India. The Supreme Court also has the right to overrule its own decisions.

DISPUTE RESOLUTION VIA THE COURT SYSTEM

Judicial Settlement

India has a single-hierarchy judicial system. There is a single national Supreme Court and a High Court for each state. The Constitution has specific provisions for maintaining the separation of powers between the executive, legislature, and the judiciary, and for ensuring judicial independence. The Supreme Court has original jurisdiction for the enforcement of fundamental rights and in interstate disputes. It has civil and criminal appellate jurisdiction from the decisions of the High Courts. It also has advisory jurisdiction. The Supreme Court may grant special leave to appeal from any judgment, decree, determination, sentence, or order in any cause or matter passed by any court or tribunal in the territory of India. The High Courts have original writ jurisdiction for the enforcement of the fundamental rights and for any other purposes and civil and criminal appellate jurisdiction over the decisions of the District/Sessions Courts. The District/Sessions Courts have original and civil and criminal jurisdiction over subcourts. Overall, the judicial review of legislation and administrative action has produced a sizable body of case law.

Arbitration

Arbitration is the reference of a dispute to an impartial third person chosen by the parties to the dispute who agree in advance to abide by the arbitrator's award. This award is issued after a hearing at which the parties have an opportunity to be heard. The Indian Arbitration Act 1940 provides for reference to arbitration in the following cases:

1. Arbitration without the intervention of the courts where parties to an arbitration agreement refer the dispute to arbitration.

2. Arbitration with the intervention of the court where the parties to an arbitration agreement may apply to the court for reference to arbitration.

3. Arbitration with the intervention of the court in a matter that is subjudice, where in a suit all of the parties agree to refer the matter to arbitration.

4. Statutory arbitration—a company under the Indian Companies Act of 1956 may refer its dispute to arbitration under the Arbitration Act.

Arbitration awards are enforceable through the courts.

India was a party to the Geneva Convention on the Execution of Foreign Arbitral Awards 1927 and incorporated it in its Arbitration (Protocol and Convention) Act 1937.

India has ratified the United Nations (New York) Convention on the Recognition and Enforcement Foreign Arbitral Awards 1958, which replaced the Geneva Convention of 1927. The New York Convention is incorporated into municipal law through the Foreign Awards (Recognition and Enforcement) Act 1961.

Ombudsman (the *Lokapi*)

Modern democracies have produced two tendencies: (1) a wide ambit of powers are conferred on governmental administrations which have extensive discretionary powers; and (2) these powers have led to abuse and misuse by administrative functionaries. Many democracies provide remedies against such abuses of powers in the form of the principle of the ombudsman. In India, the Administrative Reforms Commission in 1966 recommended adoption of the ombudsman principle in India (referred as *Lokapai*). Even though an ombudsman has not yet been established over the federal administration, eleven states have adopted the institution, known as *Lok Ayukta*. Their investigative powers extend to actions taken by ministers and other administrative agencies, including departmental secretaries, but not to actions taken by the Chief Minister. *Lok Ayuktas* may inquire to a wide range of abuse of official position and corruption. They have come to play a vital role in thwarting administrative excesses.

THE LEGAL SYSTEM IN OPERATION

The Indian legal system has the following fundamental characteristics:

- a common law;

- statutes enacted by the Legislature that are almost identical to corresponding enactments of the British Parliament;

- the organization and functioning of an almost independent superior judiciary at the Centre and the States, consisting of the Supreme Court and the High Courts;

- the applicability of the decisions of the Judicial Committee of the Privy Council as the Court of appeals over the decisions of the Indian High Courts before Independence;

- the training, traditions, privileges, and duties of the independent Indian Bar.

Before 1947, Indian courts were mostly composed of British judges who administered Common Law imposed by the British rulers, except in cases where indigenous Indian law was more appropriate, such as in matters of family law and law of succession.

Commercial Law

Commercial law during the British rule gradually assimilated English law as an integral part of Indian law. When India became independent there was nothing distinctive in Indian commercial laws. Most of them, for example the Indian Contracts Act 1872 and the Sale of Goods Act 1930, were codified Common Law. The laws relating to banking, negotiable instruments, insurance, and carriage of goods by sea were counterparts of the English laws.

Today these basic laws have not been modified to a very great extent. However, new direction and purpose have been imparted to them according to economic exigencies. Lawyers familiar with the English commercial laws will readily see the similarities between the English and Indian commercial laws, most notably that freedom of contract is not impaired.

In the case of government contracts, Article 299(1) of the Constitution provides that all contracts made in the exercise of the executive power of the Union or State shall be expressed to be made by the President and shall be executed on behalf of the President or the Governor by such person and in such manner as the President or Governor may direct or authorize. However, if the government or some other public body or their officials makes a representation or a promise and a person acts upon such promise, under the equitable doctrine of promissory estoppel the government or public body should fulfill the promise even if there is no contract in terms of Article 299.

Intellectual Property Laws

In principle, intellectual properties are protected under the Trade and Merchandise Marks Act 1958, The Designs Act 1911, the Copy Rights Act 1957, and the Indian Patents Act 1970. India is a party to the World Intellectual Property Organisation (WIPO), the Berne Union for the Protection of Literary and Artistic Works, and the Universal Copy Rights Convention as revised in Paris in 1971.

In response to complaints about persistent violation of intellectual property laws, especially regarding computer software, India has enacted amendments to the copyright law and introduced trade mark reform legislation. India's new copyright act is the most stringent legislation in the world regarding software piracy. It was designed to better protect India's software industry, which is reluctant to venture into package development because of apprehensions over adequate copyright protection. The act provides for a minimum imprisonment of seven days for violating software copyrights. The onus of proving nonviolation is on the user; formerly, only the vendor could be punished. In order to expedite prosecutions, state governments are expected to establish special courts.

Labor Laws

In the distribution of power between the Centre and the State, "Labor welfare" is included in the "Concurrent List." Consequently, even though the laws relating to labor welfare aimed at promoting industrial harmony are central laws, they are administered by the states under the direction of the central government.

The Factories Act 1948 requires a license issued by a state government before operating a factory. The act contains provisions for the health, safety, and welfare of workers and with workers' space ratio, ventilation, fixing of machinery, working hours, holidays and annual leave, and employment of young persons.

The Workmen's Compensation Act 1923 deals with the payment of compensation on the death or injury of workmen occasioning in the course of employment.

The Employees' State Insurance Act 1948 provides for the establishment of the Employees' State Insurance Corporation and compulsory insurance of employees.

The Trade Union Act 1926 provides that any seven or more persons of a "trade union," defined to include "any combination . . . for the purposes of regulating the relation between the workmen and employees," may seek registration of a trade union. A trade union has the jurisdiction for collective bargaining and enjoys immunity from law suits and prosecution for criminal conspiracy.

The Industrial Disputes Act 1947 provides the machinery for the settlement of industrial disputes, defined as "any dispute or difference between employers and employers, employers and workmen, and workmen and workmen connected with the employment, non-employment or the terms of employment, or the conditions of labor." The machinery consists of a Works Committee, Conciliation Officers, Boards of Conciliation, Labour Courts, and Industrial Tribunals. An appeal lies to the High Court and or the Supreme Court from an award of an Industrial Tribunal.

Reference to the Labour Courts and Tribunals may be made only by the government. The act requires the payment of lay-off and retrenchment benefits, and has provisions relating to strikes and lockouts. The working of the act has generated copious case law.

The Industrial Employment (Standing Orders) Act 1946 deals with the procedures for taking disciplinary action against employees.

The Payment of Wages Act 1948 deals with the payment of wages and deductions from wages.

The Minimum Wages Act 1948 provides for the establishment of wage boards and the fixation of minimum rates of wages and hours of work.

The labor movement is very zealous in India. Every political party has its own labor wing that occasionally poses difficulties in unionization. It appears that the government is considering modifying the labor laws to harmonize them with the new industrial policy.

Law of Torts

Common law of torts is operative in India but has not yet been completely codified. As a consequence of the Bhopal catastrophe, the Parliament of India enacted The Bhopal Gas Leak Disaster (Processing of Claims) Act 1985 to enable the Union of India to arrive at a settlement. It also empowered the Union of India to take over all of the litigation and conduct it in place of or in association with the individual claimants. In *Charan Lal Sahu v Union of India*, the constitutionality of the act was impugned before the Supreme Court on the grounds that the divestiture of the claimants' rights to legal remedy against the multinational for the consequence of carrying on dangerous and hazardous activities "violates the fundamental rights of equality, freedom of occupation, and the right to life and liberty." The Supreme Court upheld the constitutionality.

In M.C. *Mehta v Union of India*, a case arising from the leakage of oleum gas from one of the units of the Shriram Foods and Fertiliser Industries complex that is surrounded by thickly populated colonies, which affected a large number of persons and caused the death of an advocate, the Supreme Court laid down an unprecedented and highly controversial proposition that an Indian enterprise engaged in hazardous activities that result in death, injury, or damage to property can, under certain circumstances, be held, without exception, strictly and absolutely liable in tort to a third party. The Court also pointed out that the measure of compensation should be correlated to the magnitude and capacity of the enterprise because compensation must have a deterrent effect.

The ramifications of the *Shriram* ruling have caused consternation among foreign investors who fear that they might be held liable for damages in tort if an Indian company in which they invest is involved in a disaster that results in death or injuries to third parties.

However, in two subsequent cases, the Supreme Court held that the observations of the Chief Justice speaking in Mehta's case were only *obiter dicta*. Moreover, in the Charan Lal case the Court held that:

> On behalf of the victims, it was suggested that the basis of damages in view of the observations made by this Court . . . would be much more than normal damages suffered in similar case against any other company or party which is financially not so solvent or capable. It was urged that to make damages deterrent, the damages must be computed on the basis of the capacity of a delinquent made liable to pay and on the monetary capacity of the delinquent. The quantum of the damages awarded would vary and not be based on the actual consequences suffered by the victims. This is an uncertain promise of law. On the basis of evidence available and on the basis of the principles so far established, it is difficult to foresee any reasonable possibility of acceptance of this yardstick. Even if it is accepted, there are numerous difficulties of getting that view accepted internationally as a just basis in accordance with law. These, however, are within the realm of possibility.

POST-1991 COMMERCIAL AND INVESTMENT LAW

According to the Constitution, regulation of foreign commerce is within the competence of the Government of India. By virtue of the government's Statement of Industrial Policy, substantial changes have been effected in the laws relating to (1) industrial licensing, (2) foreign investment, (3) foreign technology transfers, (4) monopolies and restrictive trade practices, and (5) taxation.

Industrial Licensing

The Industries (Development and Regulation) Act 1951 (IDRA) regulates industrial licensing. Its First Schedule lists thirty-eight industries whose manufacture of any of the items specified in this schedule is regulated by license. License is also mandatory for (1) establishing a new industrial undertaking, (2) an existing industrial undertaking to manufacture a "new article," (3) substantially expanding the capacity of an existing industrial undertaking, (4) carrying on the business of an existing industrial undertaking that was originally exempt from the licensing provisions but which later lost this exemption, and (5) changing the location of an existing industrial undertaking.

The Government of India may, by notification in the *Official Gazette*, exempt any industrial undertaking from the above licensing requirement.

The Industrial Policy Resolution of 1956 classified industries into three categories: (a) those whose future development will be the exclusive responsibility of the state; (b) those that would be established in the private sector under the initiative of the state but would progressively become state owned; and (c) those that would be permitted to be developed through private enterprise.

Under section 29B of IDRA on July 25, 1991, the private sector can engage in any industrial activity except the industries of strategic importance listed in Schedule I. The list has been further pruned to allow private-sector activity in mining oil exploration, refining, marketing, and certain functions of the railway transport sectors.

Industrial licensing is now required only for fifteen industries of strategic, social, or environmental concern enumerated in Schedule II. Even in these industries compulsory licensing is not required in respect of the small-scale units. Listed industries may also be exempted from licensing requirements. Recently the government liberalized the medical drugs policy by abolishing production and supply restrictions on foreign drug companies. This placed them on an equal footing with domestic companies. The government also abolished the licensing requirements in regard to all drugs, barring only five basic drugs (consisting mainly of vitamins). All other industries are exempted from licensing provided that they are not located within 25 kilometers of the periphery of twenty-three listed urban metropolitan areas having a population of more than 1 million. This condition does not apply to electronics, computer, software, printing, and nonpolluting industries that may be notified from time to time, and "small-scale and ancillary industries" (i.e., undertakings with investment less than 6 and 7.5 million rupees, respectively).

Except for the manufacture of items listed in Schedules I and II, subtantial expansion of existing units is exempted from licensing. Notwithstanding the location restrictions existing units are also allowed to manufacture any new article without additional investment if the article is not otherwise subjected to compulsory licensing. Industries under compulsory licensing are notified in the Industrial Trade Classification System.

For new projects for the production of articles not covered by compulsory licensing or their substantial expansion, the only requirement is for the industrial undertaking to file a memorandum in the prescribed form to the Secretariat for Industrial Approvals (SIA). The description of the articles should be given according to the Indian Trade Classification (based on the Harmonized Commodity Description and Coding System) published by the Ministry of Commerce, Directorate General of Commercial Intelligence and Statistics.

Foreign Trade

The interdependence of technology, investment, productivity, and an outward-looking trade policy is an integral part of India' s economic reform program. Sweeping changes such as scaling down tariff barriers, virtual abolition of import and export licenses, simplification of procedures, and the liberalization of the exchange rate mechanism have been effected as a consequence of the new trade policy announced in July 1991. Under the Foreign Trade Development and Regulation Act 1992, the Central Government provides for the development and regulation of foreign trade by facilitating imports and increasing exports. It may regulate the import or export of goods and grant exemptions. An Importer-Exporter code number issued by the Director General of Foreign Trade is needed for the import and export of goods. The Central Government may formulate and announce export and import policy and amend previous policy.

For the purposes of accelerating the integration of India with the global economy, the Export and Import Policy for 1992–1997 was announced on March 31, 1992 for promoting greater freedom of trade, fewer restrictions, and administrative controls. This policy was revised on March 31, 1993 to add these features:

- It will remain stable for five years. Changes expedient for liberalization or responding to emergencies will be made, as far as possible, only quarterly.

- Goods can be imported freely except for a limited negative list of imports. Only three items (tallow, animal rennet, and unmanufactured ivory) are prohibited; eighty-six items are restricted; seven items are canalized through Central Government Corporations.

- Capital goods are not restricted; second-hand capital goods may be imported in certain sectors.

- The definition of "capital goods" is enlarged to include capital goods used in agriculture and allied activities; actual-user conditions for import of industrial inputs are removed.

- The maximum import duty on raw materials and components has been reduced to 85 percent.

India's 1994–1995 budget reduced many of customs duties. The maximum customs duty except for baggage and liquor has been reduced from 85 to 65 percent. Basic customs duty on project imports and general capital goods has been reduced from 35 to 25 percent. Import duty on parts, whether imported as parts or original equipment, or as spares, has been reduced to 25 percent from rates varying from 25 to 85 percent. Import duty on fertilizer projects continues to be nil while on power projects it is reduced to 20 percent without any countervailing duties. Duties on machine tools is reduced to 35 or 45 percent from the present varying rates of 40, 60, and 80 percent. Customs duty on steel is lowered to 50 percent from a range of 75–85 percent.

The Export Promotion Capital Goods (EPC) Scheme allows access to capital goods at a concession rate of 15 percent, subject to an export obligation of four times the c.i.f. (customs import fee) value of imports over a period of five years.

Export of goods is allowed except for items on the Negative List, consisting of prohibited, restricted, and canalized items.

Units undertaking to export their entire output can be set under the schemes of Export Oriented Units (EOUs) or Export Processing Zones (EPZs). While EOUs may be set up anywhere in the country, EPZs are in seven designated areas. The EOU/EPZ units may sell 25 percent of their output in value terms in the Domestic Tariff Area (DTA). Fifty percent sale is permitted in the DTA for the agriculture, animal husbandry, floriculture, horticulture, pisciculture, poultry, and sericulture units.

The rupee has been made fully convertible on trading account. The Liberalized Exchange Rate Management System (LERMS) has been modified with effect from March 1, 1993 to provide a single market determined exchange rate for the rupee. All export and import transactions are now conducted at the market rate of exchange. The market rate also applies to the inflow of foreign equity, and outflow in the event of disinvestment, payments in respect of repatriation of dividends, and "lump-sum" fees and royalties for technical know-how agreements.

Foreign Investment

India's Foreign Exchange Regulation Act (FERA) was originally enacted in 1947 as a temporary measure to give the Central Government wide powers to regulate foreign exchange. Its original purpose was to combat capital flight and foreign currency speculation. The Revised Industrial Licensing Policy of 1973 expanded the core sector industries and opened them to large industrial groups and foreign companies. FERA 1973 authorized the Central Government to regulate the entry of foreign investment into India by curtailing foreign shareholding in Indian companies to not more than 40 percent. Regulations on foreign investment were tightened, but controls over foreign companies themselves were loosened by various relaxation policies.

FERA 1973 has been amended substantially by the Foreign Exchange Regulation (Amendment) Act 1993. Nineteen sections were amended and two new sections added, making the following changes:

1. New Section 18A was introduced to regulate the export of goods on lease, hire, or any other arrangement other than the sale of goods on an outright basis or consignment basis.

2. Section 19 was amended to exclude the transfer of shares, bonds, or debentures between nonresidents; now such transfers do not need Reserve Bank of India permission.

3. Section 27 was deleted so that Reserve Bank of India approval is not required for an Indian company to establish a joint venture or wholly owned subsidiary abroad. Persons resident in India do not require RBI permission to be a director of an overseas company.

4. Section 29 was amended to abolish the restrictions on FERA companies relating to carrying on in India activities of a trading, commercial, or industrial nature or to establish in India a branch, office, or other place of business, that is, Indian companies (other

than banking companies) in which the nonresident interest exceeds 40 percent. Now FERA companies do not need RBI permission for acquiring the whole of or any part of any undertaking in India of any person or company carrying on any trade, commerce, or industry or for the purchase of the shares in India of any such company. FERA companies, however, are required to obtain RBI permission for carrying on any activity relating to agriculture or plantation activity, or acquiring the whole of or any part of any undertaking in India of any person or company engaged in similar activity, or purchasing shares of such a company.

5. Section 30 was amended so that RBI permission for the employment of foreign nationals is no longer necessary.

This policy made a number of changes to facilitate foreign investment in India:

- Direct foreign investment is now allowed in every sector of the economy.

- One-hundred percent foreign equity is encouraged in the power sector and the duty-free Electronic Hardware Technology Parks (EHTPs), the Software Technology Parks (STPs), EOUs, and EPZs.

- Majority foreign equity up to 51 percent is permitted in thirty-six high-priority industries, provided the foreign equity covers the foreign exchange requirement for the import of new capital goods. Companies already operating in India may also increase their foreign equity up to 51 percent for the purposes of expansion in high-priority industries.

- Foreign investment in property development is restricted to companies in which Nonresident Indians and aliens of Indian descent own 60 percent of the equity.

- With the approval of the Reserve Bank of India, foreign investors may acquire a company already in existence in India through the issue of fresh capital and/or transfer of shares or from another foreign investor.

- An Indian company acquired by a foreign investor is not subjected to any restrictions for acquiring shares in other Indian companies.

- The 51 percent of foreign equity holding applies to trading companies engaged primarily in export activities. Such companies must register with the Ministry of Commerce. For their first seven years they will be able to repatriate dividends only to the extent of their export earnings. This requirement of "dividend balancing" is now removed for all high-priority industries and applies only to twenty-three consumer industries.

- The requirement of foreign technology accompanying foreign equity is removed. Foreign brand names and trade marks may now be used for sale of goods in India.

- Foreign companies may now open branch offices in India for representing the parent or any other foreign company, conducting research, undertaking import and export trading activities, and promoting technical and financial collaborations.

- Foreign institutional investors (FIIs), including institutions such as pension funds, mutual funds, investment trusts, asset management companies, nominee companies, and incorporated institutional portfolio managers or their power of attorney holders, can now invest in Indian primary and secondary markets. These are required to register with the Securities and Exchange Board of India (the regulatory agency for security markets) before any investment can be made in the securities of the companies listed on India's twenty-two recognized stock exchanges. These must also file with SEBI another application addressed to the Reserve Bank of India for seeking various permissions under FERA. SEBI registration and RBI general permission are valid for five years and are renewable for five-year periods thereafter.

The Capital Issue (Control) Act 1947 also was repealed. With the abolition of the office of Controller of Capital Issues and administrative control over the pricing of new issues, the capital markets now enjoy a considerable degree of freedom.

The Securities and Exchange Board of India, established in 1988 through a government resolution for promoting the orderly and healthy growth of the security market and for the protection of the investors, has been made into a statutory body by the promulgation of an ordinance and later by the enactment of the Security and Exchange Board of India Act 1992. This replaced government control over issue and pricing of capital issues by guidelines announced by the Securities and Exchange Board of

India (SEBI). According to these guidelines, existing profitable companies issuing capital to augment their own capital base are free to price their issues. Any capital issue to the public is subject to a minimum limit of contributions made by the promoters. A new company organized by existing companies with a five-year track record of profitability can price its issue provided the participating companies contribute not less than 50 percent of the equity. In the case of a new company established by existing private-sector companies along with a government company or state-level agency, it will be sufficient if the private companies satisfy the five-year track record. Interest rates on fully convertible debentures (FCDs) may be freely determined by the issuer. Companies should create a Debenture Redemption Reserve (DRR) equivalent to 50 percent of the amount of the debentures issue before commencing a debenture redemption.

Indian companies can now raise equity capital in the international market through the issue of Global Depository Receipts (GDRs). These are denominated in U.S. dollars and are not subject to any investment ceilings. Because of the rapid growth of demand for Indian equities, India will now allow only power and other infrastructure companies to raise capital with overseas issue of stock and convertible bonds.

Indian direct investment in joint ventures and wholly owned subsidiaries abroad is allowed. Under the guidelines, Indian parties may invest in newly promoted or existing foreign concerns engaged in industrial, commercial, trading or service activity or in hotel or tourism industry. The total value of direct investment shall not exceed $2 million of which cash subscription shall not exceed $500,000. The remainder may be contributed by the capitalization of Indian-made plant, machinery, equipment, or proceeds of goods exported to the foreign concern; or fee, royalties, or commission entitlements.

In the latest move toward the full convertibility on current account, the Reserve Bank of India announced further measures to liberalize current account transactions.

Foreign Technology Agreements

Section 39C of the Statement on Industrial Policy envisages the granting of automatic approval for the high priority industries listed in Annexure III. Up to a lump sum payment of 10 million rupees, 5 percent royalty for domestic sales and 8 percent for exports, subject to a total payment of 8 percent of sales over a ten-year period from the date of agreement or seven years from the date of production. Permission to hire foreign technicians and foreign testing of indigenously developed technologies has been dispensed with. The procedure for automatic approval is prescribed through press releases.

Monopolies and Restrictive Trade Practices Act Amendments

In order to prevent the concentration of economic power in too-few hands, the Monopolies and Restrictive Trade Practices Act (MRTPA) 1969 came into force in 1970. Its provisions applied only to private enterprises, not to government-owned or controlled companies.

The Act sought to control the activities of (1) "dominant undertakings," that is, enterprises that either by themselves or with interconnected enterprises control not less than one-third of the total goods or services of any description, and also possessing assets of not less than 10 million rupees; and (2) "monopolistic undertakings," that is, enterprises that together with not more than two other enterprises controlled one-half of the total goods or services of any description, and whose assets exceed 200 million rupees. The Act required these undertakings to register with the Department of Company Affairs. Prior governmental approval was necessary for expansion of capital or assets and setting up or acquiring new units. The MRTP Commission was established to monitor and prevent monopolistic and restrictive trade practices.

After the announcement of the 1991 Industrial Policy the Act has been amended effective September 27, 1991, first by an ordinance and later by the enactment of the Monopolies and Restrictive Trade Practices (Amendment) Act 1991. Government owned companies are now subject to the Act. The law aims at consumer protection and at controlling only restrictive trade practices, not the size of an enterprise. All acquisitions and mergers no longer require governmental approval and are governed by the guidelines issued by the Securities and Exchange Board of India.

7

Indian History
for the Business Person

India's history is one of punctuated equilibria in which brief spurts of dramatic change occur after long periods of status quo.

Among the more readily identifiable spurts in the past are the infusion of the Aryan peoples in about 1700 B.C., the rise of economic conditions that made possible the rise of Buddhism in the fifth century B.C., the Hindu Revivalist period that began during the Gupta dynasties of the fourth century A.C., the Muslim era, the colonial period, post-independence Nehruvian socialism and *swadeshi* self-reliance, and, finally, the economic sea change set into motion by economic reforms commenced in 1991.

You are coming to India on the upswing of the latest. Enjoy the show, and learn.

FLOWER OF THE ROSE APPLE

As a regional name, "India" is somewhat recent. The subcontinent's original name (insofar as there was one) was *Jambudipa*, "Flower of the Rose-Apple Tree."

The civilization of Jambudipa grew from two taproots. One—the Indus Valley civilization—centered on the Indus River in what is now Pakistan. This was indigenous to the subcontinent. Unhappily, very little is clearly known about it. Many of its god images in artifacts like seals and burial ornaments are clear antecedents to the primal gods of India today.

The other civilization came with the incursions and eventual settlement of a warlike, nomadic Indo-European people whose original name was

Aryan. (The name "Iran" commemorates their passage through that region.)

The Aryans' various migrations and conquests influenced Europe and
Asia from the Atlantic to the Indian Oceans. One of their legacies is the
similarities in modern languages spoken from Europe to India. The Indo-
European languages include English, Greek, Latin, the modern Romance
languages, the Germanic languages, Russian, Persian, the Urdu language
of Pakistan, and Hindi and Bengali. At first, English-speaking visitors to
India will detect few familiar locutions in the rapid rattle of Hindi on the
street. However, a few remarkably familiar words soon show up, largely via
the bridge language between Western and Indian languages, Sanskrit.
Sanskrit's *ti* became Latin's *tri*, French's *trois*, German *drie*, and English's
three. The Indo-European *namen* is now French's *nom* and English's *name*.
Mussa, for "fly," became Latin's *musca* and French's *mouche*, but English
stuck to the old Nordic root "fliegen." The *vessel* that blood flows through
derived from Latin's *vascula* for "to flow" and more distantly from Sanskrit's
vas and Indo-European's *vessa* ("to rain"). *Pada* became *peda* in Latin, *pied*
in French, and by some odd routing of linguistic history arrived in English
not as "foot" but as *pedestrian*.

JAMBUDIPA BEFORE THE ARYANS

Approximately 2500 B.C., the area now known as Pakistan harbored an
advanced civilization in the valley of the Indus River. The two major cities
of this civilization, Mohenjodaro and Harappa, rivaled any cities known
to humankind at that time and for millennia afterward. Both cities were
designed around an orderly grid of streets lined with brick town houses
whose connected facades blocked the noise and dust from the street. Under
the streets ran an extensive network of drains, so that these ancient cities
were probably more hygienic than European cities were before the nineteenth century. Mohenjodaro and Harappa had ample granaries where
emergency food supplies were stored, and numerous large municipal buildings and complexes that appear to have been palaces, assembly halls,
government houses, and perhaps even schools.

Aside from the imprecise but impressive picture that the Indus archae-
ological ruins paint, the details of this ancient culture remain a mystery.
The Indus Valley civilization vanished entirely from human memory until
Mohenjodaro and Harappa were unearthed early in the twentieth century.

The Aryans perpetuated their traditions in memorized hymns that were
meant to be sung or recited; only after finally settling down in the *Aryavarta*
or "Aryan Lands" region in the region now surrounding Punjab did they

begin writing down their hymns. The indigenous native writing of the Indus civilization disappeared; during this interregnum, the religious traditions of India were passed down orally and seem to have undergone considerable change.

The Indus civilization's alphabet has not been deciphered. Our knowledge of its intellectual attainments comes from archaeological evidence such as seals, figurines, statues, and similar artifacts. The only conclusions we can draw with some certainty are a preoccupation with fertility symbols (pregnant women, stone phallic symbols) and the worship of a divinity apparently similar to the god Shiva of historic Hinduism, who was associated with the bullock and often represented by a phallic symbol. The fertility symbols imply the existence of a Mother or Earth Goddess cult and the Shiva-like males a Great Procreator/Protector.

The Indus civilization also attached religious power to certain animals, especially the tiger, buffalo, crocodile, elephant, composite creatures, trees, and auspicious symbols such as the swastika. These symbols were more than mere totems symbolizing tribal, clan, or locality identities; instead, they were icons, that is, earthly images of spiritual forces whose effect on humans could be typified by the behavior patterns of those animals. Astrological signs seem to have evolved for much the same reason.

That similar identifications of behavioral patterns with spiritual or celestial icons have occurred in so many distant cultures suggests that people the world over found it easier to think in imagistic, symbolic terms rather than abstract, philosophical ones. This is of great significance when considering the likely effects of today's icon-like ten-second television spots on India's social and economic emotions compared with wordy intellectual ideas, even if transmitted by such high-tech means as the Internet.

The Indus region's spiritual art was quite similar to the religious motifs found in Mesopotamia. To some this suggests an ultimate origin of the subcontinent's religiosity earlier and outside the Indus Valley civilization. It makes for perennial debate among Indian intellectuals whether the religion known as "Hinduism" in India today originated beyond the Indus civilization, perhaps as remote as Sumer in 7000 B.C. What is more relevant to the visiting business person trying to fathom the complexities of India today is that passing warrior bands alone seem to fully explain so complex a mix of religious art and social infrastructure as showed up in rather complete form in Mojendaro and Harappa. In short, if you think like a warrior, prepare to be absorbed rather than accepted.

The only other likely means of transmitting so many complex symbols and the ideas beneath them are long and more or less regular merchant trade. Merchants, being experts on the myriad gods and behaviors of the thousands of remote valleys and huge towns they passed through, and being the incessant chatterboxes they must have become to while away the long days under the blazing caravan sun, and being little-fooled by any chain of reasoning after a lifetime of interminable bargaining sessions in bazaars, played just as much a part in forming modern India's daily-life culture as the subcontinent's more visible priests and ascetics. India was shaped by the mix of religion with trade.

ARYANS AND THE RISE OF BRAHMINISM

Jambudipa's ancient practical religion was *sramana*, or shamanism. Shamanisms are a class of religious beliefs with similar patterns. They are little influenced by theories of good, evil, the material world, and the soul. They are largely concerned with magical control of the here and now—curing illnesses, assuring rains and good harvests, producing male heirs, and so on. No matter how preoccupied people close to nature may be with their daily concerns, they are vulnerable to nature on the grand scale—eclipses, plagues among humans and animals, sudden death, mortal illnesses that inexplicably go into remission, lightning, unexpectedly bountiful or poor harvests, flowers blossoming out of season, tropical trees losing their leaves at unpredictable times of the year, high winds occurring on cloudless days, and invasions by men who belittle them for no reason.

Ancient Indian naturopathic healers assumed that precise proportions of substances in a medicament worked because the body was similarly apportioned. Eventually they devised a theory based on three "humors" (heat, air, and bile) much like the Greeks' four humors (air, earth, water, and fire). Given that the Greek language derived in part from Indo-European roots, these similar explanations may have had a common ancestor. The word *sramana* in ancient India and the modern term *shaman* both come from the name of the magic healers of the Tungusic tribes of Central Asia, the *sramans*.

The arrival of the Aryans, whether from across Mesopotamia and Iran or over the Hindu Kush (or both), brought a major new religious force into Jambudipa that was vastly different from the Indus civilization. The Aryans' original homeland was probably the region around the Caspian Sea. Their own accounts take great pride in emphasizing over and over that they preserved their own very distinctive culture, religious concepts, nature-inspired function-gods, a ritualistic cult involving the sacrificial use of fire, and an exhilarating drink called *soma*. Some of their gods are mythologically similar to those of Iran, Greece, and Rome. Their religion was limited to persons of Aryan birth, although they tolerated the priests of others.

This religion was embodied in a collection of hymns, ritual texts, and philosophical treatises called the *Vedas*. From Aryan times down to the present, Hindus have regarded the *Vedas* as a body of eternal and revealed scripture. The earliest was the *Rig Veda*, followed by the *Yajur Veda*, *Sama Veda*, and *Atharva Veda*. This collection of hymns is the earliest body of systematized religion in India, and it was the Aryan religion, not the native.

The *Vedas* shifted dramatically away from the earlier system of trying to control nature by controlling the symbols of nature. Sacrifice and mythology began to be explained in terms of the abstractions of macrocosm and microcosm, just as business press articles today deal with the bloodletting of corporate downsizing by recommending going into business for yourself.

In times of fear, speculations about the human soul replace comforting propitiations and India, then and now, has been no different. The gods became a God: *Brahman*. The self became a soul: *Atman*. The ultimate nature of things could be satisfactorily explained only if creation and creator were different manifestations of the same thing: Atman = Brahman.

Thereafter the relationship between human thought and the causes of things blossomed quickly. Speculations along these lines were formulated by various philosophical schools in treatises collectively called *Upanishads*. Vedic literature is a study in systematic abstraction from the daily to the ultimate, the ritual fire representing security and food for the body to the fireball of Creation, from food security to soul security.

Among the various deities of the *Vedas*—still personifications of natural forces—one stood out: *Eka Deva* ("One God"), whose name was Indra. Indra was originally a real warrior hero whose exploits in conquering the Indus peoples were embellished over time from hero to legend to myth to god. Creation originated when Indra, now no mere bully with a sword but the champion of the celestial gods, killed the serpent demon Vritra, who enclosed the waters needed for human life. The waters were released and life could begin. Indra then set the sun in the sky and established a cosmic order (*rita*) under the god Varuna. Gods and humans were assigned specific functions to perform to fill this cosmic order. After death, those who had fulfilled their *rita* obligations went to a heavenly realm presided over by Yama, the first mortal. Two mythical dogs guarded the righteous on the path to this region. Those who violated the order of *rita* were chained and devoured by demons.

The ideas that descend into today from this myth are that obedience to a celestial order of things determines one's fate, and that to act outside the boundaries of one's duties brings endless woe. It is useful to reflect on these things when making one's adjustments to the Indian bureaucracy.

Vedic cult practices developed an elaborate ritual based on a fire sacrifice. Agni's voice was the crackling of the fire. This ritual necessitated a highly specialized priesthood. Great significance became attached to the chanting of hymns and invocations by the human priest as the sole access to divine solace. The ritual of sacrifice rather than the lesson of sacrifice came to be viewed as the most important, and the point of it all switched from gaining spiritual solace to gaining material comfort. Ritual's exact procedures could impart a magical power that could bend the will of the gods to the will of humans. The spiritualization of want through ritual sacrifice is a core idea of early Indian religious thought.

The generic name for this is imitative magic, and it is a fairly widespread practice among all the world's behaviors. As a theory of religious behavior it seems abstract until one begins to look closely at the rituals of the shares markets and law courts. Hence it is very useful for visitors to India to step aside from romantic awe at the exoticism of its ways to look at India as drinking, too, from our common cup of need.

THE GODS GO BEGGING

The seventh to fifth centuries B.C. found India in great flux. Village republics were evolving into urban commonwealths. States were accruing military power to protect trade and rulers alike. Wealth from trade produced a need for regional security that the subsistence village did not need. Iron replaced bronze, which had implications for wielders of both plowshares and swords. The development of organized states and the advance of material well-being stimulated new ideas. Land cleared of dense forest for paddies and fields opened limitless horizons, and with them many people's view of the world. The earth goddess was slowly shunted aside by the war god. The sense of village commonwealth was replaced by the fear of want inherent in impersonal commodity economies. The self-governing character of village gatherings slowly evolved toward despotic kingdoms in which individuals lost control of local authority. The intelligentsia became increasingly dissatisfied with the dull mindlessness of priestly ritual. The pragmatic populace at large was disgusted with the high fees brahmins demanded. The lower caste chafed under social rules which stated, among other things, that their shadow must not cross that of a brahman under penalty of death.

More important, the brahmins were failing at one of their primary duties. The original function of their poetic, magical priestcraft was to offset the mythology of destruction brought by the Aryan warriors. Hundreds of years after the Aryans first settled down, warriors were slaughtering again, this time in the name of taxes. The brahmins had nothing to offer by way of counterbalance. Militarization of India's gods came as Shiva the destroyer surpassed Vishnu the preserver. Indra, the ancient conqueror, was slowly forgotten. Along with the warlords' virile massacres of weaponless cultivators came a decline in the status of the feminine regenerative goddess of the earth. The alley's profane prostitute replaced the temple's *Deva dasi* or sacred consort. The rise of states all but eliminated matriarchal common sense in community affairs. Women became cows and, like the cow, were revered for their nurturing and their docility. These changes could not help but produce religious ferment.

Siddartha Gautama was the son of the chief of one of the small local republics, Shakya, that dotted what is now the Bihar region surrounding modern Patna. Most of these republics were politically and economically minuscule. They depended on the large kingdoms of Kosala and Magadha south of the Ganges for their security and trade.

In Gautama's home region north of the Ganges, a confederation of republics called the Vajjian Confederacy was governed through a titular chief by a republican assembly of tribespeople. For those who wonder why modern India opted for democracy while so much of Asia went in for petty potentates, the history of the Vajjian Confederacy makes for a good read.

The Vajjian administrative infrastructure consisted of chiefs of the various tribes; Gautama's father was one of them. For much of Gautama's life political stability enabled him and many others to either chase after the good life or pursue the truth, to whichever they were inclined. Gautama as Buddha chose both: the middle way between glutton and ascetic, intelligence tempered with pragmatism.

India was a plentiful repast for those hungry for ideas. Of the many being bandied about resulting from dissatisfaction with Brahminism, one had become common currency—reincarnation. Spiritual rebirth is as old as religion, but the idea of reincarnation in India supposed a mechanism by which one's future fate was decided not by the gods but by this life—*karma*.

Karma linked activity in this life with what occurs in the next. Before the Buddha, the mechanism of karma was by no means certain. The most philosophical form of the idea was articulated by Mahavira, the founder of the Jain sect. Jain philosophy holds that the human self consists of a soul enmeshed in physical matter. *Moksha*, or salvation, occurs by liberating the soul from matter so that it becomes pristine again and can thus achieve perpetual bliss. Mahavira thought of karma as a specialized form of matter flowing into the soul through the body's senses. Cruel and selfish acts result in unhappy karma-matter, which results in unhappy rebirths. Good acts are free of karma-matter and therefore produce no weightiness. Suffering sponges away bad karma-matter from the soul.

Mahavira realized his complete doctrine after years of naked wandering. He appealed to the percentage of the populace whose daily suffering was not a great deal less than the naked *sramanas* or ascetics who wandered about looking for moksha. The elaborate sacrifices demanded by brahmins were alien to people who knew all too well the intensive labor demanded by field and animal. They must have harbored quite a few resentments at the golden-girdled *arrivistes* from Punjab who cozied up to the kings and demanded that the lowly burn their own best produce to propitiate the gods while nature, in the villagers eyes, seemed to behave no different than before.

When the autocratic brahmins aligned themselves with Magadha and Kosala's emerging principalities south of the Ganges, their rituals evolved to satisfy the grandiosity of these new autocrats. The brahmins became more aligned with the throne than ever. In a piquant play on words, villagers altered the term *balipatigga haka* (literally "tax demons") applied to the king's tax farmers to *balipanigga haka* ("torture demons") and applied it to the brahmins. Both words alluded to the equal indifference of brahmins to the suffering of animals being sacrificed by having their throats cut and the suffering of people whose purses were slit. Their real point was that priests and princelings had become coequal tyrants.

The brahmins were in fact a whipping boy for deeper social ills that no one could articulate because few if any understood their causes. Kings could not expand their territory if they were restrained by the slow, self-protective deliberations of tribal leaders. Kings developed the idea that they as *individuals* had the right to rule (an idea apparently introduced by brahmins), whereas the populace had always considered the *office* of ruler as preeminent. Unrighteous rulers could be stripped of their symbolic regalia (a white parasol, whisk of yak-tail's hair, conch, trident, spear, and headdress) and replaced. Today politicians bear different regalia, but they are still briskly swept out the office door when they forget the mandate that it is the office that rules.

Along with these kings came a new class of people who lived in towns and engaged in the trade of surplus commodities for personal gain. Their economy was a significant departure from the tribal ethos of equal distribution of excess commodities and property rights in common. Town merchants looked to kings to protect trade routes from the tolls imposed by countless tribal leaders. The kings hired mercenaries, who led to the institution of universal taxation in place of specific levies for specific purposes. The *Lokayata* of Professor Chattopadhyaya published in New Delhi in 1957 paints a vivid picture of life under this system:

> If the subjects did not pay willingly, or if the King wanted (as seemed often to happen), the King sent his officials who used force to fill the coffers of the King. Oppressed with taxes, the inhabitants lived in forests like beasts with their wives and children. Where there was once a village, there no village stood any more. The men could not, for fear of the King's people, live in their houses. They surrounded their houses with hedges and went before sunrise back into the forest. During the day the *rajapurisa* ("King's people", i.e., mercenaries) plundered; at night the thieves. (p. 476)

All of this has the distinct air of rural life in the days of Richelieu in which the surest way to lose wealth was to display it. However, more serious issues than oppressive taxation preoccupied the philosophers like the Buddha and Mahavira. Theirs were philosophies partly spawned by frustration in the face of ancient and, to them, noble institutions being replaced by forces of injustice and abuse. If one sees mirrored the fate of the Congress Party in this, it is useful to reflect on the timeless quality of righteousness in India.

The Vajjian world of sudden economic affluence was beset by ills which were not really all that different from those before. The symbols mythified by Gautama's first encounters with the world outside his palace never changed: illness, age, and death. Suffering has causes that no one has ever completely understood. To people of Gautama's time, resignation and fatalism seemed the only cure.

The Buddha's solution was vastly different. He examined causes, not effects. The causes were in each individual's behavior toward other individuals. The solution was personal, not group, responsibility.

BUDDHA'S REVOLT

Gautama was raised within the context of tribal republicanism during the emergence of royal states, so he was familiar with the virtues and defects of each. Brahminism had not achieved the preeminence in the young Siddartha's region that it had achieved elsewhere. Indeed, Aryanism's diffusion through India was not the hasty affair many think it was. It seeped slowly eastward from the Punjab down the Ganges, becoming more tenuous as it did, and never penetrated the Dravidian south.

The young prince's religious upbringing probably encompassed as much folk belief from the kitchen fires as Brahminism from the sacrificial fires. He was certainly acquainted with the asceticism of the time, for when he decided to adopt this path for himself he knew exactly what to do, even to the rituals of crossing a river and cutting off his own hair.

The story of Gautama's escaping the paradaisal confines of a palace full of *nauch* girls and feasts to see the "real" world may have a certain delicious fantasy, but later Buddhist mythifiers were no less apt to trim off the unpleasant edges of fact than their Brahminist ancestors. In actual fact, the Buddha accompanied his father on the republic's business many times and even won archery competitions. The lands of the Shakya state were hardly huge, and its economy was as rice-reliant as it is now. Moreover, its population was perhaps one-fifth to one-tenth of what it is now. Hence Gautama's "palace" was more likely a two- or three-floor extended house with outbuildings not much different than the average rural Indian moneylender's house today, although without so many armed guards and dogs—and mercifully without those toadish little Ambassador autos favored by today's farming elite.

At the age of twenty-nine Gautama came to feel that there must be something greater in life than listening to the endless squabbles of a petty state's populace and the hourly updates of a young wife with a new son. He forswore all to become a wandering ascetic. After five years of this (he was down to one grain of rice a day for awhile) he realized that asceticism would reveal to him no ultimate answers. He determined to acquire ultimate wisdom by meditation. Under a ficus tree on a full-moon night in May 529 B.C., he penetrated into a state of understanding and bliss that surpassed all of his previous experience.

He carried his message into the world, meaning the rising middle class of the then-emerging provincial towns. Over time he gained many adherents and a few implacable enemies. After forty-five years of preaching and good works, he passed away between two *sala* trees in the village of Kusinara, not far from his birthplace. His message was simple: The unexamined life is not only not worth living, but you have to live it again and again until you do examine it. When you do you will discover that the solution was there all along: Do all in moderation and think about why you are doing it.

At the time of the Buddha the ideas of karma and reincarnation were taken for granted by all strata of society. The historical record is unclear about how these two ideas came into common currency. Probably the bottom castes, the *sudras* and the *candalas* (or untouchables), had always grasped at some form of psychological life buoy that promised redress. But in an era when society was quickly advancing both spiritually and materially despite the accompanying disagreeabilities, it is difficult to understand why so many relatively well-off people should be attracted by a philosophy like reincarnation that promised no immediate benefit, but only life after life after life for indefinite eons into the future.

The concept of escape from this life by migration to another was not alien to people's minds when the Buddha set the wheel of the Dhamma ("The Path") in motion in 529 B.C. The writers of the *Upanishads* sought release by way of knowledge. The Buddha emphasized the way of deeds: People cannot always achieve a life of great wisdom, but they can certainly perform good deeds. The Buddha's behavioral philosophy of *dana* (giving), *metta* (unreserved love), and *karuna* (compassion) stood in stark contrast to the brahmins' reverence for money-making above all else. The Buddha replied to god religions that gods are irrelevant. Salvation can only come from within, through one's own efforts. Earthly thinking, faced with suffering, death, and the idea that nothing about life can ever be truly and enduringly satisfying, is an illusion.

At first this idea took hold slowly. Then the emperor Ashoka was converted to the Buddhist ideal in about 250 B.C. Much of India went along, to the point where Buddhism, Brahminism, and the old folk beliefs coexisted amiably for some half a millennium. Starting in the fourth century A.C., the theologians of the dynamic Gupta dynasty re-examined the age-old Brahminist beliefs, changed them to suit the times, and the resulting Hinduism swept over India, this time all the way to the Dravidian southern tip. Buddha was transformed into one of the many reincarnations of Vishnu (Krishna of *Bhagavad Gita* fame was another), tribal marauders from over the Hindu Kush wiped out every "bald brahmin" they could, Islam converted many Buddhists with Sufi's lyrical mysticism, and that was that. Today Buddhism comprises less than 0.4 percent of India's religious followers. Despite—or perhaps because of—its absence of concern with fate, it suffered the fate of any belief system that fails to provide a god.

BRAHMINISM, BUDDHISM, AND BUSINESS

Certain facile conclusions are often drawn from all of this. One is that India has a sociological predisposition to polytheism and that dissenting belief systems are either re-garbed in old clothes or politically and economically marginalized.

Perhaps. What India's long history of religious stolidity demonstrates is the truly enduring power of the notion behind *Atman = Brahman*, that the one is the all and the all is the one. The metaphor that best illustrates India's mindset about the way things work is Indra's Net. According to this, all existence is like the webwork of a vast net. At the juncture of each strand is a splendid jewel of a multitude of facets. Each facet reflects itself, every other jewel, every other facet of every other jewel, and, finally, the whole of the net itself.

Indra's net, if one looks at it as a metaphor, can be glimpsed in a remarkable number of venues. India's *kovils* (Hindu temples), with their vast panoply of gods, sum to a god of the gods. There is a fire within. Indeed, if you attend during the hour of worship when the bell tolls, people will whisk the smoke from the flaming bowl carried by the priest across their faces, cleaning themselves with fire. Agni speaks.

It is also useful to think of Indra's Net when exasperated with the labyrinthine complexities of India's bureaucracies (now in the private sector, too) and the seeming impossibility of ever discerning how and by whom a decision is actually made. In India, all things reflect all things. It is simply a matter of time before you happen to be looking in the right direction for the right thing, and then illumination occurs. Atman, indeed, is Brahman.

Finally, there is a fathom-filled gulf between the wants of the individual and the need of the self. Reincarnation theory has it that there is no ultimate individuality. The karma one inherits, adds to, and passes on carries no person with it. There is no "you," only a summation of deeds; there is no soul, only an accumulation of effects. Individuality is ego and ego is always in flux. It changes from day to day, depending on what happens to us and how we feel. Being impermanent, individuality brings with it the craving for something permanent. It is a lifetime filled with wants, none of which are deeply satisfying. Individuality, to the Indian, is like the frosting on a cake: tasty, but no one would want it for every meal.

Self, on the other hand, is the deeds one adds to one's karma. It has no identity, no soul, no abiding "me." But it does have a need: release from its own limits. Hinduism proposes that release comes through wisdom, through physical and mental discipline, or through devotion to the deities. Buddhism proposes that it comes through a life of reflective moral behavior.

TEN CENTURIES OF CHANGE

Hindu fears raised by the extent of Buddhist influence encouraged a brahminist military officer to initiate a coup that led to the collapse of the

Ashokan Empire in 184 BC. India entered a period of political fragmentation that lasted for 500 years.

India being so vast, events taking place in one part of the subcontinent did not always affect other parts. Kingdoms that rose, flourished, and fell in one region had little impact on life in other regions. Despite periods in which a ruler or succession of rulers unified the country, Indian history is marked by political alliance and then fragmentation, all of which perpetuated regional fiefdoms with deep linguistic, cultural, and religious differences. This appears in modern times as the unity of Nehruvian socialism and the Gandhi dynasty crumbles into political fragmentation, democratic enough to be sure, but still producing considerable disparities in the economic status of India's states.

By the early fourth century A.C., the western region that is Pakistan today had fallen to the Persian Sassanians. In 319 A.C., in the eastern part of India, Chandragupta II founded the Gupta Empire, beginning the first phase of the imperial Gupta period that lasted until 606 A.C. During this period, the arts and literature flourished. Toward the end Buddhism and Jainism had declined considerably as a Hindu tide swept through the third to ninth centuries. At the end of the Gupta period, northern India had broken into several Hindu kingdoms and was not unified again until Islam arrived.

ISLAM'S GREAT FLOWER

In the early eighth century Islam began to exert a mercantile presence in India. Overland traders brought it by caravan and southerly traders by dhow. By 1206, Islam had established a sultanate in Delhi that lasted 300 years. By 1226, the entire Ganges basin was Muslim in name if not control. The Hindu kingdom of Vijayanagar, founded in 1336 in southern India, was the strongest Hindu kingdom of the time.

The Muslims converted only about 25 percent of India's population. They brought Hindus into the bureaucracy, and Urdu-Persian vocabulary and Hindi grammar written in an Arabic script became the lingua franca of aristocracy and commerce. English is the counterpart today.

The Delhi sultanate successfully protected the Indian subcontinent from the Mongols, who had a record from China to Baghdad of invading fiercely and then settling in peaceably, acquiring local civilizations in the process. In the early sixteenth century there was established a dynasty which created the most enduring architectural ideas that typify India today. Because of their passion for architecture, art, literature, and grandeur, the Moghuls had a significant impact on the cultural landscape of India.

Akbar (1556–1605) is held to be the greatest Moghul emperor. A strong military commander and a fair, cultured, wise, and religiously tolerant man, he astutely observed that the Hindus were impossible to subjugate. So instead he integrated them into the bureaucracy of his empire, and, based on their ability to pursue their own religion as they wished, they lived long and memorably in peaceful coexistence. Shah Jehan (1627–1658) built the Taj Mahal in honor of his late wife, assuredly the most enduring thing a man has ever erected for a woman.

Aurangzeb (1658–1707) was the last of the Moghuls. He attempted to extend the boundaries of his empire, but succumbed himself to internal dissension based on religious zealotry. Remembering little of Akbar, he destroyed Hindu temples and put mosques on their sites. This alienated the Hindu bureaucracy, which revolted. His blind fundamentalism more than 350 years ago fuels the furies between Hindus and Muslims today, as Ayodhya and its subsequent riots testify. This is all the more ironic since Hinduism and Islam have a common belief that underlies Brahman and Allah: Nothing happens by accident.

Islam's loss of rule was not only its alienation of the Hindu masses. The squabbles of other rulers—notably the Marathas and the Rajputs—also contributed. The Rajputs were a warrior caste with a fanatical devotion to bravery in battle (an attitude similar to the knights of medieval Europe). For a time, they successfully opposed all foreign incursions, but they were unable to effectively unite and eventually spent more energy battling each other than their common foreign enemies. Perhaps today's Europe uniting and India's fragmenting are simply where they are at the moment on the turning cosmic wheel.

Another group, the Marathas, originated in what is today Maharashtra. They rose to power under Shivaji, who between 1646 and 1680 made great renown for himself with his military cunning and heroism. He continues to be idolized by many Maharashtrans today as a sort of local-hero Indra, up to the legend level but not quite a myth. Shivaji is particularly admired because he came from a lower Hindu caste, thus proving that great leaders did not have to be ksatriyas, the legatees of the ancient warrior caste. Today's Phoolan Devi, the *dalit* "Bandit Queen" who rode into political office on the coattails of her fearsome reputation as the vengeant murderess of twenty-four petty local lords who raped her, is yet another heroine on the way to being mythified.

THE ARRIVAL OF EUROPE

The first Europeans to settle in India were the Portuguese, under the leadership of Vasco da Gama, who landed in 1498 on the coast of modern-day Kerala. In 1510, the Portuguese captured Goa, which they controlled until 1961. In 1600, Queen Elizabeth I granted a charter to a British company, giving them a monopoly on British trade with India. For the next 250 years, British affairs in India were not handled by the British government, but by the British East India Trading Company. In 1612, the British made their first permanent settlement at Surat in the state of Gujarat, subsequently adding trading posts at Bombay, Madras, and Calcutta. The Dutch and the French also established trading posts.

When the Moghul Empire disintegrated in the seventeenth century, India fragmented, due, yet again, to the absence of an assertive centralizing leader. The British took advantage of India's political rivalries, winning war after war against India's local rulers. The British were preoccupied with trade; they were not especially interested in converting the Indians to Christianity. It was hard enough to swallow the idea of Scots or Irish nearing the hallowed portals of Westminster Abbey, to say nothing of those creatures in turbans.

Religious indifference, however, gave the British an advantage over the Portuguese, who thought that since the sword and the cross looked the same, they should act the same. They were wrong, and eventually they had only tiny Goa to wave their flag. For almost a century, the French and British competed for control of Indian trade, often playing local rulers against one another and manipulating relationships between royal family members within the same kingdom. Both hired and trained Indian *sepoys*, local police, to guard their forts and serve in their armies. The French pursued a partially successful policy of buying the favor of India's rulers in the south, but this strategy became too expensive and was eventually abandoned.

In 1757 the British, under Robert Clive, the governor of the British East India Company in India, defeated the Indian ruler Siraj-ud-daula and his French supporters in Calcutta, thereby cementing the power of the East India Trading Company. India's future was now in Great Britain's hands. In 1803, the British finally defeated the Marathas. In 1849, Punjab, the last state under local rule, was conquered and a little later, Nepal. British respect for the military prowess of Nepal's Gurkha soldiers led them to recruit and maintain separate Gurkha regiments.

The British profited immensely from Indian trade, and in its furtherance built a strong, well-organized bureaucracy and an extensive railway network, roads and bridges, irrigation systems, and other infrastructure projects.

The British East India Trading Company focused primarily on commerce and did not interfere with Indian culture, beliefs, or religions. They controlled India through a combination of direct rule in certain provinces and indirect rule in others, often using their traditional divide-and-rule approach that worked so pyrrhically well in the short term in their colonies most everywhere. They allowed Indian rulers to remain on their thrones but retained control of trade policy and other economic issues. By the middle of the nineteenth century, the British East Indian Trading Company had recruited, armed, and trained more than 300,000 Indians, forming an army that was used to fight and subdue other Indians.

In 1799, Ranjit Singh, a Sikh, became governor of Lahore. Eventually he came to control most of what is now modern Pakistan plus Punjab, Kashmir, and the Peshawar Valley. The British eventually annexed this small empire and incorporated the Sikh soldiers into their army. The British were less successful in conquering what is now the Northwest Frontier Province in modern Pakistan.

In 1857, Indian battalions of the Bengal Army stationed near Delhi revolted against British control. Their mutiny sparked similar revolts against the British throughout northern India. Because the rebellion was fragmented, and because no one leader emerged to coordinate it, it died out within a year. In the end, the revolt achieved exactly the opposite of its ambition: The British government assumed direct control over India. The subcontinent, comprising today's India, Pakistan, and Bangladesh, became the Asian revetment of Britain's global empire, providing it with all of the profits and prestige that England needed to become suffocatingly self-satisfied.

After the 1857 Mutiny, the British reorganized their Indian armies, mixing units by race, caste, and region to ensure that individual ethnic groups would be less likely to unite and rise in mutiny again. The Indian leaders, devastated by their impotency against British firepower, adopted an interim stance of complacency, realizing that they would have to transform themselves before they could successfully challenge British rule.

The sons of India's upper classes were often sent to Great Britain to receive a Western-style education. A small but steady flow of Indians went off to Europe, were inculcated with modern, liberal ideas, and brought those ideas home to India. A nationalist movement, with two schools of thought, began to form. The radical group wanted to rid India of the British as soon as possible. The moderate group believed that, before India could accept the responsibilities of self-rule, all Indians had to learn to treat each other more humanely and engage in social reform.

By the turn of the century, Indian opposition to British rule began to intensify. The Indian National Congress, which had been created in 1885 to promote more self-rule for Indians, assumed the leadership role in the struggle for independence. Gradually the Indians were given more opportunities for participation in India's administration. In 1906, the All-India Muslim League was founded in Dacca as a counterbalance to the Indian National Congress, for many Muslims feared Hindu domination. During this same period, Hinduism began another era of revival and adjustment, having lost much of its mass appeal during the Moghul and early British period. This became a unifying point within India's population.

MAHATMA GANDHI

In 1915, Mohandas Gandhi, who was later given the honorific title "Mahatma," meaning "Great Soul," returned from South Africa, where as a lawyer he had devoted himself to fighting racial discrimination. Upon his return to India, he became involved in the struggle for independence, particularly after the Amritsar massacre in 1919, during which British soldiers fired on an unarmed crowd of protesters. Gandhi was successful in expanding the independence struggle from a concern of the small middle and upper classes to one involving India's great peasant masses. He led boycotts against British textiles and the salt tax. He was often jailed, as were other leaders, but his policy of *satyagraha*—passive resistance and noncooperation—gained him global recognition and sympathy. He was a fervent advocate of equality and tolerance, and worked to rid the Hindu religion of discrimination in its caste system. His ideas of self-reliance and "home-grown" encouraged Indians to purchase Indian-made products and reduce their reliance on foreign products. This was the foundation for an attitude that would permeate India's future political and economic policies all the way to mid-1991.

INDEPENDENCE AND CONGRESS

By the end of World War II, it was apparent that Indian independence was inevitable. The war destroyed the myth of European superiority. England no longer had the financial resources to support a far-reaching global empire.

However, not all Indians supported Gandhi's methods and policies. The Muslim minority realized that an independent India would be Hindu-dominated as the Muslim minority lost its British protectors. There was a rapid and sometimes violent growth of communalism. Mohammed Ali Jinnah, leader of the Muslim League, vowed to divide India into two nations. The Congress party, led by Jawaharlal Nehru, vowed to maintain a united India. Lord Mountbatten tried unsuccessfully to reconcile the two sides. The Congress party's fight for an independent greater India and Jinnah's egotistical bid for power over a separate nation brought India close to civil war.

Hence the decision to divide India was made, resulting in India and Pakistan. India's independence was declared on August 15, 1947. The division resulted in violent and widespread communal unrest. Today the division is still a sore spot for many Indians who view it as a betrayal of their nation. Gandhi opposed the division, but always advocated peace as the primary objective. Sadly, he was murdered on January 30, 1948, by a fanatical Hindu member of the right-wing Rashtriya Swayamsevak Sangh (the RSS) group, which advocated Hindu supremacy through force.

In his efforts to promote communal harmony and mutual respect, Gandhi often read from both Hindu and Islamic scriptures and was thus accused by fanatical Hindus of being a Muslim-lover and traitor to his own religion. Dividing India proved as difficult as contemplating it, since Muslim enclaves were scattered throughout the country. The two main enclaves were on opposite sides of the country and became East and West Pakistan, separated by 1,000 miles of Indian territory. Twenty-five years later, a war brought independence to the eastern enclave, today's Bangladesh.

Many of India's Muslims fled their home region for refuge in Pakistan, while many Hindus and Sikhs in the new nation of Pakistan fled in the opposite direction. With almost 10 million people changing sides, it was arguably the largest transfer of misery in human history. Violence broke out as Hindu-Sikh and Muslim mobs preyed on each other. At least one million people were killed. What should have been a time of national rejoicing became a period of chaos, death, and despair.

A 1949 United Nations cease-fire gave Pakistan control over one-third of the Kashmir region, while India retained control over the remaining two-thirds. The two clashed over Kashmir in 1965 and 1971. In 1971, India came to the aid of East Pakistan's independence efforts and fought against Pakistani forces, defeating them and thereby enabling East Pakistan to become Bangladesh. Between 1847 and 1971 was but a century and a quarter in India's immense span. However, it is the one everyone would like most to forget, and cannot.

At independence, India's administrative system was more efficient and less corrupt than that of most other former colonial countries. Jawaharlal Nehru, the first prime minister, promoted a policy of global nonalignment and is recognized as one of the founders of the Nonaligned Movement. Eventually, geopolitical issues brought India to align itself with the former Soviet Union in response to the regional threat posed by China and the United States's support for Pakistan because of its location next to Afghanistan and the former Soviet Union.

In 1962, India and China fought a war over a border dispute, leaving India humiliated and shaken by the Chinese aggression. India still claims sovereignty over areas that were taken by the Chinese. The two Asian giants remain wary of each other to this day.

Nehru died in 1964 and was succeeded briefly by Lal Bahadur Shastri, who died in January 1966. Nehru's daughter, Indira Gandhi, was appointed prime minister in the same month by the Congress party chiefs, who assumed that she would be easy to manipulate. Were they ever wrong.

Mrs. Gandhi (no relation to Mahatma Gandhi) had two sons, Sanjay and Rajiv. A shrewd, calculating, and very capable politician, Mrs. Gandhi became one of India's strongest leaders and is often referred to as "Mother India." She held power for more than sixteen years. She preserved India's role as the leader of the Nonaligned Movement. This came at some cost in friendly relations with the small countries that India borders, and Indian politicians often meddled in their internal affairs by trying to bring about political alignments that they felt were best for India. Sri Lanka in particular rankles at India's Big Sister approach—indeed, Indira Gandhi had made plans to invade Sri Lanka and install a puppet government more to her liking, but the plans' troop trains turned back when she was assassinated.

India's domestic problems were no less than its external ones. Many relate to uncontrolled population. In the early 1970s, the oil crisis combined with droughts to ignite strikes throughout the country. In 1975, Mrs. Gandhi declared a state of emergency, suspended basic rights, and jailed her opponents. During the emergency her eldest son, Sanjay, tried to implement a forced sterilization program throughout the country, which cost her the election two years later. Sanjay was killed in an air accident in 1980, and many feel that Mrs. Gandhi's political judgment began to unravel thereafter.

The 1977 election was a testimony to the strength of India's commitment to democracy. Morarji Desai, the leader of the Janata Dal opposition party, became prime minister. The Janata Dal was disorganized, and he ruled for only three years. The economy suffered terribly. Mrs. Gandhi was reelected in 1980 by an overwhelming majority. Her younger son, Rajiv, then became the heir apparent.

The early 1980s were characterized by communal unrest, the most notable of which was the demand by militant Sikhs that an independent Sikh state called Khalistan be split off from the state of Punjab. In 1983, Mrs. Gandhi sent the Indian Army into the Golden Temple in Amritsar, the holiest temple for Sikhs, to arrest a cell of heavily armed radicals. This resulted in riots and violence all over the region. Mrs. Gandhi was assassinated by her own Sikh bodyguards in October 1984. Stability in Punjab is fragile to this day.

Rajiv Gandhi was swept into power as the result of the sympathy vote. He brought a fresh, pragmatic vigor to the prime ministry. His drive for modernization inaugurated the economic overhaul we witness in India today. Indeed, the three themes of his plan are still the core of liberalization today: eliminating import restrictions, encouraging modern technologies, and creating new industries and businesses. Their initial momentum was during Rajiv's administration by accusations of bribery and corruption, particularly the so-called Bofors Scandal. In this it was alleged that a Swedish arms manufacturer bribed various prominent Indians, most of whom were close friends of the prime minister. Rajiv was forced out of power in 1989.

He was succeeded by V. P. Singh, who lasted as prime minister less than a year. Singh was succeeded by Chandra Shekar, who also barely lasted a year. During the 1991 elections, while on a campaign stop in the state of Tamil Nadu, Rajiv Gandhi was assassinated by a suicide bomber sent by the Tamil Tigers, a radical Tamil group demanding a separate state in Sri Lanka. This second change of government by bullet points up India's problem with its leaders becoming personality cults, particularly members of the Nehru family, which has provided three of India's seven prime ministers.

A solitude-loving, somewhat dour academic named Narasimha Rao assumed leadership of the Congress party after Gandhi's assassination and led it to victory in 1991. His government initiated widespread economic reforms, including reducing export and import barriers, dismantling some of the swollen bureaucracy, making the currency partially convertible, and eliminating the black market for foreign currency and gold. Efforts were also made to privatize or increase the efficiencies of unprofitable state companies. Finance Minister Manmohan Singh has been successful in beginning to dismantle the License Raj, India's intricate system of govern-ment control of the economy through permits and quotas. (Since this is the most important subject for this book, the purely economic aspects of the Rao-Singh reforms are discussed in greater detail below.)

Economic improvement was dramatic for India; not so political. Kash-mir again became an issue as Pakistan-backed secessionist militants rose against the Indian army, accusing the army of over-zealous activities, including human rights abuses against the militants and protesters in the region. A near war in early 1992 was barely avoided by diplomacy. Today, Kashmiri militants remain strong; the Kashmir issue is not likely to be resolved soon.

Other internal problems also plague India. Hindu–Muslim rivalries have been exploited by some political parties, primarily the BJP (Bharatiya Janata party), a staunch *hindutva* or Hindu supremacist. The BJP and its paramilitary RSS advocate religion-based policies that would elevate the position of Hindus at the expense of Muslims and other minorities. Many outsiders sense that much of the BJP's emphasis on age-old Hindu values is in part a rebellion against the market reforms being made by the Rao government.

In December 1992, the BJP led Hindu mobs who destroyed a mosque in Ayodhya, a small town in central Uttar Pradesh. Because of its identity as the birthplace of the god Rama, Hindus had long vowed their intention to rebuild a temple on the same site. The Hindus believed that centuries before, Moghul emperors razed several Rama temples to build mosques in this area. The destruction of the Babri Mosque sparked riots between Hindus and Muslims all over India, notably in Mumbai, where hundreds died on both sides. Later, no evidence was found that a Rama statue had ever existed on the mosque site, although one may have existed nearby.

The BJP's fervent call for a pure Hindu state was overwhelmingly rebuffed by the Indian voters in the December 1993 elections. While religious tensions, from all evidence of history, will never really dissipate, their source today is more a matter of ambivalence or even hostility at the ideas of equal economic opportunity for all and the replacement of spiritual gain with material gain.

India has been obliged to address its policies of reserving spaces in colleges and government jobs for lower caste Hindus, Muslims, and other minorities. As more Indians vie for limited education slots and government jobs, the fuse of minority favoritism is never far from the religious flame.

Despite—or perhaps because of—India's social tensions and external border disputes, India is moving forward economically. Foreign investment has poured steadily into the country, and Indian companies are competing more strongly in global markets. Economic gains have made possible improved standards of living for nearly everyone, although whether they will be achieved socially is an entirely different matter. Rao retained power through several no-confidence votes because his economic policies have brought clear and tangible improvements.

HISTORICAL THEMES THAT AFFECT BUSINESS TODAY

Indian business is preoccupied with three themes that do not enter much into business thinking elsewhere. These are (1) the proper role of power and punishment in preserving social order, (2) foreigners ignoring the fact that Indians successfully transited over 1,000 years ago the market and globalized economy phases of business development that most visiting business people fancy as "modern," and (3) the disastrous consequences of misapplying Western theories to Indian life, as exemplified in the License Raj that nearly ruined India's economy.

These are complicated issues, and they mandate a fairly thorough look if one is to understand the philosophy of business evolving in India today. Without understanding India as India, the whole point of doing business there will be missed. India is not a market. It is an education in the disasters that can befall anyone once they stop being true to their roots.

Power and Social Order

The origins of India's complex modern concepts of power and control can be traced to early Indian ideas underlying the gods as kings (*devarajas*) and the state as the theater of power play. Both of these ideas are central to the various Indian theories of power that have emerged over time.

According to Brahminism, the individual is born into a station in life in which he or she has to follow precise rules of conduct, deference to superiors, and of avoidance of contamination by subordinates. The Indian caste system decreed that certain people could be *rajas*, or rulers, but that they need not at the same time be religious figures. Of the four *varnas*, the brahmins, in their role as religious/educational leaders, were the elite, but this gave them neither political power nor material benefits (even today there are many quite poor brahmins). The Brahmins were supposed to pursue their religious obligations without the need for social burdens, although many very definitely lined their pockets from their teachings and sacerdotal acts.

The ksatriyas, or princes and warriors, were distinctly second in the social hierarchy, even though it was their *varna* to govern society, a seemingly omnipotent role. The Brahminist concept of kingship made a distinction between the sacred role of priests and the godlike role of kings. Indian gods are very strong in image content but much weaker in power content. The rules of duty and obligation for everyone are determined by their *Dhamma*, their fate as determined by their obedience to those selfsame rules in previous incarnations. The specifics of conduct may vary according to the station of the individual, but the ideal of behavior itself was to adhere to one's own particular varna and *jati*—one's caste category and subcaste group—and not some universally admired or other-worldly standard, as is so often the case in Middle Eastern and European cultures.

According to India's most ancient and seminal code of laws, the *Law of Manu*, "It is better to discharge one's own appointed way incompletely than to perform the appointed way of another; for he who lives according to the law of another caste is thereby instantly excluded from his own."

The caste system had one liberating effect: It separated status from power to a degree unknown in other Asian societies. People who belonged to a high caste or subcaste could (and very often still do) have less power than those of lower status. Indeed, the brahmins, who had the highest status, clearly had less physical power than the ksatriyas. The gap between power and status was possible because Hindu culture was more explicit in declaring that gradations among people should be based on the boundary lines between purity and defilement, between cleanliness and abomination.

In most cases, the dividing line between *jati* (subcaste) categories was that of family and food. One could only marry a member of the same *jati*. One's food had to be prepared by a certain type of person, and, more particularly, there were rules for who could give and who could receive food—that is, who could nurture whom. Superiors had the right to be served first, but they were expected to pass on their leftovers to subordinates—wives, children, servants, and other dependents.

Today, one of the most intact and functioning relics of this system is the Buddhist clergy in Sri Lanka. When the early followers of Buddhism discovered that better survival was to be had by cozying close to kings rather than begging as the Buddha himself did, they inaugurated a long institutionalization process that ended up with them monasticized to such a degree that they forbid themselves to have any contact with everyday people. They went from asking for the street's leftovers to asking for the king's, then supping with him, and finally demanding his food to be served to them first, but separately from his table. Centuries of removal from powerful kings has rendered Sri Lanka's Buddhist clergy more attuned to the repasts that come with pastoral care, but they still eat on a high dais, first before others, only the best, and seated on a white cloth that no one else may use. There is not an iota of power in these roles, yet prime ministers and haughty politicians fumble and fawn to serve them thus.

The distinction between status and power in Indian culture made it possible for rulers to be pragmatic to the point of self-serving ruthlessness. Free of the constraints of having to appear holy (roles reserved for the brahmins), ksatriyas could concentrate on managing power. Since it was their Dhamma to be rulers, ksatriyas were expected to be masters in using force to uphold the social order. It was above all their duty to punish in order to make sure that people adhered to their caste-determined roles. As the *Law of Manu* puts it, "The whole world is kept in order by punishment, for a guiltless man is hard to find. Through the fear of punishment the whole world is called to enjoy its blessings."

The *Law of Manu* emphasized that kings should harshly punish transgressors not because it was in their nature to be harsh by virtue of their Dhamma, but because maintaining social order required a temporal force to uphold the divine laws of the universe. The *Law of Manu* decrees, "If the King did not, without tiring, inflict punishment on those worthy of being punished, the stronger would roast the weaker, like fish on a spit, the crow would eat the sacrificial cake, and the dog would lick the viands, ownership would not stay with anyone, the lower would usurp the place of the higher."

All of this without a shred of actual evidence that things really happen this way.

The ruler's obligation to coerce through punishment was the basis of the rules of punishment or *danda*. These were deemed necessary to uphold the social order and to help people achieve their Dhamma. If carried out properly, punishment could hasten along *moksha*, or salvation.

According to traditional Brahminic thought, the state has six basic functions: (1) protect the people from internal and external dangers; (2) maintain the common law as embodied in the customs and usage of the land; (3) uphold the social order; (4) levy taxes; (5) promulgate laws and resolve conflicts; and (6) promote the people's happiness by performing the proper rituals and sacrifices.

The concept of *danda* stressed punishment and the ruler's power to coerce. Indeed, there was a great enthusiasm by the author of the *Laws of Manu* for the idea that rulers needed to punish people for their own good: "Punishment alone governs all created beings, punishment alone protects them, punishment watches over them where they sleep; the wise declare punishment to be identical with the law."

This legitimation of violence and coercion lies at the core of the Brahminic concept of power. Yet it would appear to stand in sharp contrast to the spirit of nonviolence that runs through so much of Indian religious thought. How can these two ideals of behavior and power be reconciled?

The Indian idea of power insists that there should be a division between religion and politics. Religion was the supreme force that held society together and dictated people's obligations and duties. The place of politics was more ambivalent. On one hand, power was the ultimate force needed to uphold social order; hence rulers had to perform society's dirty work using coercion. On the other hand, because of the ruler's obligation to use *danda* to uphold the social order, there could be no limits to the power of the state. Because rulers had to be concerned about whether their subjects were following their Dhamma, they were permitted to pry into the private lives of their people.

This is why the Indians did not develop the notions of personal life, privacy, or individual rights until the British introduced them.

While early Indians could think of power and politics as matters of only secondary importance to spiritual attainment, they could at the same time accept the right of power to penetrate every aspect of their lives and to dispense punishment from which there could be no appeal: "Whatever a king does is right. That is a settled rule because the world is entrusted to him on account of his majesty and his benignity towards living creatures. As a husband though feeble, must constantly be worshipped by his wives, in the same way a ruler, though worthless, must constantly be worshipped by his subjects."

Manu himself, who lived about 1900–1800 B.C., was the first philosopher in this tradition. The tradition ended with one of Asia's great masters of political thought, Kautilya (c. 400–320 B.C.), the prime minister to Chandragupta Maurya, founder of the Mauryan empire, and one of India's greatest, geographically as well as culturally.

Kautilya based his philosophy on the Brahminic notion that the state was created by divine and not human action. Hence the ruler's duty in applying *danda* was helping people achieve their Dhamma. In his key work, the *Artha Shastra*, Kautilya asserted the need for deception and trickery. He did not believe in mere force or the ruthless application of laws. In fact, he praised explicitly the value of voluntary support: "The acquisition of the help of local communities is better than the acquisition of an army, a friend, or profits."

Kautilya viewed the objective of state power as the creation of a strong, centralized government, supported by an extensive bureaucratic machine but sensitive to local usage and customs. Such a power structure was necessary to protect against external and domestic enemies and to guard against the uncontrollable horrors of "fire, flood, pestilence, famine, rats, tigers, serpents, and demons."

The key idea in Kautilya's thinking is the idea that, while governments may be troublesome, not to have them brings disaster. The absence of government would mean anarchy and brute power, but more important (to him), the abomination of living in a society without castes or divinely ordained distinctions. The pure and the impure might mix, and all of the evils of contamination would appear as taboos were violated: "A kingdom without a sovereign is like a river without water, a forest without vegetation, a cow without a cowherd. No man loves his own kind in a rulerless state, but each slays and devours the other daily, like fish. Atheists and materialists exceed the limits of their caste, assume domination over others, there being no king to exercise control over them. The king, discerning good and evil, protects his kingdom, for bereft of him, the country is enveloped in darkness."

Power and punishment have come to be seen in Indian history as necessary to each other as rulers and ruled.

The Ignorant Colonials

When the British imposed themselves over the huge Indian subcontinent, they assumed that Indian society was impervious to technical and economic progress. Hindus, living within a rigid caste system and following ancient traditions, seemed to authorities such as Lord Cromer as "people living on a lower plane," who were ill-suited for the adoption of new industrial forms and technologies.

Such sentiments came naturally to Europeans, who were shocked by the political decay as well as massive and deplorable poverty of the society they now commanded. They did not reckon with an India that, in the years dating at least to the time of Alexander the Great, attracted the brightest minds of China, Korea, and Arabia to study mathematics, medicine, and philosophy. Traditional European and American conceptions of India as a permanently backward and inwardly focused society ignore the reality that India was a successful business and mercantile civilization 1,000 to 3,000 years ago, just as Islam produced the first scientific revolution a half-millenium before Copernicus and Newton came along.

In the industrial arts as well, particularly the manufacture of spices and textiles, India developed strong export markets as far away as the Roman Empire. After the fall of Rome, Indians also established strong commercial ties with their Byzantine, Persian, and Arab successors, forming a wide-ranging array of trading partners in Europe and, most particularly, the Middle East. By the thirteenth century, Indians also had developed world-class spinning wheel technology, and some of their products, such as Kashmiri shawls, were prized even by the emperors of China.

India's influence in Asia grew from early trading ties established by fourth-century Dravidians with southern China and much of Southeast Asia. These traders brought with them not only products but also irrigation techniques and cultural influence, first in the formats of Buddhism and Hinduism and later Islam. By 1500, an estimated 1,000 Gujerati merchants had settled in Malaysian Melaka, which emerged as a critical center for trade in spices, foodstuffs, handicrafts, and textiles from Arabia to Indonesia and China. By this time Southeast Asia, in at least cultural and economic terms, was essentially a part of a "greater India."

But, as in the case of China, various forces—some political, some cultural—began to retard India's technological and economic progress. Under the Mughal empire, which came to power in 1526, the suppressed Hindu elites clung increasingly to the religious and caste systems as a means of excluding the new rulers from dominant social institutions and maintaining their own superiority over other Hindus. "Although the Muslim ruled the infidels," notes historian Romila Thapar, "the infidels called them barbarians."

The growing influence of the caste system sharply limited the progress of a market-based economy. High-caste Indians stayed largely outside the commercial sphere altogether, and virtually every activity was broken down into ever more specialized categories. The overall lack of mobility—an unwillingness even among Muslims to break the caste patterns—hindered the progress of many of the very classes such as artisans who in Britain, continental Europe, and Japan played critical roles in commercial and industrial development. Under the caste system, for example, even interest rates for the vaishyas (traders) and shudras (artisans) were set at twice or higher than rates for the brahmins, who generally disdained new commercial ventures.

The enormous relative wealth of India, as it did in China, also deflected interest in foreign trade, often a critical element in spurring both technical improvement and changes in the social order. The Mughal emperor, noted an Italian traveler in 1624, was indeed a "great and wealthy king whose tax revenues at the time of the great Moghul emperor Akbar were more than fifteen times greater than those available to Britain's James I." Even as late as 1757, the British conqueror Lord Clive compared the silk-producing city of Murshidalvad in Bengal, now little more than a small village north of present-day Calcutta, favorably to London in size, population, and wealth of its merchant class.

Again like China, India's loss of economic control began first at its periphery. European power grew, but Indian traders, lacking the aggressive backing of their state, were reduced to serving as middlemen for newcomers such as the Portuguese, whose state actively promoted their activities through both missions of exploration and direct military action.

The European states also increasingly took advantage of their growing technological lead, sometimes improving on innovations and knowledge that originated in India. The very ships that the Portuguese explorer Vasco da Gama used to circumnavigate Africa employed both Indian navigational technology and a pilot from Gujarat whose experience with sailing African waters exceeded that of his European counterparts.

Perhaps even more critical was the widening gap in spinning technology. As late as the eighteenth century, India's textile industry, using the traditional spinning wheel technology, was still competitive enough to export products to Europe, as well as to serve a vast domestic market. But by the early nineteenth century, technological improvements pioneered by the manufacturers of Manchester—as well as new restrictions on the import of Indian textiles—were bringing on the virtual annihilation of an entire class of native weavers, whose bones, the British governor general would report in 1835, were "bleaching the plains of India."

The British hegemony, which started in the latter half of the eighteenth century, transformed India far more than such peripheral trading diasporas as the Dutch or the Portuguese. The empire needed modern ports and cities to service its expansion, and within a century British-developed cities such as Bombay and Calcutta had all but eclipsed the older centers of urbanization, remaining the leading centers for Indian economic life to this day.

British commercial dominance also overcame the last elements of influence held by Indian merchants throughout Asia, essentially detaching the subcontinent from direct access to its traditional markets. Even more important, British imports, most particularly textiles, swamped Indian markets, devastating the huge village-based economy that, as recently as the early nineteenth century, had been exporting its products to England.

Soon one of the world's oldest trading civilizations had become little more than a satellite of Great Britain. The imperial interest controlled major industries from jute to coal mining and treated the Indians as if they existed purely to further British commercial advantage. Between 1834 and 1934, roughly 30 million Indians were sent out as indentured servants to work on the empire's plantations, in the mines, and on other projects, often being subject to the most deplorable conditions.

India's overall domestic economy received similarly one-sided treatment. Despite the favored position of British industrial products, India ran a huge trade surplus with the imperial metropolis and the rest of the world. By 1914, according to estimates by economist Susan Strange, these surpluses were essentially propping up the entire financial structure of the empire itself. British interests carried away the profits from India's vast natural resources and agricultural products. Bullion earned in India found its way into the coffers of London and from there was reinvested in the expanding British world economic network.

Thus the indescribable mix of humiliation and fear when in 1991 Indians saw the near-last of their bullion entering an airplane for London. London *again*. Indians realized that they had gone disastrously wrong in the most fundamental aspects of economic thinking. How did this happen?

The License Raj and the Failure of Trying to Think Western

The first place Indians looked was the License Raj. Manmohan Singh, Prime Minister Rao's new finance minister, had way back in the early 1980s written a series of trenchant critiques of the License Raj. His analysis—and variants published by others—was roughly that socialism was not a native idea from any of India's ancestral cultures. India has always been republican, even in the time of strong kings. Socialism was Western in origin and suppositions, going back as far as medieval monastery days. Misapplying a Western social ideal to India had the same effect as placing a brick on a balloon: The balloon will not burst, it will distort into a grotesque shape.

For a long time after Independence, technology and innovation were not perceived as essential elements to economic growth. Only in the past decade or so has there come to be a generally held view that companies must continuously reinvent themselves, discard old ideas, withdraw or change products according to the needs of the market, try new approaches to different management problems, and change organizational structures.

Throughout the License Raj era, the organized sector of Indian industry saw little use for innovation. The modern use of the term—"creation and introduction of new ways of doing things, better use of goods, and improving the efficiency of services and systems"—was not part of the business

260 Doing Business in Today's India

ethos. The emphasis was not on markets and customers, but on achieving safe positions of monopoly in the market. Much effort went into institutionalizing this belief in license terms—pre-empting production capacities, closing the market to other entrants, and so on. Factories were intentionally set up for suboptimal production to intimidate competitors from planning too big. Companies grew by diversification rather than expansion in response to the threat of limitations that might be imposed by the government.

The upshot was that industries failed to develop core competencies; instead they developed defense competencies. They did not invest in research and development or experiment with new ideas and methods; they invested in lawyers and bribes. Manufacturing took a low place in the hierarchy of corporate functions—again that distant echo of the Brahminist control mechanism that mind was better than matter. Production was a relatively low-level function in most companies; the liaison manager in Delhi was much more important in the scheme of things, and after him the finance manager.

There was no reason for any meaningful attempt to control costs or to improve systems and processes. Pricing was based on cost—plus formulas over which the consumer had no choice—yet another distant echo, this time to the centuries-ingrained thinking of petty traders in the marketplace who saw nothing beyond buying low and selling high. Because production capacities were so limited, most businesses concentrated on premium segments of markets, not the mass markets. To this day, many Indian businesses look on the consumables sector as low and petty.

The carryover into financial thinking was just as unproductively elitist: There was little experiment with new ways of raising finances, alternative methods of working capital management, and even less interest in international markets or managing foreign exchange.

All of this had a smothering effect the further down the business ladder all of this corpulence descended. Small industries had no safe harbor provided by government controls; they had to fight in the market with each other and with much larger producers. They were—the small business entrepreneurial spirit being what it is—much more innovative out of expediency than the famed companies whose names still dominate India's business news pages. Some targeted specific products at special market segments, others devised novel means to maneuver money out of the taxman's view, and still others developed innovative distribution and communication methods. Some embraced the socialist ideals by increasing worker participation in all of the activities of the organization.

The defect of family management—people managing organizations be-cause of parentage and not their ability—did not adversely affect small business as devastatingly as it did the corporate sector. Small industries had to perform in an environment where there were many local imitators and competitors. If they could not compete, they did not survive. This was not so in the organized sector because corporations there enjoyed relatively guaranteed markets and powerful barriers protecting them. This encouraged the perpetuation of inefficient family members in top management positions in the organized sector. Many are still there. Today the combined effects of attrition from age and the market economy are weeding them out.

THE HISTORICAL IMPORTANCE OF THE 1991 ECONOMIC REFORMS

Today's market reforms arose as abruptly and appear to be proceeding as inexorably as the Buddha's religious reforms in the fifth century B.C.—and for some of the same reasons.

Recall that the first time a substantial middle class arose in India was during the Vajjian Confederacy, during the time of the Buddha. The known economic causes for this development were a broader and more even distribution of wealth resulting from the rise of regional identities, a protectorate idea of governance, a tax system inspired by the need for mutual defense, the increasing meaninglessness of the rigid brahminical caste system, and sizable increases in regional trade. Some economists regard these as essential conditions for the rise of a middle class, since one of their consequences is removing monetary and commodity controls from the hands of a priestly class and placing them in the hands of traders. Certainly that happened in the Vajjian/Magadha days, and it could be loosely argued that they have arisen in India today since the demise of Indira Gandhi.

With the economic changes of the Vajjian era there also came a profound new attitude toward religion. Buddhism, Jainism, and the trans-formation of Brahminism into Hinduism all seem to have resulted from a major shift in social consciousness from priest-centered to royalty-centered and from deity-centered to goods-centered.

In India of the 1990s, reaction against priestly religion has not been the major catalyst for change that it was in the past; instead, the catalyst is the stimulus of international imagery, especially via television. Before 1991, so much economic activity in India was government-manipulated and so many jobs the grist of political mills that secrecy and intrigue became become an ever-present way to extract a share of the spoils. Religious politics simply made economic politics more shrill (to say nothing of becoming steadily more entertaining).

Between the assassination of Indira Gandhi and 1991, the biggest single religious divide in India had come to be between the upper caste Hindus (of whom there are some 525 million) and the Muslims (110 million). Its roots lay in the Kashmir and Pakistan residues after independence, but matters slowly heated to the boiling point as Hindus felt their control on power, and the proper social structure as they saw it, erode through economic change and the aspirations of the non-scheduled castes for real power. From these sprang one of the two principle challenges to rule of the Congress party.

The other root was the wretched excesses of local politicians shamelessly mulcting the public purse for their own families' welfare. Religious politics are always dangerous in India, but they have relatively little effect on economic change. Pouring the public purse into one's own pocket is very different: It can turn the cry for political change not only into economic change but also class change. Today's reforms are as much attributable to the rise of India's middle class as to the blaggarding (blackguarding) of the culprits who lined their pockets with public office. While the BJP is often thought of as the party representing the values of the impecunious Hindu small-shopkeeper class, its real effect is to favor economic reforms deregulating the domestic economy, which work to the net benefit of the mobile and professional middle class.

Many people who become aware of the nuances of India's complex society are surprised that today's internationalized upper middle class professionals ("Maruti yups" in their own self-parodying terminology) are attracted to the seemingly yesteryear-worshipping BJP. One would assume them to be unimpressed with any political policy that hinders their economic mobility. Indeed, if foreign firms were not permitted in India (an oft-stated BJP ideal), the middle-class segment would have to relinquish their ideal of self-motivated market-astute wealth-building and revert to the old, now odious, practice of wealth-building through patronage.

Class Mobility and Caste Change

There are several reasons for this. One is that affirmative-action policies are as mistrusted by some classes of Indians as they are by their counterpart classes in the United States. Both of these classes tend to be self-motivated, entrepreneurial, and hostile to government bureaucracies. In the run-up to the 1996 elections, both Congress and the BJP suffered from the divisions raised by attempts to ameliorate the old, deep antagonisms of the caste system. The ideas and practices of caste that penetrated throughout Indian society from their relatively innocuous origins in the *varna* system of Aryan days have today come to thrive on some 3,000 minute caste classifications based solely on parentage. In all-too-common cases caste dictates whom people can marry and what sorts of work they can do.

The Congress party attacked the problem with a remedy that turned out, politically if not economically, to be worse than the disease. Congress set aside university admission quotas and government jobs for *dalits* (outcastes) whom Hindi society considered too contemptible to even allow into the caste system.

Whether good or bad in intent, in actual fact the Congress quota system for these scheduled castes happened to arrive at a very bad time economically. Four decades of slow-growing socialist economics had been strongly outpaced by fast-growing populations, and among the fastest growing were the *dalits*. The economy's slow growth made sinecures of any kind extremely valuable by the late 1980s. When the *dalits* pressured for more set-asides, the upper castes resisting vehemently.

By 1990, pro-quota parties whose power base of lower caste Hindu and Muslim votes began beating both the Congress party and the BJP in state elections in the Hindi belt. The administration of Prime Minister V. P. Singh was outsted. This handed free-market reformers in the central government a genuine dilemma: If people were convinced that wealth flows only from patronage and it is their turn at the trough, it will be very difficult to convince them of the virtues of a market economy that rejects patronage of any kind. Hence no matter what showers of praise were falling on India from the pages of the international business press, at home the reforms were on very shaky ground.

July 1991

In the spring of 1991 India was an economic wreck. For years the country's politicians had sustained its tepid growth by borrowing from abroad. Two attempts at reform, one in the late 1970s under Indira Gandhi and the other in the mid-1980s under her son Rajiv, did not address the economy's most critical shortcoming: productivity. By May 1991, India's foreign exchange reserves were down to $1 billion—enough for barely twenty days of imports. India's politicians, despite decades of lip service to the principles of socialism and democracy, acted almost entirely at the behest of special-interest groups—most notably themselves.

The mentality of co-opting social unhappiness with subsidies has a long history in India. The kings of Magdha and Kosala in the Buddha's time granted merchants monopolies in exchange for loyalty—and then charged them taxes to pay for the armies that protected the monopolies. Today, India's state and local governments spend about 60 percent of their budgets on salaries for civil servants while stinting on the infrastructure and services that benefit society at large.

Now they are looking to overseas investors to come to the rescue to accomplish what they did not do themselves. Of the national government's budget, two-thirds is sidetracked to service debt. India's system of regulation, union, and trade protection has enriched favored companies and certain pampered work forces at the expense of the multitudes of firms without political clout. For the moment it is politically inexpedient to change things, and the 1996 budget reflects that in continued subsidies to those who enjoyed them all too well in the past—labor, farmers, bureaucrats.

Having taken a long look at what foreign investment did for Asia's tigers, some politicians think that the same thing is certain to happen in India merely by loosening trade and investment restrictions.

That hope is far from assured. In the 1960s, India's industrial output rose 5.5 percent a year—about one-half of the rate in neighboring Pakistan, less than one-half of the rate in Thailand, and one-third of the rate in South Korea. Throughout the 1970s, India continued to underperform its Asian neighbors. Although its performance picked up in the 1980s, the increase came from capital efficiency, not dramatic increases in labor productivity. Between 1960 and 1985, India's manufacturing productivity declined by an average of 0.4 percent a year. By the late 1980s, much of India's ruling elite complacently asserted that India was doing rather well. The "Hindu rate of growth" (a phrase coined to describe India's 3 percent annual GNP growth) had, after all, been nearly doubled during the 1980s.

India's overstretched credit line in the 1980s reached its effective limits by 1991. In June of that year, Indians saw on television their precious gold bullion being trucked from the Central Bank for shipment to the Bank of England as loan security. The psychological blow was devastating. Gold is the very last thing a traditional Indian family parts with in the face of catastrophe.

Subcontinent Supernova: India First Implodes, Then Explodes

Indians love conspiracy theories. They are, after all, free entertainment. One of them is that the media's lavish extensive coverage of the bullion heading to sea was part of a strategy by India's leaders to attack central planning at the passion level rather than the rational level. India has always changed more dramatically and quickly that way. Many of India's new wave of opinion leaders were media people with a significant interest of their own in globalization.

For whatever reasons, the system they wanted to demolish was as untenable as the Soviet Union's. Its four cornerstones were socialism, secularism, nonalignment, and democracy. Its socialism originated as the brainchild of the most advanced theories of economic development fashionable in the West during the 1950s—meaning that the ideas themselves were largely framed by young men back in the 1930s who had finally risen to power by the 1950s.

The theory of this system was that India's scarce resources needed to be directed to the country's socially most productive uses: poverty alleviation and industrialization. The Indian capital markets could not be trusted to work in the public's interest, and even less trustworthy were the international capital markets.

The three main pillars rising from this belief were (a) a high degree of government ownership of industry and banks, (b) high levels of government regulation of privately owned industrial businesses, and (c) tight controls on foreign trade and investment. India in essence tried to grow by eliminating competition.

Government ownership of industrial enterprises in India came to be the most extensive in the noncommunist world. A number of business categories were designated "core industries" in which only government-owned firms would be allowed to operate. These included defense, atomic energy, railways, airlines and aircraft building, electricity generation, and the distribution of coal, iron, steel, and heavy machinery. Two waves of bank nationalization, in 1969 and 1977, added virtually all of the financial system to the government's portfolio.

These measures had numerous counterproductive economic consequences, two of which were devastating. First, state firms continued to put a big dent in India's public finances. In 1991, nearly one-half of the state-owned firms were in the red. Government money was siphoned away by both direct and hidden subsidies. In 1991, about 30 percent of the capital investment in state-owned heavy industry was financed not by businesses but by taxpayers.

Second, many of the state industries were so basic to the economy that their inefficiencies were transmitted to the rest of the economy through high prices, bad products, and poor services.

The License Raj

The private sector was not much better off. The government had set up a system that required industrial firms to obtain a government-granted license before they could set up a production line, add equipment, refurbish capital goods, or convert a plant into one making an even slightly different product because of technological change or shifting market demand. This License Raj stifled India throughout the 1970s and 1980s.

To the License Raj requirements were added special restrictions designed largely by politicians to benefit their friends. Big firms had to get clearance from an anti-monopoly regulator before they could apply for an industrial license. They often had to wait two or three years for this single signature. Small firms encouraged protections designed to thwart anyone else from making competing products.

Even worse, anyone in business was assured that, no matter how much money it lost, the business could not legally be shut down without the consent of its entire workforce. "Sick units" (as bankrupt companies are officially called) numbered almost 225,000 in 1991. Since bankruptcy was next to impossible, many sick firms were palmed off on a government agency that, handily enough, employed local politicians' family members and friends. Many others were simply abandoned. Their owners stripped what assets they could, leaving their still-employed workers with nothing to make and, conveniently enough, no equipment with which to make it. The main beneficiaries of the License Raj were the bureaucrats who devised it.

Government domination of industry was guaranteed by laws which made sure that foreigners did not bring in unneeded products or divert needed resources. Imports were curtailed as much as possible. Imported consumer goods were flatly outlawed, to the anguished howls of Coca Cola. Capital and intermediate goods faced a phalanx of restrictions. Anything that made it through these restrictions was burdened with some of the world's highest tariffs: over 100 percent on every kind of good, reaching as high as 400 percent on some. FDI was minimized through a licensing regime that was even more draconian than what Indian bureaucrats foisted off onto their own countrymen.

This program was perversely successful. By 1990, India was less tied to the world economy in terms of exports, imports, foreign investment, and technology transfer than any other country in Asia—except North Korea.

Mr. Singh's Reforms

When Rao became prime minister in June 1991, he appointed as finance minister an immaculately bearded and beturbaned Sikh named Manmohan Singh who on television, in the press, and in global financial meetings looked, breathed, and talked the very soul of financial probity.

Dr. Singh was an academic economist who had worked at the World Bank. As early as the 1970s he had written a book asserting that India's anti-foreign bias was harmful. He went on to serve in high posts in several Indian governments that had staunchly backed—and even added to—the very system the Rao government set out to dismantle. Singh knew it so well that he knew exactly where to begin: the License Raj.

Not to steal from his credit, India's macroeconomic crisis of 1990–1991 would have demanded decisive action from whatever government took power after the mid-1991 elections. India's overseas creditors—the IMF, commercial bankers, and grant-in-aid governments—would probably have demanded macroeconomic adjustments anyway.

Mr. Singh's emergency budget of July 1991 launched a direct assault on India's most grotesque economic distortions. He took direct aim at the License Raj, the ultimate source of India's budgetary problems. He whittled away at India's entire central-planning system over the next few years.

During the first two years the Indian economy barely grew in real terms. Manufacturing output actually shrank in 1991–1993. But by 1995, real economic growth had reached 6 percent and was accelerating. Industrial output was up to 8 percent a year. The dollar value of exports rose by more than 20 percent in 1994, and by the end of that year the country's foreign exchange reserves had zoomed to more than $20 billion. India faced the irony of foreign confidence becoming so high that too much money was pouring in, making it hard to keep the rupee and the money supply from pushing inflation upward. Overseas investment in equities and factories was $100 million in 1991 and $1.5 billion in 1995. Indian companies, until 1992 forbidden to raise money in the international capital markets, raised more than $2.4 billion in 1994.

Reforming India's Government

Prime Minister Rao's labors were more ponderous and difficult to measure. His initial problem was communicating the reformist spirit at the top to the labyrinthine administration of the government below. The bonfire of the License Raj barely singed the piles of paperwork mounded up awaiting bureaucratic approvals. Although central-government approval for an investment was no longer required for many business procedures, the forms, and form-filling, still awaited the many that remained.

However, Rao faced a more serious matter: State bureaucratic power still thrived in India's federal system and was very hard to exterminate. Each Indian state mimicked the old central-government control apparatus, although the licenses required by the states focused on practical matters such as sewage and telephone connections rather than complying with the decrees of economic planners. The ability of state politics to sidetrack central-government reforms was (and still is) daunting. In 1995 a survey by the Confederation of Indian Industry found that a power-plant project required seventeen approvals by nineteen different government agencies.

Trickling Up

The pathos of Indian socialism was how little it did to improve the lot of the poor it was supposed to relieve. Income inequalities in the rural areas widened over Indian socialism's 45 years, while there was only modest improvement in the lives of almost everyone else. As an old joke puts it, one-half of the people did terribly and the other one-half got by on badly.

One surprise accompanying the liberalization of the 1990s was how quickly the structures of Indian society and business were transformed. One reason was that those with any affluence at all to speak of possessed a great deal more of it than the official statistics reported. India's black-market economy cheerfully takes advantage of this, varying between 20 and 50 percent of the official GNP.

The 1990s-era economic changes were even quicker in the cities, especially those most exposed to the world beyond India. None was more exposed than Mumbai, and hence it is a good example of the potential of urban India elsewhere. With 13 million people, Mumbai is India's financial and commercial capital. It has always been money-focused to a much greater degree than the rest of India. After the post-1991 reforms, Mumbai moved out of India's cost-of-living orbit into those of the Middle East and East Asian financial capitals. Business and finance multinationals poured into Mumbai and bid up the prices of the international quality office space and living rentals. Between 1993 and 1996, office and home rents in neighborhoods frequented by expatriates rose 100–150 percent, and few were quoting rupees any more. Selling versus rental prices for office space in the best areas of Mumbai rose tenfold between 1986 and 1996, reaching around $900 per square foot.

Salaries went the same way. Branch managers of local financial companies whose maximum annual salaries reached barely $12,000 were snapped up by foreign financial firms for starting salaries of $40,000. Indian industrial firms faced with manager demands for commensurate salaries complained that the multinationals were in a position to wipe out their profits. The response to this unanticipated talent inflation was twofold. Local companies said the whole thing was a bubble economy and would expire with the next burst of inflation. Business people with a longer view noted that highly skilled labor in Bangalore (computer software) and Hyderabad (drugs, electronic engineering, and automation) were still bargains by world standards and likely to stay that way. This opened up some surprising labor markets, for example, the heavy use of satellite links to tap the talents of Indian software writers who like semi-Western incomes but like them better in Bangalore.

The appetite of regional centers for national-level products and services, especially consumer and financial ones, is growing as fast as Mumbai's rents. In mid-1996, more than 22 million Indians owned shares in companies listed on the country's nineteen shares markets (as stock markets are called in India). A significant portion of these shares are owned by mutual funds.

India's consumer boom has given birth to entirely new modes of financial growth that would have been unheard of a decade ago. Many financial firms today got their start in consumer finance as they emerged (often on the fringes of legality) to meet demands for car, consumer-durables, and retail finance.

Rural Change

The countryside also is changing. City populations have been swelling in part because people are leaving the parched and unproductive land around them—hardly news to urban demographers. What is surprising them is that economic betterment has reached some hitherto pretty neglected places. Migration is but one cause. More important, however, is that the spinoff success of the green revolution raised incomes until many villages could afford electricity and tractors. In Northern India, this spinoff effect was first noticed in the Punjab region, where the canal network the British left behind created transport-vectored wealth spread to Uttar Pradesh, Gujarat, Haryana, and Karnataka. By the early 1980s, farm labor from the desolate, overpopulous, backward Bihar region began migrating to Punjab, where incomes averaged fifty times (*times*, not percent) higher in search of casual work. Today Biharis comprise 85 percent of the work force in Punjab's multitude of bicycle factories. Punjabis promptly took their savings and headed for Mumbai to carve out a minor market niche driving and then owning local taxis. Today Punjabis own fleets of them.

This may be no consolation while arguing with a Mumbai taxi driver over a fare, but he is a ripple on the waves stirred by the rain of poverty in Bihar.

More exalted are the returning NRIs (nonresident Indians) who went away to university and stayed there a generation or more, making reputations for Indian competence and work ethics that give the lie to the lazy-wallah image. NRIs from locales as diverse as Uganda and Kenya, Silicon Valley and Fremont, and the Midlands today have begun to return in numbers sufficiently worthy to inspire property developers to put up retirement villas—guards at the gates and all—near enough to cities to enjoy their conveniences but just far enough from them to enjoy the contentments of the countryside. With touching irony some of the most desirable locations around Hyderabad and Bangalore are the villages recently deserted by the poor on their way to the city.

Population shifts like these inspire shifts in the service industries. Private hospitals have been built in rural areas of the states of Andhra Pradesh and Tamil Nadu by NRI doctors who see enough demand from affluent Indians to support world-class medical care in India itself. The same may be said of the makers of "white goods," the consumer durables (no longer painted white) like washing machines and refrigerators that comprise one of the most sought-after consumer market niches in India, and is all the more volatile because of the furious attention.

Star-TV and Friends

The single biggest influence on the changing views of ordinary Indians has been the rise of television in general and satellite television in particular. It is hard to think of any other country in the world with an economic baseline as low as India's where television had such an enormous impact on people's perception of the way things can be compared with the way they are. By the mid-1990s, perhaps 600 million Indians were watching television on an average day. More often than not it was black-and-white with only a handful of channels, but even watched in community settings, television today reaches 80 percent of India's villagers.

By 1993, India had at least 60,000 cable-television operators. (The actual number is difficult to pin down because of the many illegal operators tapping cables from neighborhood phone poles to feed a few dozen subscribers.) Hong Kong-based Star-TV was avidly eaten up by perhaps 20 million households. Zee TV in Mumbai did Hindi-language programming for Star-TV and then began its own cable networks. Even the state channels responded to competition instead of trying to suppress it, improving their programs and letting India in on the fact that the world did not look, talk, and act like old Hindi movies. In 1996, 72 percent of India's total "adspend" went to television.

All of this is certainly a welcome change from the tepid growth and mediocre quality of consumer products in India when the old-line politicians held sway. These pundits are no less shy when it comes to acknowledging their role as in large part responsible for India's consumer revolution.

The large numbers would not have mattered much had Indian television remained the state monopoly it was in the late 1980s, when exotic, cultured, eons-old India produced some of the most lusterless television in the world. People with even the most modest appreciation of the depths of Indian culture went away shaking their heads. Satellite television changed that.

In years to come, academics and marketers will probably acknowledge that more social change emanating from television affected rural India than urban. In the early 1990s, three-quarters of Indians still lived in some 550,000 villages whose economic and literacy sophistications varied widely but whose ability to absorb visual imagery was the same everywhere. In those days, about one-third were wholly outside the money economy, approximately 40 percent wholly in it, and the rest in between. Today, those with above-subsistence cash levels are so multitudinous—above 300 million— that the absolute size of India's rural market for many products exceeds that of the aggregate city market. In 1984 only 28 percent of the packaged goods sold in India were bought in the countryside, in 1989 the share was 37 percent, and in 1996 it was roughly 55 percent for many high-volume low-yield product categories such as detergents, hand soap, and packaged tea. For other, lower turnover but higher margin products, rural sales are estimated to reach more than 50 percent before the year 2000.

As city dwellers grew richer they substituted purchases of quartz wristwatches for mechanical, VCRs for radios, and so on, leaving manufacturers to refocus their marketing budgets on the rurals. One result was more sophisticated marketers, and another was more sophisticated rurals. These two developments coincided with the rising rural purchasing power. In 1984, rural families spent 87 percent of their budgets on food, clothing, and shelter. By the early 1990s, that share was down to 67 percent. A 1992–1993 survey, barely a year after reforms had had a chance to exert a significant impact, found wealth growth in the countryside to be both accelerating and widening. The better-off farmers were able to buy VCRs and tractors. Washing machines—unheard of in the countryside in the 1980s—were owned by one in ten rural households by 1995.

The atomized nature of India's markets still required innovative marketing. Hindustan Lever, which sells packaged consumer goods such as soap and tea, found that about ten villages are needed to sustain one of its outlets. This meant settling on the largest village in any given aggregation of ten; and that meant, in turn, locating villages with access roads for the distributors' trucks. HL then discovered to their surprise that given sufficient local income levels and the necessary paved roads, rural consumers at any given disposable income level were inclined to buy almost exactly what their urban counterparts did.

This testified to the truly revolutionary change in aspirations that television commercials brought to the countryside. By 1996, low-income rurals accounted for 18 percent of India's lipstick sales, 20 percent of face creams, and 33 percent of nail polish. This level of luxury sales testifies to how thin the veneer of socialism really was. The academics and idealists were never much for market surveys, and when these were eventually made, the results surprised everyone. This is one reason why continuing with liberalization is high in every politician's mind. No matter what they say to the media, they still have to go home and face the voters, who have been watching the world on television.

Reinventing Business

Hand in hand with a changing society, the post-1991 reforms brought major rethinking to Indian business.

The economic policies of 1950–1990 distorted Indian business, especially its industrial structure. Anti-monopoly laws reinforced by the government's ban on foreign competition encouraged the creation of large, high-wage, capital-intensive businesses. Since few Indian companies did business abroad, profits in the domestic market were artificially easy. The result was a preoccupation with management over marketing. Management theories came into existence that were at considerable variance with the productivity and profit motives. The License Raj put a high reward on political and bureaucratic contacts and monopolies. Companies would diversify into lines of business in which they had no interest simply to preempt a competitor getting a license.

Government regulation also imposed a capital structure on firms that separated the interests of the owner-managers from those of the shareholders. As in most of Asia, Indian firms are dominated by the families that founded them. What was good for them is good for the firm. But in India, the family that founded and generally ran a firm rarely owned the majority of the shares. Instead, many of those shares were publicly held, with the government almost always holding the biggest concentration.

This shares transfer was accomplished through the state-owned banking system. Before 1991, every bank loan to a private company contained a clause allowing the state-owned bank to convert the loan into equity in the borrower whenever it felt like it. This was the state equivalent of a hostile takeover. The result was that the controlling family's goals changed from maximizing their capital appreciation and dividends to keeping the government's board representatives quiet enough so that the family could retain management control and draw out its income that way.

Hence many firms grew by turning into keen diviners of the politicians' idea of what was good for the economy. Too often that meant the politicians' personal economy. Since the government also owned many industrial and financial firms, the result was co-option rather than competition.

Up until their final turning out from office in 1996, Congress's industrial management was inefficient at best. At worst it resulted in wholesale looting of firms through false transfer pricing between government and family-owned parts of a firm, and by inflating the book value of assets far above their real worth and then pocketing loans based on the difference.

Here, too, just as in marketing, changing demographics had a hand in changing the old ways of doing things. One factor was that the aging and passing away of the founding generations opened the way to the rise of professional and non-family managers with international MBAs and computer spreadsheets. Another was the breakup of firms along family fault lines. A third was that many industrialists had become frightened that two generations of cozy political protection had made Indian business too flabby to compete amid the very clear market-orientation the world was taking.

Even labor unions had become jittery. They had a few MBAs on their staffs, too, who knew how to do serious budgeting and project planning. Without any particular sense of cooperative survival, both labor and industry realized that the License Raj was doing no one any good except the bureaucrats who sponged off the proceeds of putting the proper signature on the proper piece of paper.

One result was larger industrial firms selling off subsidiaries that did not fit their goals. Joint ventures with foreign firms increased sharply, especially in investment banking. This meant outside shareholders with very different ideas of the shareholder's role. The blossoming of the capital markets introduced the shareholding category of owner-managers. These were more sensitive to the interests of shareholders in general, and hence the needs of the firm itself rather than the needs of its political allies.

Three Transitions Today

The 1996 elections bequeathed India and the world the honorable Deve Gowda and P. Chidambaram. Their engaging personalities aside, the political, social, and economic transitions they represent are more basic to India's system than mere party alignments. Their success, should it come to be, will advance three existing trends.

First, they will mark a clear shift of political power from the forward castes to the backwards and the dalits. The unforeseen rise of the backward castes in the early 1990s presaged the breakdown of the coalition dominated by Congress.

Second, they have made coalition governments tenable to the center. This fact is readily acknowledged in many states, including West Bengal, Kerala, and Maharashtra.

Third, they underscore what the economic reformers have known for years—the country's mindset has changed with regard to economic management. Reforms are here to stay despite all the kicking and screaming they inspire from vested interests.

The destruction of the Babri mosque in December 1992 proved a watershed that the Bharatiya Janata Party (BJP) did not anticipate. It divided the country into two clear camps on the issue of *hindutva*, or Hindu nationalism. The side that never liked them now can point an accusing finger unequivocally. The other side, which might have been willing to be their allies, now wants nothing to do with a match so close to the fuse of uncontrollable violence that might burn them as well. Unless the BJP can end its political isolation or somehow dramatically increase its voter appeal, it is likely to pass many futile days warming the opposition benches.

It is impossible to predict if coalition machiavellis might bring down the next government. But if the political players involved manage to rustle up the required world view, coalition governance may actually prevail this time. The two fundamental changes of 1990–1996 are that the Narasimha Rao government took Indian democracy away from the dynastic hands of the Nehru-Gandhi family, and the government now looks to take it away from a Congress-dominated democracy.

The future of economic reform now seems assured. The Congress talked reform but lined pockets instead. The BJP promised reform, but burning mosques somehow did not seem the right way to begin.

Now the United Front is actually reforming. Virtually all of the hues in the political spectrum are committed to making the economy less statist and more market-driven. Privatization has been accepted as an idea, delicensing is to be extended in industry, reform is to be enlarged to include agriculture, fiscal discipline has been stressed (again), and the need for foreign capital is recognized.

Business Can Improve India—and India Can Improve Business

The importance of the effect of historical punctured equilibrium—the notion that irregular but powerful changes attempt to insert themselves into the values of a culture—is not that the changes succeed. They often do not, as the failures of colonialism and socialism have amply demonstrated in India.

India's core culture has managed to reassert itself in patterns of thinking and behavior that eventually defeat almost every external force that has come along. The notable exception is Islam.

Whether India's obduracy is good or bad is a judgment that is absolutely worthless. India is India. Any visiting business or other person interested in whether Indians are likely to buy their products has to understand that India is not a market. It is a time capsule of its own culture. Open it every thousand years or so and it will still be the same. India has swallowed markets whole, gnawed political systems to bones, turned conquerors into co-religionists, and invented more gods than all other cultures combined. When all is done, India is still India, older and wiser. No other surviving archaic civilization can make that claim.

What has instead happened is that India changes other cultures more than they do India. The British are a lot more sentimental about India than the Indians are about Britain. Perhaps the most sage, needed, and ignored advice that can be given about India is to unlearn everything you are coming to teach and learn what India can teach you. It has been around a lot longer than the market economy. In fact, India invented most of what we call the modern globalized market economy long before Christ walked the earth.

Appendix A: Useful Addresses

BUSINESS ADDRESSES

Business Organizations in the United States

U.S. India Business Council
1615 H Street, N.W.
Washington, DC 20062-2000
Tel: (202) 463-5492

India American Chamber of Commerce
P.O. Box 2110
Grand Central Station
New York, NY 10185-2110
Tel: (212) 755-7181

U.S. Trade Department of Commerce
International Trade Administration
India Desk
Room 2308
14th & Constitution Avenues, N.W.
Washington, DC 20230
Tel: (202)482-2954

Business Organizations in India

American Business Council of India
R-50 Hotel Hyatt Regency

New Delhi 110 066
Tel: (11) 688-5443

Associated Chambers of Commerce
Allahabad Bank Building
17 Parliament Street
New Delhi 110 001
Tel: (11) 310-749

Chief Controller of Imports and Exports Ministry of Commerce
Udyog Bhawan
Maulana Azad Road
New Delhi 110 001
Tel: (11) 301 1938/301 1275
(Deputy Chief Controller), 331-8857 (Licensing)

Confederation of Indian Industries
23, 26 Institutional Area
Lodhi Road
New Delhi 110 003
Tel: (11) 462-9994

Export Import Bank of India
Centre One, Floor 21
World Trade Centre
Cuffe Parade
Mumbai 400 005
Tel: (22) 218-5272, 218-6801

Foreign Investment Promotion Board
Prime Minister's Secretariat
South Block
New Delhi 110 011
Tel: (11) 301-7839, 3040

India Investment Centre
Jeevan Vihar building
Sansad Marg
New Delhi 110 001

Indo German Chamber of Commerce
Maker Tower E, 1st Floor
Cuffe Parade

Mumbai 400 005
Tel: (22) 218-6131

Industrial Credit and Investment Corporation of India

63 Backbay Reclamation
Mumbai 400 020
Tel: (22) 2022535
In Delhi: (11) 331-9611, 12

Indo-U.S. Joint Business Council

c/o Federation of Indian Chambers of Commerce and Industry
Federation House
Tansen Marg
New Delhi 110 001
Tel: (11) 331-9251

Ministry of Commerce

Udyog Bhawan
New Delhi 110 011
Tel: (11) 301-0261

Ministry of Finance

(Economic Affairs)
North Block
New Delhi 110 001
Tel: (11) 301-4452 (Joint
Secretary for Investments)
301-2883 (Director)

Ministry of Industry

Udyog Bhavan
New Delhi 110 001
Tel: (11) 301-1487 (Protocol),
301-0261 (Export Promotion),
301-4005, 1983 (Investment
Promotion and Project
Monitoring)

Secretariat for Industrial Approvals

Ministry of Industry
Udyog Bhavan
New Delhi 110 001
Tel: (11) 301-0221, 1983

Banking and Financial Institutions

Reserve Bank of India (RBI)
New Central Office Building
Fort
Mumbai 400 023
Tel: (22) 266-5726,
286-1602 (Approvals)

Reserve Bank of India
Central Office Building
Shahid Bhaqat Singh Road
Mumbai 400 023
Tel: (22) 266-1602, 266-0604
Telex: 011-82318, 82455
Fax: (22) 266-2105

Export Credit Guarantee Corporation of India Ltd.
Express Towers, 10th Floor
Nariman Point
Mumbai 400 021
Phone: (22) 202-3023, 202-3046
Telex: 011-83231
Fax: (22) 204-5253

Export-Import Bank of India
Centre One, Floor 21
World Trade Centre
Cuffe Parade
Mumbai 400 005
Phone: (22) 218-5272
Telex: 011-85177 EXIM IN
Fax: (22) 218-8075

General Insurance Corporation of India
Suraksha, 170
J.T. Road
Churchgate
Mumbai 400 020
Tel: (22) 233-3046, 285-2041
Telex: 011-83833
Fax: (22) 2897-4129

Industrial Credit & Investment Corporation of India Ltd.
ICICI Building
163, Backbay Reclamation
Churchgate
Mumbai 400 020
Tel: (22) 202-2535
Telex: 011-83061
Fax: (22) 204-6582

Industrial Reconstruction Bank of India
19, N.S. Road
Calcutta 700 001
Phone: (33) 209 941-45
Telex: 021-7197
Fax: (33) 207 182

Industrial Development Bank of India
IDBI Tower
Cuffe Parade
Mumbai 400 005
Tel: (22) 218-9111, 218-9121
Telex: 011-82193, 84812
Fax: (22) 218-0411, 218-1294

Industrial Finance Corporation of India
Bank of Baroda Building
16, Sansad Marg
New Delhi 110 001
Tel: (11) 332-2052, 332-1013
Telex: 031-65444, 66123
Fax: (11) 332-0425

Life Insurance Corporation of India
Yoyaksnema
Jeevan Bima Marg
Mumbai 400 021
Tel: (22) 202-8267, 202-2151
Telex: 022-82327

National Bank for Agriculture and Rural Development
Sterling Centre
Dr. Annie Besant Road
Mumbai 400 018
Tel: (22) 493-8627

Telex: 011-73770 NAB IN
Fax: (22) 493-1621

National Housing Bank
Hindustani Times House
18-20, Casturba Gandhi Marg
New Delhi 110 001
Tel: 371-2036-37
Telex: 031-66486
Fax: (22) 371-5619

Security and Exchange Board of India
1st Floor, Mittal Court,
B Wing
24 Nariman Point
Mumbai 400 011
Tel: (22) 223-886
Fax: (22) 202-1073

Shipping Credit Investment Corporation of India
141, Maker Towers F
Cuffe Parade
Mumbai 400 005
Tel: (22) 218-0800
Telex: 011-85721
Fax: (22) 218-1539

Small Industries Development Bank of India
Nariman Bhavan
227 Vinay K. Shah Marg
Nariman Point
Mumbai 400 021
Tel: (22) 202-7726
Telex: 011-85016
Fax: (22) 204-4448

Unit Trust of India
13, New Marine Lines
Sir Vithaldas Thackersey Marg
Mumbai 400 020
Tel: (22) 206-8468
Telex: 011-82365
Fax: (22) 266-3673

Trade Service Organizations

All India Manufacturers Organization
DHP Regional Board of AIMO
AIMO House
E1/11, Jhandewalan Extension
New Delhi 110 055
Tel: (11) 528 848

All India Shippers Council
Federation House
Tansen Marg
New Delhi 110 001
Tel: (11) 331-9251

Associated Chambers of Commerce and Industry (ASSOCHAM)
Allahabad Bank Building
17, Parliament Street
New Delhi 110 001
Tel: (11) 310 704, 310 749, 310 779
Fax: (11) 312 193

Confederation of Indian Industry (CII)
23-26 Institutional Area
Lodi Road
New Delhi 100 003
Tel (11) 615 693, 462-1874
Fax: (11) 694 298

Directorate-General of Commercial Intelligence & Statistics
1 Council House Street
Calcutta 700 001
Tel: (33) 283 111

Federation of Indian Chambers of Commerce and Industry (FICCI)
Federation House
Tansen Marg
New Delhi 110 001
Tel: (11) 331-9251
Fax: (11) 332-0714

Federation of Indian Export Organizations (FIEO)
PHD House, Opp. Asian Games Village

New Delhi 110 011
Tel: (11) 686-4624, 686-1310
Fax: (11) 686-3087

Indian Council of Arbitration
Federation House
Tansen Marg
New Delhi 110 001
Telo: (11) 331 9251

Indian Investment Centre
Jeevan Vihar Building
Sansad Marg
New Delhi 110 001
Tel: (11) 373-3673
Fax: (11) 373-3673
Fax: (11) 373-2245

India Trade Promotion Organization (ITPO)
Pragati Bhawan
Pragati Maidan
New Delhi 110 001
Tel: (11) 331-8143
Fax: (11) 331-8143, 332-0855, 331-7896

World Bank India
P.O. Box 416
New Delhi 110 001

EXPORT COUNCILS AND COMMODITY BOARDS

Agricultural Processed Food Products Export Development Authority
3rd Floor
Ansal Chambers II
Bhikaji Cama Place
New Delhi 110 066
Tel: (11) 487-2141
Fax: (11) 487-5016
Telex: 82061 FEDA IN

Apparel Export Promotion Council
15 NBCC Tower

Bhikaji Cama Place
New Delhi 110 066
Tel: (11) 688-3351, 688-8300
Fax: (11) 688-8584
Telex: 031 72196, 72442

Basic Chemicals, Pharmaceuticals & Cosmetics Export Promotion Council
Jhansi Castle
4th Floor
7 Cooperage Road
Mumbai 400 039
Tel: (22) 202-1288, 202-1339
Fax: (11) 202-6684
Telex: 011 84047 BCPC IN

Cashew Export Promotion Council of India
P.B. No. 1709
Chitoor Road
Ernakulam South
Cochin 682 016
Tel: (48) 436-1459, 435-3357
Fax: (48) 437-0973
Telex: 0885 6677 CPPC IN

Carpet Export Promotion Council
110-A/1 Krishna Nagar
Street No. 5
Safdarjung Enclave
New Delhi 110 029
Tel: (11) 602-742, 601-024
Fax: (11) 601-024

Chemicals & Allied Products Export Promotion Council
World Trade Centre
14/1-B, Ezra Street
Calcutta 700 001
Tel: (33) 258-216, 258-219
Fax: (33) 255-070
Telex: 021 4368

Coffee Board
1, Dr. Ambedkar Veedhi

Bangalore 560 001
Tel: (80) 262-917, 260-250
Fax: (80) 226-5557
Telex: 0845 8281

Coir Board

P.O. Box No. 1752
M.G. Road
Ernakulam South
Cochin 682 016
Tel: (484) 351-788, 354-397
Fax: (484) 370-034
Telex: 0885 6363

Cotton Textiles Export Promotion Council

Engineering Centre
5th Floor
9, Mathew Road
Mumbai 400 004
Tel: (22) 363-2910, 361-1793
Fax: (22) 363-2914
Telex: 011 75466 TCIL IN

Electronics and Computer Software Export Promotion Council

PHD House
3rd Floor
Khelgaon Marg
New Delhi 110 016
Tel: (11) 655-103, 655-206
Fax: (11) 485-3412
Telex: 031 73333 ESC IN

Engineering Export Promotion Council

World Trade Centre
3rd Floor
14,1 B, Ezra Street
Calcutta 700 001
Tel: (33) 250-442, 250-443
Fax: (33) 258-968
Telelx: 21 5109

Federation of Indian Export Organizations (FIEO)
PHD House
3rd Floor
Khelgaon Marg
New Delhi 110 016
Tel: (11) 6853-1310, 685-1312
Fax: (11) 686-3087
Telex: 031 73194

Gem and Jewellery Export Promotion Council
Diamond Plaza
5th Floor
391-A, Dr. D.B. Marg
Mumbai 400 004
Tel: (22) 385-6916, 388-8005
Fax: (22) 386-8751
Telex: 011 75360

Export Promotion Council for Handicrafts
6, Community Centre
1st & 2nd Floor
Basant Lok
Vasant Vihar
New Delhi 110 057
Tel: (11) 600-871, 687-5377
Telex: 031 72315

Handloom Export Promotion Council
18, Cathedral Garden Road
Nungambakkam
Chennai 600 034
Tel: (44) 827-8879, 827-6043
Fax: (44) 827-1762
Telex: 41 7158 HEPC IN

India Trade Promotion Organization
Pragati Bhavan
Pragati Maiden
New Delhi 110001
Tel: (11) 331-9560, 331-7534
Fax: (11) 331-8142

Indian Silk Export Promotion Council
62 Mittal Chambers
6th Floor
Nariman Point
Mumbai 400 021
Tel: (22) 202-7662, 204-9113
Fax: (22) 287-4606
Telex: 0118 3190 SILK IN

Council for Leather Exports
Leather Centre
53 Sydenhams Road
Periamet
Chennai 600 003
Tel: (44) 589-098, 582-041
Fax: (44) 588-713
Telex: 041 7354 CLE IN

Marine Products Export Development Authority
P.B. No. 1663
MPEDA House
Panampilly Avenue
Cochin 682 015
Tel: (484) 311-979, 311-901
Fax: (484) 313-361
Telex: 0885-6288

Overseas Construction Council of India
H 118 (11th Floor)
Himalaya House
23, Kasturba Gandhi Marg
New Delhi 110 001
Tel: (11) 332-7550, 332-2425
Fax: (11) 331-1296
Telex: 031 65588 OCCI IN

Plastics and Linoleums Export Promotion Council
Centre 1, Unit 1, 11th Floor
World Trade Centre
Cuffe Parade
Mumbai 400 005
Tel: (22) 218-4474, 218-4474

Fax: (22) 218-4819
Telex: 011 83940

Rubber Board
P.B. No. 280
Sastri Road
Kottayam 686 001
Tel: (481) 563-231
Fax: 481 564-639
Telex: 888 205

Shellac Export Promotion Council
World Trade Centre
4th Floor
14/1 b Ezra Street
Calcutta 700 001
Tel: (33) 254-556, 255-725
Fax: (33) 248-2070
Telex: 021 7622 23021

Sports Goods Export Promotion Council
1-E/6, Swami Ram Tirath Nagur
New Delhi 110 055
Tel: (11) 525-695, 529-255
Fax: (11) 753-2147

Spices Board
P.B. No. 1909
St. Vincent Cross Rd.
Cochin 682 018
Tel: (484) 353-837, 353-578
Fax: (484) 370-429
Telex: 0885 6534

Synthetic & Rayon Textiles Export Promotion Council
Resham Bhavan
78 Veer Nariman Rd.
Mumbai 400 020
Tel: (11) 204-8797, 204-8690
Fax: (11) 204-8358

Tea Board
14 Biplabi Trailokya
Maharaj Sarani

Calcutta 700 001
Tel: (33) 260-210
Fax: (33) 260-218, Telex: 021 4527

Tobacco Board
Srinivasa Rao Thota
G.T. Road
P.B. No. 322
Guntur 522 004
Tel: (863) 30399, 32993
Fax: (863) 33032
Telex: 071 264 TOBD IN

Wool & Woollens Export Promotion Council
612/714 Ashok Estate
24 Barakhamba Road
New Delhi 110 001
Tel: (11) 331-5512, 331-5205
Fax: (11) 331-4626

EMBASSIES AND CONSULATES

American Embassy
Shantipath
Chanakyapuri
New Delhi 119921
Tel: (11) 600651

American Consulates
Lincoln House
78 Bhulabhai Desai Road
Mumbai 400026
Tel: (22) 363-3611

5/1 Ho Chi Minh Sarani
Calcutta 700071
Tel: (33) 242-3611
220 Mount Road
Chennai 600006
Tel: (44) 827-3040

British High Commission
Chanakyapuri

New Delhi 110021
Tel: (11) 601371

Canadian High Commission
7/8 Shanti Path
Chanakyapuri
New Delhi 110021
Tel: (11) 687-6500

Canadian Consulate
41/42 Maker Chambers VI
Jamnalal Bajaj Marg
Nariman Point
Mumbai 400021
Tel: (22) 287-6027

French Embassy
2/50E Shanti Path
Chanakyapuri
New Delhi 110021
Tel: (11) 604300

French Consulate
Bacon
7th Floor
Madame Cama Road
Mumbai 400021
Tel: (22) 202-1217

German Embassy
6/50G Shanti Path
Chanakyapuri
New Delhi 110021
Tel: (11) 604861

German Consulates
Hoechst House
10th Floor
Nariman Point
193 Backbay Reclamation
Mumbai 400021
Tel: (22) 232422

1 Hastings Park Road
  Alipore
  Calcutta
  Tel: (33) 711141

22 Commander-in-Chief Road
   Chennai
   Tel: (44) 471747

Appendix B: Additional Readings

WEB SITES

The Hindu (India's best daily newspaper available online):
http://www.webpage.com/hindu

India World business directory:
http://www.indiaworld.com/open/biz/index.html

India Business Directory (gov't):
http://www.webindia.com/india.html

Software Technology Parks of India:
http://www.stph.net

Gov't of India NYC office business facts:
http://www.indiaserver.com/biz/dbi/MEA2.0.html

How to Invest info:
http://www.indiaserver.com/biz/dbi/MEA3.0.html

Doing Business with India:
http://www.indiaserver.com/biz/dbi/dbi.html

Insider News:
http://www.globalindia.lcom/index.htm (still sparse yet)

General Info:
http://www.indiacomm.com

Economic Times (daily news):
http://www.economictimes.com/today/pagehome.html (e-mail: times@giasdl01.vsnl.net.in)Economic Times, Times House 7 Bahadurshah Zafar Marg, New Delhi 110 002, India
Phone: +91-11-3312277 Fax: +91-11-3715832

Business Services Syndicate consultants:
http://www.indiagate.com/commerce/busi.html

Indian Economy:
http://www.webcom.com/%7Eprakash/ECONOMY/ECONOMY. HTML

BUSINESS AND DOING BUSINESS IN INDIA

Books

India Fast Forward, 12 chapters aimed at foreign investors and overseas partners interested in commerce with India; a broad look at the effects of liberalization and the reforms undertaken since 1991. Mumbai: Business India Book Club (14th Floor, Nirmal, Nariman Point, Mumbai 400 021 (Fax: 91-22-287-5671).

India Means Business, a portfolio of brochures prepared by the Economic Co-ordination Unit of the Ministry of External Affairs and Arthur Andersen & Co., Inc. available through Indian trade affairs officers in Indian Embassies, and from Arthur Andersen & Co. and affiliated offices. Official propaganda versus real life, but highly informative between the lines.

Balachandran, S., *Managing Ethics,* New Delhi, Sangeetha Associates. A comparison of the various management systems in general use in India and the ethical dilemmas they face.

Dandekar, V. M., *The Indian Economy: 1947–92,* New Delhi, Sage Publications. Analysis of the conditions that led to the 1991 liberalization program.

Kakar, Sudhir, *the Inner World: A Psychoanalytic Study of Childhood and Society in India.* Oxford: Oxford University Press. Mainly of use to business people in the advertising and marketing communities, This is also a good background read for anyone doing business in India.

Ninan, Sevanti, *Through the Magic Window: TV and Change in India,* New Delhi: Penguin. From tool of the government to satellite dishes, CNN, and MTV, television has influenced India in incalculable ways. This is a populist book rather than a serious study, but it's the only one on the subject available and at least an introduction to India's TV scene.

Pant, Manoj, *Foreign Direct Investment in India: The Issues Involved,* New Delhi: Lancers Books. Based on interviews with academics, government officials, and expatriate business people, this is a thorough and balanced look at the issues involve din investing in India.

Sen Gupta, Bhabani, *India: Problems of Governance*, New Delhi: Konark. A summation of now accepted conventions of change in India: market-friendly economic policies, the defects of *Hindutva*, reinventing government, and the need to serve the people rather than the people in power.

Singh, Mina, *Business Etiquette, a Book of Modern Manners for the Indian Office*, New Delhi: Rupa & Co. A useful guide for the person who will be doing quite a bit of interfacing and networking with Indian counterparts.

Srinivas, M. N. (editor), *Caste: Its Twentieth-Century Avatar*, New Delhi: Viking Penguin India. An anthology of essays which looks at the modern caste system from many different perspectives, from academic to polemic, with many shades of attitude between. A basic thread running through is that caste makes a person part of a social network which controls inside information, resulting in a monopoly on a privilege.

Vakil, Tarjani, *Achieving Excellence: Case Studies of 6 Indian Export Companies*, New Delhi: Tata McGraw-Hill.

Business Periodicals That Will Airmail Overseas

Business India, B-24 Maheshwari Towers, Road No. 1, Banjara Hills, Hyderabad 500 034. Fax: (91) 842 390-233. (Airmail: US$ 110/yr.)

Business Today, Subscriptions, Post Box 247, New Delhi 110 011. Fax: (91) 11 331-6180/331-08385. E-mail: btoday@giasdl0l.vsnl.net.in (Airmail: $125/yr.)

Business World, 10th Floor, New Delhi House, Barakhamba Road, New Delhi 110 001. Tel: (91) 11 372-2684-85. (Airmail: US$110/yr.)

India Today, Post Box 115, New Delhi 110 001. Fax: (91) 11 331-6180. Telex: 31-62634 INTO IN. (Airmail US$120/yr.)

HISTORY AND POLITICS

Brown, Judith M. *Gandhi: Prisoner of Hope*. New Haven: Yale University Press.

Crossette, Barbara. *India—Facing the Twenty-first Century*. Bloomington: Indiana University Press. Reflections by one of America's most astute journalists, a long-time *New York Times* correspondent in India. This is probably the most important and informative book on life in India after Liberalization.

Embree, Ainslie T. *Sources of Indian Tradition, Vol. 1; From the Beginning to 1600*. New York: Columbia University Press.

Galbraith, John Kenneth. *Ambassador's Journal*. Boston: Houghton Mifflin.

Gandhi, Mohandas. *The Essence of Hinduism*. New Delhi: the Navjivan Trust.

Kapoor, Sanjay. *Bad Money: Bad Politics: the Hawala Story*. New Delhi: Alka Paperbacks (Har-Anand Publications).

Radhakrishnan, Sarvepalli. *The Hindu View of Life*. London: Unwin Paperback. London.

Salgaocar, Ranjana. *The Pleasure of Your Company*. Pyramid Books.

Sisson, Richard, and Leo E. Rose. *War and Secession: Pakistan, India and the Creation of Bangladesh*. Berkeley and Los Angeles: University of California Press.

Thapar, Romila. *A History of India* (2 vols.). London: Penguin Books. A broad, non-academic history covering cultural subjects as much as political and religious ones.

Zakaria, Rafiq. *The Widening Divide: an Insight into Hindu-Muslim Relations*. New Delhi: Viking Penguin. A painstaking analysis of the tempestuous relations between these two religious groups.

TRAVELING IN INDIA

Alberuni. *Alberuni's India*. New York: Norton. Fascinating account by the traveler, adventurer and chronicler in 13th century India.

Al Rasham. *The Wonder That Was India*. London: Sidgwick & Jackson. Survey of Indian history, society, music, art and literature from 400 B.C. to the coming of the Muslims.

Bose, Sunil. *Indian Classical Music*. New Delhi: Vikas Publishing House. The emotions and history behind Indian classical music.

Boyce, Mary. *Zoroastrians: Their Religious Beliefs and Practices*. London: Routledge. A Survey of Zoroastrian secular and religious history.

Cole, W. O., and P. Singh Sambhi. *The Sikhs: Their Relgious Beliefs and Practices*. London: Routledge.

Crann, Roy. *Indian Art*. London: Thames & Hudson. The most reasonable and concise general introduction to Indian art, from Harappan seals to Moghul miniatures.

Davidson, Robyn. *Desert Places*. New York/New Delhi: Viking Penguin. A thrilling account of the life of the desert nomads of Gujarat and Rajasthan.

Fishlock, Trevor. *India File*. London: John Murray. The latest edition of this now classic analysis of contemporary Indian society brings the picture up to date with essays on the Golden Temple siege and the rise of Rajiv Gandhi.

Frater, Alexander. *Chasing the Monsoon*. New Delhi: Penguin. Frater's wet-season jaunt up the west coast and across the Ganges plains is a great monsoon read for those who don't like being wet all day long.

Gombrich, Richard. *Theravada Buddhism*. London: Routledge & Kegan Paul. A history of Theravadin beliefs and practices from their beginnings to the present.

Khokar, Mohan. *Traditions of Indian Classical Dance*. New Delhi: Clarion Books. Detailing the religious and social roots of Indian dance, this lavishly illustrated book, with sections on regional traditions, is an excellent introduction to the subject.

Lewis, Norman. *A Goddess in the Stones*. London: Pan Macmillan. This veteran English travel writer's account of his trip to Calcutta and around the backwaters of Bihar and Orissa includes some vivid insights into tribal India. One of the more accomplished travelogues of recent years.

Naipaul, V. C. *India: A Wounded Civilisation*. New Delhi: Penguin. Naipaul, a Trinidadian Indian indicts India for narrow-mindedness and barbaric selfishness amid debilitating poverty and misguided faith.

O'Flaherty, Wendy. *Hindu Myths*. New Delhi: Penguin. Translations of popular Hindu myths, providing an insight into the foundations of Hinduism.

Reat, Noble Ross. *Buddhism, A History*. Fremont, California: Asian Humanities Press. A thorough account of the history of Buddhism from the historical perspective.

Rippin, Andrew. *Muslims—Their Religious Beliefs and Practices*. London: Routledge. The essential guide to Islamic history and religious beliefs.

Spear, Percival. *History of India Volume II.* London: Penguin. Covers the period from the Moghul era to the death of Gandhi.

Tagore, Rabindranath. *Selected Works*. London: Penguin. Poems, prose, and mystical verse by the Bengali Nobel Laureate.

Thapar, Romila. *History of India Volume I*, London: Penguin. Concise paperback account of early Indian history, ending with Delhi Sultanate.

Tully, Mark. *No Full Stops in India*. London: Penguin. Personal anecdotes and first-hand accounts of political events over the past twenty years by an almost legendary BBC correspondent. (Note: "Full stop" in India means the same as "period" as at the end of a sentence. Used as a term of emphasis it conveys the sense of ". . . . and that's *final*.")

Wade, Bonnie. *Music in India: The Classical Traditions*. New Delhi: Manmohar. A thorough catalogue of Indian music, outlining the most commonly used instruments, with excellent illustrations and musical scores.

Zashner, R. C. *Hinduism*. Oxford: Oxford University Press. Lively, accessible and often amusing catalogue of Hinduism and Indian society.

THE DAILY AND WEEKLY PRESS

Economic and Political Weekly, Mumbai
Frontline, Chennai
India Abroad, New York
India Magazine, Mumbai
India Today, New Delhi
Inside-Outside (architecture and landscape design), Mumbai
Mainstream, New Delhi
New Quest, Mumbai
Sunday, Calcutta

Index

Goenka, Vivek, 11
Golden Temple at Amritsar, 24, 250
Goldman Sachs, 50
Goldstar, 62
Gopalkrishnan, K., on labor, quoted, 142
Governance, by favored friends, 98
Government: as a motherly protectress, 83; consumption, 57; -controlled corporations, 206; employees, 27; spending, 57
Government of India Act of 1858, 213
Gowda-Chidambaram government, 99
Greater Bombay, 70
Greece, 234
Greenfield regions, 142
Greetings, upon meeting, 205
Group consensus, 136
Growth capital, sources of, 96
Grundig Auto, 73
Guangdong, China, 45
Gujarat, 20, 33, 69, 73
Gujerati merchants, 257
Gummidipoondi, 74
Gupta dynasties, 231
Gupta Empire, 243

Hajj (Muslim pilgrimage to Mecca), 110
Harappa, 232
Harmonized Commodity Description and Coding System, 223
Haryana, 86
Hawala (bribery), 22; 1996 corruption scandal, 33
Hazardous activities, legal consequences of, 221
HCL, 81
HDFC Bank, 107
Head & Shoulders shampoo, 63
Heavy machinery sector, 62

Henkel, 62
Hero Cycles, 116
Hewlett Packard, 81
Hidden takeovers, 101
Hierarchical management, 129
High Court, 215, 220
High priority industries, 177
High-tech sectors, 68
Higher education, government spending on, 117
Himalayas, 123
Hindi language, 14, 22, 83, 84, 147, 232; press, 11; TV programming, 270
Hindu: body language, 137; concept of supremacy through force, 248; nationalism, 32, 274; rate of growth, 264; revivalism during Gupta Dynasty, 231; temples, 127
The Hindu, 70
Hindu Kush, 234, 241
Hindu–Muslim rivalries, 251
Hinduism, 7, 41, 127, 241, 246
Hindustan Lever, 62, 76, 86, 120, 272
Hindustan Motors, 73
The Hindustan Times, 11, 12, 14
Hindutva, 274
Historical behavior patterns in India, 126
Hitachi, 62
Hi-tech agriculture, 104
Hitler, Adolf, 33
Holding companies, 170
Holidays, public, list of, 211
Hong Kong, 14, 17, 40
Hoover vacuum cleaners, 62
Horlicks, 84
Hospitals, 24
Hosur, 73
Hotel industry, 160
Hours of work, 220
Human development, 24
Hyderabad, 14, 20, 70, 269

About the Author

DOUGLAS BULLIS is a writer, editor, and currently owner of Atelier books, a full-service book production firm serving international publishers with interests in the Southeast Asian market. His clients include major publishers here and abroad. Mr. Bullis has written and published more than 200 articles on topics ranging from art and cultural history to business, country investment, and technology transfer. He also is author of *Selling to India's Consumer Market* (Quorum, 1997).